# Climate Justice and Geoengineering

# Climate Justice and Geoengineering

## Ethics and Policy in the Atmospheric Anthropocene

Edited by
Christopher J. Preston

ROWMAN & LITTLEFIELD
INTERNATIONAL

London • New York

Published by Rowman & Littlefield International, Ltd.
Unit A, Whitacre Mews, 26-34 Stannary Street, London SE11 4AB
www.rowmaninternational.com

Rowman & Littlefield International, Ltd. is an affiliate of Rowman & Littlefield
4501 Forbes Boulevard, Suite 200, Lanham, Maryland 20706, USA
With additional offices in Boulder, New York, Toronto (Canada), and Plymouth (UK)
www.rowman.com

**British Library Cataloguing in Publication Data**
A catalogue record for this book is available from the British Library

ISBN: HB 978-1-7834-8636-6
      PB 978-1-7834-8637-3

**Library of Congress Cataloging-in-Publication Data**

ISBN 978-1-78348-636-6 (cloth : alk paper)
ISBN 978-1-78348-637-3 (pbk. : alk. paper)

♾ ™ The paper used in this publication meets the minimum requirements of American
National Standard for Information Sciences—Permanence of Paper for Printed Library
Materials, ANSI/NISO Z39.48-1992.

Printed in the United States of America

# Contents

v

# Introduction

## Climate Justice and Geoengineering[1]

### Christopher J. Preston

The publication of this collection of essays on climate intervention comes a mere 10 years after Nobel Prize-winning chemist Paul Cruzten broke the international taboo on talking openly about this controversial topic. In a widely cited article in the journal *Climatic Change*, Crutzen made the case that, in the absence of effective progress on emissions reductions, it was time to start a serious discussion about artificially cooling the planet using stratospheric aerosols (Crutzen 2006). Even though Crutzen was fully aware of the reason for the taboo, namely that starting this discussion appeared to create a risk of distracting attention from the critical work of greenhouse gas mitigation, he concluded that simply hoping against all evidence that adequate mitigation would arrive in time was starting to look more and more like a 'pious wish' (Crutzen 2006: 217).

Three years after Crutzen opened the discussion, the UK's Royal Society suggested in an equally widely cited report that the barriers to geoengineering deployment were as much 'social, legal, ethical, and political' as they were 'technical and scientific'(Shepherd 2009: xi). In other words, while the science and engineering required to deploy geoengineering might at some point be mastered, the social and ethical dimensions looked like they would provide more lasting challenges. After the Royal Society report, there was no hiding from the fact that the ethics of climate engineering was going to be enormously complicated and controversial.

One of the unusual features of climate engineering among emerging technologies is that even those who advocate for concerted research tend to be completely upfront about the fact that the proposals raise difficult social and ethical challenges. The most enthusiastic researchers all recognize that for humans to insert themselves intentionally into processes as basic to planetary function as atmospheric chemistry and solar irradiance is a massive step that generates widespread unease. All other things being equal, most advocates acknowledge, we should not even be thinking about it. David Keith, one of the foremost proponents of research into solar radiation management (SRM)—and a contributor to this volume—famously told *Foreign Policy* magazine on hearing his interviewers' reaction to one technology: 'You are repulsed? Good. No one should like it. It's a terrible option' (Wagner and Weitzman 2012). On *The Colbert Report* in front of a wide television audience, Keith called the whole idea he was promoting 'horrifying'. In this regard, the climate engineering discussion has been from the start considerably more self-reflexive and cautious than the discussion around some other globally significant technologies such as nuclear power and early agricultural biotechnology.

The Royal Society's pronouncement about social, legal, ethical and governance issues quickly unleashed a veritable tidal wave of attention to climate engineering from those in the social sciences and humanities. Before 2009 there was probably only one article written by an academic philosopher on the ethics of climate engineering (Jamieson 1996). Since the Royal Society report came out, ethicists, legal scholars, governance experts and social scientists have quickly compiled an extensive archive of books, papers and reports devoted to the social and governance issues that the Society anticipated would be so challenging.[2]

The speed at which this work has accumulated is an indication of just how gripping, difficult, yet critically important these issues are. From an ethical point of view, the thought of intentionally manipulating the whole planet challenges the whole segment of environmental thinking that suggests humans need to be stepping back from their interference with nature, rather than ratcheting it up. From a legal point of view, experts are tortured by the question of what sort of international mechanism or framework could possibly be adequate for regulating planetary-scale interventions such as the ones proposed. From the perspective of the social sciences, researchers struggle over how the views of all affected populations could possibly be included in decisions about the design and implementation of the technologies. Across each of these domains, the different forms of climate engineering present depressingly difficult challenges to existing frameworks. Climate policy expert Mike Hulme, for example, has suggested rejecting stratospheric forms of climate intervention on the grounds that they are quite simply 'ungovernable' (Hulme 2014).

## JUSTICE

A large proportion of the ethical challenges presented by climate engineering involve considerations that are directly related to justice. There are two main reasons for this. The first is that since climate engineering is supposed to push back against a warming phenomenon that is clearly *global*, by definition it is an engineering project that will impact everybody on Earth. This creates important and highly complex demands of procedural justice, that is, demands over ensuring fairness about how research and deployment decisions would take place. Admittedly, not every person on Earth is vulnerable to climate change—and so has a stake in the efforts to fix it—in exactly the same way or to exactly the same extent. While some affluent members of developing nations may simply have to turn up their air conditioning while enjoying new crops that previously would not grow in their area, those in low-lying Pacific Islands are likely to find their homeland and their very existence under existential threat. Yet despite the differences in the severity of impacts, everyone on the planet has some stake in climate engineering.

The second reason that justice issues are so prevalent is that it is widely acknowledged that attempts to cool the climate using the management of solar radiation or the rapid removal of greenhouse gases, while potentially helpful overall, will likely have somewhat uncertain and uneven impacts on different populations across the globe. This means that while many people are likely to be made better off, a small minority are quite likely to be made worse off. A subset of those made worse off will be the people already most vulnerable to—and often least responsible for—climate change. This creates painful demands of distributive justice, that is, demands about ensuring fairness over how the benefits and burdens of climate engineering will be distributed. In some cases—including the Pacific Islands and certain parts of sub-Saharan Africa and Asia—these burdens could quite literally be matters of life and death.

These procedural and distributive obstacles offer significant challenges in their own right. But when it is recognized that both the procedural and the distributive challenges have intergenerational elements to them, the ethical ratchet clicks upwards a few more notches. For it is not only the current generation living with the threat of climate change for whom procedural and distributive justice concerns arise with climate engineering. The time lags built into the climate system due to the longevity of carbon dioxide in the atmosphere and the thermal inertia of the oceans mean that actions today will invariably have consequences tomorrow, and in fact over many decades and centuries to come. This means that one must not only consider procedural and distributive justice within the current generation. One must also consider it for future generations, generations who are not only unable to participate in today's deliberations but whose very existence and composition might be affected by the decisions made today. It is easy to see why the 'perfect moral storm' of climate change (Gardiner 2011) risks becoming an unprecedented moral typhoon with the addition of climate engineering. Justice, in sum, looms extraordinarily large in the kind of social and governance challenges that the Royal Society warned about.

In view of the importance of justice, the primary focus of the essays in this volume is the matter of how climate engineering impacts climate justice. Can climate engineering restore some measure of justice in a world increasingly impacted by climate change, or will it pile on ever more injustices? The current book is not the first to consider justice in relation to climate engineering. Other collections of essays that take justice into account have been published since the Royal Society report (Preston 2012, Burns and Strauss 2013). But this volume is the first to focus on what might be called a "second generation" of ethical investigation into the justice issues surrounding climate engineering.

## A SECOND-GENERATION ANALYSIS

What makes these essays represent a second generation is the *comparative* nature of the analysis offered. In the first generation, the various climate engineering technologies were mostly scrutinized noncomparatively. Noncomparative considerations of climate engineering consider the proposed technologies entirely on their own terms as if all other things were equal. For example, in addition to making much of the procedural and distributive challenges facing climate engineering discussed above, authors in the first generation warned against the overconfidence or hubris that some advocates of the technology appear to display (Hamilton 2013). They expressed concern about what might happen if an albedo modification technique proceeded for a number of years and then had to be stopped for unanticipated political or environmental reasons (Svoboda et al. 2011). They raised questions about the ecological impacts of large-scale carbon removal infrastructure (Axon and Lubansky 2012). They voiced concern about the potential for a climate engineering solution to distract from what is viewed as a more desirable mitigation solution (Lin 2012). They warned against vested interests that might steer the global community down a type of deployment path that serves only the interests of a few (Long and Scott 2013). And they expressed caution about the massive sense of perpetual responsibility that climate engineering could create if its deployment lasted beyond the short term (Preston 2016).

What has been peculiar about this first generation of ethical reactions to climate engineering is the extent to which authors looked at the idea of climate engineering more or less entirely on its own terms, in isolation from other options for dealing with climate change. They poked and probed the various climate engineering techniques for what might be their individual weaknesses and often found the technologies to be wanting from an ethical point of view.

Considered solely on their own terms, many forms of climate engineering do indeed appear outlandish, as David Keith's comment to *Foreign Policy* magazine conceded. In this first generation of analysis, it was perhaps too easy to find ethical problems with the whole idea.

It is when climate engineering is considered in relation to the other available options that the ethical landscape starts to shift. In the two decades since the Kyoto Protocol was approved and representatives from 192 nations formally acknowledged that something needed to be done about the emission of greenhouse gases, a disappointingly small amount of meaningful action has occurred on the ground. Regrettably, this means that many of the best options for dealing with the escalating climate problem are no longer on the table. The options that remain are increasingly far from ideal. What might have been a slow and orderly transition to a low-carbon economy will now have to be a rapid and lurching one. What might have been a timely and balanced research and development path away from fossil fuels and towards clean technologies will now have to be an almost impossibly quick one. Where climate engineering once looked outlandish or even repulsive, it is now becoming increasingly credible to growing numbers of observers.

Realistic or not, in this post-Paris era the global community has expressed a commitment to limit temperature increases to 'well below 2°C above pre-industrial levels' and to 'pursuing efforts to limit the temperature increase to 1.5°C' (UNFCCC 2015). These goals are highly ambitious given the nearly 1°C rise in temperatures that has already occurred. While the discussions in Paris did not entertain the possibility that reaching this target would necessarily involve solar geoengineering, there was an understanding that it would likely involve the artificial enhancements of sinks and the deployment of carbon capture technologies, two strategies that are often considered part of the carbon dioxide removal (CDR) category of climate engineering. If climate engineering is not already on the global agenda, it is certainly now knocking loudly on the door.

Due to this shifting landscape, there seems to be little point in evaluating the ethics of climate engineering in isolation. It no longer seems reasonable to ask the question 'All other things being equal, would climate engineering be desirable from a justice perspective?' Clearly all other things are not equal. The so-called 'ambition gap' between the nationally determined contributions pledged by close to 190 countries in Paris and what is required to keep temperature increases below 2°C suggests that achieving the stated goals of the global community will require significant as yet undeveloped technologies. The inclusion of a discussion of climate engineering in the Intergovernmental Panel on Climate Change's Fifth Assessment Report (Fischedick et al. 2014) suggests that, even if climate engineering is not yet being taken as seriously by the global community as Paul Crutzen intended in his 2006 essay, it is getting ever closer to the mainstream.

The essays in this volume are all devoted to putting the justice issues at stake in climate engineering into dialogue with the justice issues already being presented by the harms of climate change and various other proposals for tackling those harms. For example, the collection asks whether the potential injustices that might befall certain nations under a radical emissions reduction scenario would be greater than the potential injustices that might befall them under a climate engineering alternative (Baatz and Ott, Horton and Keith). It asks whether procedural injustices are more likely to occur under climate engineering than under mitigation and adaptation (Hourdequin). It asks whether the threat to food security presented by climate change exceeds the threat to food security that might arise under geoengineering (Kortetmäki and Oksanen). It asks how engineering the climate stacks up from a justice perspective against adaptation and compensation (Baard and Wikman, Habib and Jankunis). It probes the key ideas and mechanisms by which a just deployment of climate engineering might emerge out of current climate policy (Long). It investigates whether climate engineering is being properly framed with respect to the mitigation and adaptation options that are still on the table (McLaren, Fragnière and Gardiner).

This comparative dimension found in the essays that follow supplies a much needed *second-generation* analysis of the ethics of climate engineering. While the ethical issues uncovered in the first generation of work on climate engineering remain relevant, this second generation promises to be more useful for policy-making. It now seems certain that any solution to the climate change problem is going to be non-ideal from an ethical perspective (Morrow and Svoboda 2016). If ethical compromises have to be made, it is desirable to compare the possible compromises as even handedly as possible. This is what the essays collected here endeavour to do.

The 13 essays included in the volume are written by philosophers, economists, climate policy experts, discourse analysts, geographers and sustainable development theorists. In addition to being thoroughly interdisciplinary, the collection is also thoroughly international and atypically gender diverse for this territory. Contributors originate from the Netherlands, Nigeria, Finland, Scotland, Sweden, Canada, England, Kenya, United States, Switzerland, Italy and Germany. The essays offer a range of theoretical and practical viewpoints. Roughly one-third of them are oriented primarily around philosophical and ethical theory. Another third are more practice and policy focused. The final third offer a range of frames, models and scenarios through which to think about geoengineering justice alongside climate justice. The organization of the book reflects this coarse breakdown of categories.

## THEORIZING GEOENGINEERING JUSTICE

Toby Svoboda's contribution shows how, even if climate engineering carries the risk of distributive injustice, it is philosophically plausible that it may yet be the right thing to do. He comes to this somewhat sobering conclusion by peeling apart what he calls 'axiological justice' from 'deontic justice'. An axiological use of distributive justice considers both the morally valuable and morally disvaluable consequences of stratospheric aerosol injection. Due to concerns about precipitation and the uncertainty over the spatial distribution of projected impacts, it is highly likely that there will be some disvalues from an axiological standpoint resulting from the deployment of SRM.

A deontic approach to distributive justice, however, would determine which course of action might be permissible, or even obligatory, regardless of the axiological injustices it might contain. After all, the situation to be faced is not ideal. A policy, in other words can be 'unjust in the axiological sense while being just in the deontic sense' (p. 6) while viewed from the point of view of distributive justice. The distinction Svoboda explores in some ways gets to the heart of what separates the two generations of ethical analysis of climate engineering. As a comparative analysis, the second generation necessarily evaluates climate engineering relative to what else is on the table. This distinction between axiological and deontic justice also seems to be required if ethical analysis is to avoid paralysing conclusion that all courses of action are wrong and none are permissible.

Augustin Fragnière and Stephen Gardiner take on the common characterization of stratospheric aerosol injection as a Plan B response to climate warming when Plan A—emissions reduction—has failed. They point out that there are many different ways of talking about such 'insurance' types of claims, ranging in the first instance from insurance as a means of compensation to insurance as a method of prevention. In a lot of these cases, the 'insurance' is not necessarily the second-best option but an ethically dubious option ahead of which there might be a number of preferable alternatives. The Plan B framing of climate engineering can obscure this and make climate engineering sound misleadingly attractive while at the same time ignoring the reality of the political and cultural context in which it is being offered. For a host of reasons that Fragnière and Gardiner unpack throughout the chapter, climate engineering is unlikely to be a Plan B but potentially something closer to a Plan X, Y or Z. As an option this low down the list of preferences, there might be some serious questions about whether such a last resort can meet any reasonable standard of moral decency.

One of the important acknowledgements contained in Fragnière and Gardiner's chapter is that the Plan B framing does not adequately represent the views of even its most plausible advocates. The framing of climate engineering as a Plan B eclipses the way that most of its plausible advocates only promote climate engineering as one part of a portfolio of responses to the harms of climate change. Stratospheric aerosols, Fragnière and Gardiner point out, are not a 'plan' at all but a technology or a tool. This tool would never stand alone. Presenting it otherwise distorts any comparative lens that one might be attempting to employ. Assessments of climate engineering need to be much more integrative (i.e. combined with discussion of attendant policies of mitigation, adaptation and carbon removal) than they have thus far been.

Marion Hourdequin looks at the question of how to ensure just procedure in climate policy. She identifies the goal of securing adequate 'recognition' as a key criterion for a just process. Recognition, Hourdequin suggests, demands 'receptivity and openness rather than imposition and presupposition' (p. 35). If all parties with a stake in a decision are accorded equal recognition, then we can be confident of 'participatory parity'. She compares mitigation, adaptation and stratospheric aerosol injection for how well (or poorly) they can ensure recognition of the needs of stakeholders, with particular attention paid to the most vulnerable.

While she finds that recognition is a challenge to secure in almost any climate policy, there are reasons why stratospheric aerosols create particularly acute challenges. These include inadequate political forums for representation when the affected population spans the whole globe, enhanced risk and uncertainty about precise outcomes, the novelty of the technology and the polarized nature of the existing discussion. Adequate recognition, Hourdequin concludes, should be the measure of climate policy and especially a policy that includes climate engineering.

Patrik Baard and Per Wikman-Svahn investigate the question of whether engineering the climate might remain an important residual obligation for the developed nations when those country's primary obligations to mitigate and provide adaptation assistance are not adequately fulfilled. They compare solar geoengineering with financial compensation as two possible candidates for fulfilling the residual obligations that most people would agree fall upon the high-emitting countries for their greenhouse gas emissions. They reveal both some advantages and some disadvantages of SRM in comparison to financial compensation, concluding that there are other residual obligations that should be prioritized over SRM.

With the idea of solar geoengineering as an adequate way to satisfy a residual obligation undermined, Baard and Wikman consider various other types of residual obligation that might be more appropriate to pursue alongside mitigation and adaptation. These include (at a minimum) obligations to better communicate failures and to accurately assess damages and (more pro-actively) obligations to pursue CDR alongside more traditional mitigative measures.

Also considering justice through the lens of compensation, Allen Habib and Frank Jankunis look to the 'middle to distant future' (i.e. greater than 100 years) and evaluate different forms of climate engineering as potential forms of 'compensation' for the climate harms that are already built into the system. When considering capital transfer as the most typical form of compensation, Habib and Jankunis find it coming up short on multi-century to millennial timescales. Whether the type of capital being considered is financial, manufactured, social, natural or human, the authors find in each case various practical and theoretical obstacles (e.g. durability, commensurability, decay) that stand in the way of the successful transference of value from the current generation to the future. How might climate engineering as a form of compensation compare?

Even though climate engineering strategies presumably are intended to prevent harm from occurring before it can become something that warrants compensation, Habib and Jankunis suggest that various theoretical and legal views commonly consider the remediation of a future harm (or its cause) to be a preferable form of 'compensation' for a future generation to the transference of capital. They accordingly consider the two main branches of climate engineering as forms of compensation that 'pay forward'. SRM is found to suffer from some of the same forms of 'decay' through the generations as many forms of capital transfer. CDR, on the other hand, lessens damage, does not suffer from decay and pays back indefinitely. Furthermore, the moral character of CDR as a form of 'polluter pays' is also attractive given that the global community is likely to need to pursue a drawdown of existing atmospheric carbon dioxide even after emissions have been reduced to zero.

## GEOENGINEERING JUSTICE IN PRACTICE

Joshua Horton and David Keith build an ethical argument for researching climate engineering based on the stark reality of the climate harms now facing the world's poor. Though not created by these populations, these very real harms already bear down disproportionately on many of those living in poor nations. They argue that when comparing the climate policy options of mitigation, carbon removal, adaptation and solar geoengineering through the lens of both their near and long-term costs and benefits, the consideration of distributive justice 'entails a moral obligation to conduct research on solar geoengineering' (p. 80). This is particularly clear when the near-term interests of the poor are taken seriously.

Two arguments are commonly levelled against addressing the harms of climate change with solar geoengineering. Horton and Keith label them the 'Hurts the Global Poor' argument and the 'Shirks Responsibility' argument. Against the first, they point out that the evidence provided by modelling that solar geoengineering would create additional harms for the global poor is vanishingly slim, especially when multiple variables and all regions are considered. Against the second, they point out several flaws in the suggestion that solar geoengineering unfairly enables the rich countries to evade their responsibility for mitigating greenhouse gases. Evidence that the carrot of solar geoengineering causes people to lose interest in mitigation is sketchy and even if it did, the relevant question would be what sort of trade-off between near and long-term benefits is appropriate. Furthermore, Horton and Keith sense that the Shirks Responsibility argument tends to subordinate the need to reduce harms to the *a priori* preferences of its advocates for other climate strategies such as cutting emissions or even reigning in capitalism. It is clear to Horton and Keith that justice in the short term obliges the rich countries to conduct concerted research into solar geoengineering.

Christian Baatz and Konrad Ott argue towards the opposite conclusion. Much of the discussion of solar geoengineering proceeds on the assumption that dramatic mitigation is simply too costly or too challenging to happen in time. If this assumption becomes entrenched, the debate over the ethics of researching and deploying climate engineering is inevitably tilted. Pushing back against this assumption, Baatz and Ott argue that what they call 'fast and far-reaching' emissions reductions do not unduly burden a rich country such as their native Germany and thus remains a primary obligation, whatever additional strategies are adopted. Assuming that some harm is now unavoidable, they add that in addition to emissions reductions, certain additional compensatory duties also fall on high-emitting countries.

Anchoring their argument on the assumption that no individual ought to emit more than their historically weighted fair share of emissions, Baatz and Ott find—in keeping with the intuition of many climate ethicists—a substantial obligation falling on governments in developed countries for emissions reductions of the order of 60–90% over the next 50 years. They use a combination of economic, political and technological evidence to suggest such reductions put individuals in these richer countries nowhere near a 'sufficiency threshold' that would make those reductions unreasonable or unfair. They suggest CDR is quite likely to be required for a pathway that minimizes harms and even that SRM may under some circumstances be permissible. However, they deny the possibility of substituting these technologies for emissions reductions. They also deny that researching these technologies in any way reduces the primary obligation to reduce emissions. Since few countries are yet on a pathway where these 'fast and far-reaching' mitigation obligations are being met, they suggest consideration of climate engineering (CE) research currently lacks moral justification. By the end of their chapter, Baatz and Ott hope to have 'raised the bar for convincing justifications of CE research programs' (p. 102).

Jane Long is a noted expert in energy policy and was co-chair of the task force that produced the Bipartisan Policy Center's 2011 Report on Climate Remediation Research. Long clearly lays out the technical and economic obstacles that stand in the way of a quick transition to a low-carbon economy and suggests that climate engineering may be one of the tools required for making what currently looks like a very rocky road into a just transition. She presents climate engineering as essential to a 'strategic portfolio' of policy options that rising temperatures will demand. It is clear in her argument that she does not think SRM could ever be a replacement for strong mitigation. Yet she suggests that it will most likely be a necessary accompaniment and that certain steps should start being taken to prepare for that reality.

Long discusses two changes that will be necessary for a strategic portfolio that includes SRM to be enacted. One of these steps is cultural, the other is political. The cultural step requires shifting over to more widespread acceptance that humans have an active management role of major ecosystem processes to play in the emerging Anthropocene epoch (Waters et al. 2016). Accepting that role would open the door to more widespread and less-contested research of climate engineering. The political step is the formation of something like a World Council on Climate Engineering that would govern what Long anticipates to be an incremental drift towards intentional climate management. She envisions this incremental drift as likely to occur when regional attempts to respond to (or to pre-empt) climate emergencies become more frequent. The formation of such a council would be a prerequisite for procedural justice if future climate engineering moves towards implementation.

Teea Kortetmäki and Markku Oksanen become the first to tie the discussion of climate engineering into the discussion of food justice. They give two important reasons why this tie needs to be made. The first is that no solution to climate change is likely to be acceptable if it compromises food security. Food justice, which they define as 'securing the right to food and ensuring that food system activities … are fair in their distribution of benefits and burdens' (p. 121), is simply a ground-level condition for just climate policy. The second reason is based on agriculture's climate impact. Since the production of food creates 25–30% of greenhouse gas emissions (when land-use change and energy demands are taken into account), any solution to the climate problem is highly likely to require significant changes to the global food system.

Kortetmäki and Oksanen come at the link between agriculture and climate justice through three different lines of inquiry. The first line involves the possibility of agriculture being used as a climate engineering strategy itself. This might happen through genetically engineering crops to have a higher albedo or through designing agricultural crops to sequester carbon. The second line involves agriculture being transformed so that it becomes a dramatically less-carbon-intensive practice. The third line involves looking for the impacts on food production and food justice of non-agriculturally based methods of SRM and CDR—for example, stratospheric aerosols or direct air capture of carbon with 'artificial trees'. In each case, the authors consider the potential impacts of the strategy on food justice. At the end of the chapter they create a tableaux of the different options, their potential impacts on climate and their impacts on food justice and security. Their analysis provides an important reminder that the justice considerations of any climate strategy, whether climate engineering or more traditional mitigation options, will have to take into account the basic necessity of the provision of food.

## GEOENGINEERING JUSTICE IN FRAMES, MODELS AND SCENARIOS

Duncan McLaren analyses the existing discourse frames surrounding both climate change and climate engineering and finds a worrying trend. Borrowing from the work of John Dryzek, McLaren finds within climate change three types of common discourse which Dryzek had labelled 'Promethean', 'eco-modern' and 'green radical' (Dryzek 2013). He compares them to the frames currently found within the climate engineering discourse.

While McLaren finds the climate engineering technologies of SRM and CDR tending to fit within two different discourse frames—the Promethean and the eco-modern—neither of them connect comfortably with the green radical discourse, the only one that makes justice issues central. He suggests that climate engineering is mostly treated as a 'post-political' endeavour, offering little chance of justice being given due consideration. He suggests that if climate engineering were not given an artificially 'clean sheet' framing, where the only contrast offered is between climate engineering and unabated climate change, then there would be more chance of justice being taken up as a primary concern. While McLaren does not rule out climate engineering as part of a portfolio of climate responses, he suggests that keeping justice front and centre would helpfully focus attention on the salient issues in governance, research and funding that are most ethically relevant.

One of the commonest calls for justice in the geoengineering literature surrounds the need to ensure justice for those already most vulnerable to and simultaneously least responsible for climate change. Luwesi, Doke and Morrow employ a scenario planning methodology to look at how different countries on the African continent are likely to respond to increasing climate stress on water supplies. After establishing this 'base scenario', these responses are compared to how they might respond to a developed world climate intervention employing stratospheric aerosols, while keeping in mind a certain amount of uncertainty about the intervention's effects of water.

African countries are in very different positions to respond to the prospect of stratospheric aerosol deployment based on their relative water wealth and their varying national capacities to adapt and respond. Four different types of reaction are predicted from four clusters of countries. Each of these reactions bears on the prospect of climate justice for the populations of the nations involved. After identifying the potential responses to stratospheric aerosol deployment's burdens and potential benefits, the authors consider several different types of climate justice and injustice that are salient in each cluster of countries.

The authors know their projections are both speculative and broad, but the work provides two important reminders. First, Africa is a diverse continent with dramatically different ecological conditions, national capacities and political tendencies that might emerge when responding to a future climate intervention initiated by rich countries. Second, as the authors gently probe the territory for each cluster, it becomes clear that it is far too simplistic to suggest that a stratospheric aerosol intervention will either ameliorate or exacerbate climate injustice in Africa as a whole. Identifying different clusters of responses to potential future deployment makes possible a more nuanced discussion about the required adaptive, compensatory and capacity-building mechanisms that will be part of Africa's future. This includes the approaches to governance that might ease the arrival of these mechanisms.

Johannes Emmerling and Massimo Tavoni's contribution to the volume assesses the potential for integrated assessment models (IAMs) to reveal the justice dimensions of CDR and SRM. These IAMs place economy, energy, land use and climate components into a unified framework enabling the creation of scenarios from which it is possible to view the trade-offs that occur with particular climate strategies. While these are early days for the incorporation of many forms of CDR and SRM in IAMs due to significant uncertainties about costs, effectiveness and side effects, Emmerling and Tavoni sift through initial results and find certain instructive ethical lessons emerging.

While CDR is now widely agreed to be a precondition of a 2°C target, a target that likely already assumes an overshoot in atmospheric carbon followed by a drawdown, the models point out how this strategy shifts the burden for mitigating climate change from present to future generations. The degree of this shift depends on both the degree of discounting of the future that is employed and the degree of optimism about the technology and the global economy. As well as the potential for intergenerational injustice, the assumption of the availability of huge negative emissions later tends to also favour the high-emitting countries in the current generation since they are required to do less in the near term.

While projections of the consequences of employing SRM are hard to determine from IAMs because of current uncertainties, Emmerling and Tavoni find that the likely high degree of variability of SRM's effects between regions creates incentives for coalition building between those similarly affected. This creates knock-on challenges for governance and the risk of overprovision of SRM's goods. This makes SRM particularly risky from the justice point of view and places further emphasis on the need for governance structures that would avoid both noncooperative deployment and deployment that is not tied to significant mitigation and adaptation strategies.

It has long been appreciated that countries have different amounts to gain or lose through the deployment of geoengineering strategies to cool global temperatures. Richard Tol uses an economic model to estimate how geoengineering plus compensation of losers might work both efficiently and equitably. Tol analyses 27 sets of data drawn from existing studies on the welfare impacts of climate change for each country of the world and gets numbers for loss of welfare for a certain temperature rise relative first to per-capita income and relative next to the country's starting temperature. As one might expect, less is at stake for richer countries and less for countries that start off cooler. Tol then calculates two different global optimal temperatures that, on average, maximize welfare depending on whether countries are weighted by population or by GDP. He establishes the costs of temperatures falling above or below these optima.

What these numbers allow Tol to track is the different gains and losses in welfare for various countries under a certain amount of globally optimal cooling through geoengineering. If it is assumed that countries doing worse than optimal after this geoengineering deployment would have to be compensated in an economically efficient global regime, Tol can see how the money would have to flow between countries.

Depending on the type of starting assumptions, some interesting differences emerge. If we assume that a country is entitled to any benefits they might have gained from unbridled climate change and that they should be compensated for the warming they do not experience after climate engineering by those who gain more, then money generally flows from the poor to the rich. If, on the other hand, we assume that a country is entitled to the exact amount of climate change they would most benefit from and then compensate them for what they don't get with globally optimal climate engineering, then money generally flows from the rich to the poor. If decreasing existing global inequity is seen as a desirable condition of geoengineering deployment, then it is clear which starting assumptions need to be imported into any compensatory mechanism. Tol's analysis helpfully quantifies winners and losers under different temperature scenarios and highlights how the starting assumptions for a future compensation regime are absolutely crucial.

## CONCLUSION

By the end of the volume, the complexity involved in attempting to make comparative evaluations between climate engineering and other climate policies is abundantly clear. Simplistic suggestions that climate engineering would either reduce or increase climate injustice are unhelpful. Fortunately, as Augustin Fragnière and Stephen Gardiner's contribution makes evident, the choice ahead is not an 'either-or'. Almost all the authors agree that under no circumstances would a climate engineering strategy be even remotely plausible unless it were accompanied by substantial and long-range efforts directed at emissions reduction and adaptation.

What does emerge out of the second-generation analysis is that the portrayal of the bevvy of problems identified in the first generation of climate engineering analysis can start to take on a different hue when put into a more realistic context. The situation the global community finds itself in now is far from ideal. While significant ethical challenges still clearly attend climate engineering, the arguments of a number of the authors in this collection do not preclude the possibility that *some* form of climate engineering will make *some* contribution to climate justice in the future under certain highly constrained circumstances. Of course, the devil is in the details and these details are of rapidly increasing importance. Given the incendiary nature of the whole idea of climate engineering, this volume might serve as a reminder that the discussion ahead needs to be deeply contextualized, richly detailed and thoroughly democratic. It should also serve as a reminder that matters of justice are perhaps the primary consideration that should drive any discussion of climate change and any serious recommendations about how to tackle it.

## NOTES

1. Publication of this volume was supported in part by a grant from the Baldridge Book Subvention Fund in the College of Humanities and Sciences at the University of Montana.

2. Internet sources for these works include the Online Resource Center at the University of Montana (http://www.umt.edu/ethics/resourcecenter/default.php), the Oxford Geoengineering Programme Geolibrary (http://www.geoengineering.ox.ac.uk/geolibrary/index) and the Kiel Earth Institute's Climate Engineering News (http://www.climate-engineering.eu).

# BIBLIOGRAPHY

Axon, C., and A. Lubansky. 2012. 'Stripping $CO_2$ from Air Requires Largest Industry Ever.' *New Scientist*. https://www.newscientist.com/article/mg21428593-800-stripping-co2-from-air-requires-largest-industry-ever/.

Burns, Wil C. G., and Andrew L. Strauss. 2013. *Climate Change Geoengineering: Philosophical Perspectives, Legal Issues, and Governance Frameworks*. Cambridge, MA: Cambridge University Press.

Crutzen, Paul J. 2006. 'Albedo Enhancement by Stratospheric Sulfur Injections: A Contribution to Resolve a Policy Dilemma?' *Climatic Change* 77 (3–4): 211–20. doi:10.1007/s10584-006-9101-y.

Dryzek, John. 2013. *The Politics of the Earth: Environmental Discourses*. 3rd ed. Oxford, UK: Oxford University Press.

Fischedick, Manfred, Joyashree Roy, Adolf Acquaye, Julian Allwood, Jean-Paul Ceron, Yong Geng, Haroon Kheshgi, et al. 2014. 'Climate Change 2014: Mitigation of Climate Change. Contribution of Working Group III to the Fifth Assessment Report of the Intergovernmental Panel on Climate Change. Technical Report.' Cambridge, United Kingdom and New York, NY, USA: Cambridge University Press, http://www.ipcc.ch/report/ar5/wg3/.

Gardiner, Stephen. 2011. *A Perfect Moral Storm: The Ethical Tragedy of Climate Change*. Oxford, UK: Oxford University Press.

Hamilton, Clive. 2013. *Earthmasters: The Dawn of the Age of Climate Engineering*. New Haven, CT: Yale University Press.

Hulme, Mike. 2014. *Can Science Fix Climate Change: A Case Against Climate Engineering*. New York, NY: Wiley & Sons.

Jamieson, Dale. 1996. 'Ethics and Intentional Climate Change.' *Climatic Change* 33 (3): 323–36. doi:10.1007/BF00142580.

Lin, Albert C. 2012. 'Does Geoengineering Present a Moral Hazard.' *Ecology Law Quarterly* 40 (673): 673–712.

Long, J. C. S., and D. Scott. 2013. 'Vested Interests and Geoengineering Research.' *Issues in Science and Technology* 29 (3). http://issues.org/29-3/long-4/.

Morrow, David R., and Toby Svoboda. 2016. 'Geoengineering and Non-Ideal Theory.' *Public Affairs Quarterly*, 30 (1) 85–104.

Preston, Christopher J. 2016. 'Climate Engineering and the Cessation Requirement: The Ethics of a Life-Cycle.' *Environmental Values* 25: 91–107. doi:10.3197/09632 7115X14497392134964.

Preston, Christopher J. 2012. *Engineering the Climate: The Ethics of Solar Radiation Management*. Edited by Christopher J. Preston. Lanham, MD: Lexington Press.

Shepherd, John. 2009. 'Geoengineering the Climate: Science, Governance, Uncertainty.' London. https://royalsociety.org/~/media/Royal_Society_Content/policy/publications/2009/8693.pdf.

Svoboda, Toby, Keller Klaus, Goes Marlos, and Tuana Nancy. 2011. 'Sulfate Aerosol Geoengineering: The Question of Justice.' *Public Affairs Quarterly* 25 (3): 157–79.

UNFCCC. 2015. 'Adoption of the Paris Agreement.' http://unfccc.int/resource/docs/2015/cop21/eng/l09r01.pdf.

Wagner, Gernot, and Martin Weitzman. 2012. 'Playing God.' *Foreign Policy Magazine*. http://foreignpolicy.com/2012/10/24/playing-god/.

Waters, et al. 2016. 'The Anthropocene Is Functionally and Stratigraphically Distinct from the Holocene.' *Science Magazine* 351 (6269).

*Part I*

# GEOENGINEERING JUSTICE IN THEORY

*Chapter 1*

# Solar Radiation Management and Comparative Climate Justice

Toby Svoboda

Solar radiation management (SRM)—that is, any climate engineering technique that would reduce the fraction of incoming solar radiation absorbed by the planet—is a very interesting subject for distributive justice, or the type of justice that concerns how benefits and burdens should be apportioned among various parties. On the one hand, SRM techniques carry risks of substantial injustice to present and future parties, and ethicists interested in climate engineering have tended to focus on these possible injustices. On the other hand, SRM has the potential to manage current and impending injustices due to anthropogenic climate change, including risks of unjust harm to the global poor. This points to the possibility that, for all its potential ethical problems, a climate policy involving deployment of some SRM technique might perform better than other available options in securing distributively just (or minimizing distributively unjust) outcomes, at least in certain future contexts.

In line with Christopher Preston's argument in the introduction to this volume, I argue here that, although it is helpful to identify potential injustices associated with SRM, it is also crucial both to evaluate how SRM compares to other available options and to consider empirical conditions under which deployment might occur. In arguing for this view, I rely on a distinction between two types of questions: (1) whether SRM would produce just or unjust outcomes in some case and (2) whether it would be just to deploy SRM in that same case. The former question pertains to whether some distribution of benefits and burdens is morally good or bad, whereas the latter pertains to whether some action or policy is morally permissible, impermissible or obligatory. Although related, these two uses of justice do not come to the same thing. It may be that some climate policy involving SRM carries risks of substantial distributive injustice and yet is permissible or even obligatory. This is because, as I argue, considering what would be just to do should be comparative, taking into consideration both empirical conditions and the morally valuable and disvaluable features of alternative climate policies. To put this in a more intuitive manner, rightness and goodness can come apart— sometimes the right course of action produces bad outcomes. I will return to this distinction in greater detail below.

I consider a prima facie case that some climate policies involving SRM could come out well on such a comparative perspective, given that a commitment to dangerous climate change due to past emissions may limit the effectiveness of policies relying on mitigation and adaptation alone. Notwithstanding, the Paris agreement reached at COP 21, given the insufficient progress on cutting global emissions to this point, it is plausible to expect that, at some point in the future, all available climate policies will exhibit substantial inadequacies when it comes to securing just outcomes. In such cases, the morally disvaluable features of SRM might not be decisive in counting against the permissibility of deployment. In one sense of the term, we might think of this as a 'lesser of two evils' argument, for my claim is that SRM, despite serious problems, could be morally permissible in cases in which it compares favourably to all the alternatives. However, although not technically incorrect, using this language of 'lesser evils' potentially invites misunderstanding. Usually, 'lesser of two evils' arguments are broadly consequentialist in nature, claiming that some policy is to be favoured despite serious costs or harms, and this because its ratio of benefits to costs or harms is better than the ratios of the alternatives. My argument is quite different, because it does not involve merely weighing up the aggregate costs and benefits of various climate policies. Instead, my focus is on the *distributions* of such costs (or burdens) and benefits, and I argue that some policy involving SRM can be a just thing to do if its distribution of burdens and benefits is better than that of any alternative policy. In order to avoid the false impression that my argument hinges on aggregate costs and benefits, I will forego using the 'lesser of two evils' language.

## DISTRIBUTIVE JUSTICE AND CLIMATE CHANGE

Anthropogenic climate change raises important questions of distributive justice, because climate change will involve substantial benefits and burdens, as will any policy meant to deal with it. Importantly, these benefits and burdens will be differentially distributed on each policy, with some parties enjoying a greater share of benefits or suffering a greater share of burdens. Moreover, specific distributions will vary depending on what responses are adopted. Potential climate-related burdens are driven by many factors: an increased frequency of extreme weather events, sea-level rise, the spread of disease to new regions and so on. Potential benefits of various climate policies include curbing these burdens and perhaps avoiding them altogether. This could be achieved through mitigation of greenhouse gas emissions, adaptation to changing climatic conditions, climate engineering through either carbon dioxide removal (CDR) or SRM techniques or some combination of these responses.

Anthropogenic climate change and climate policy are matters of justice because, unlike natural phenomena, they are driven by human activity, such as the emission of greenhouse gases and the deliberate policy choices made by human societies. Those who suffer a disproportionate measure of the burdens of climate change are victims of injustice, for they have been wronged due to the actions or inaction of others. Such injustice can include actions that merely put others at *risk* of suffering climate-related burdens, even if those risks are not realized. In his recent work on climate change justice, Darrel Moellendorf relies on the following reasonable principle: 'If a person is especially vulnerable to very bad things happening due to the actions and omission of others, that person has a prima facie claim to have the vulnerability reduced' (Moellendorf 2015: 182). The idea is that imposing such vulnerability on others is unjust and that the victims of this injustice have a legitimate claim against other parties (e.g. high emitters) to reduce or eliminate the amount of vulnerability that has been imposed on them. By contrast, a victim of mere misfortune (e.g. a genuinely natural disaster) does not have the same type of legitimate claim, because no one has wronged her by either causing or culpably allowing the burden she suffers. Moellendorf argues that justice, therefore, requires cutting emissions, as doing so decreases the vulnerability of various parties to climate-related burdens. At the same time, justice requires that emissions continue to some extent, as they are currently necessary for the pursuit of many goods, including reducing global poverty via relatively affordable fossil fuels. As Moellendorf notes, how emissions entitlements get distributed is itself a matter of justice. For example, distributive justice might favour differential emission entitlements, with less-developed countries receiving larger entitlements than more-developed countries, the latter of whom have already benefitted from substantial historical emissions and can more readily afford large-scale transitions to renewable sources of energy.

## JUSTICE AS A VALUE AND JUSTICE AS A DUTY

Considerations of distributive justice can help us think about potential climate policies in at least two ways, corresponding to the two uses of justice I noted earlier, which I will refer to as axiological justice and deontic justice. First, consideration of distributive justice can highlight morally valuable and disvaluable features of such policies. This is what I call the 'axiological' (from the Greek *axiā*, meaning 'value') use of distributive justice, for it identifies morally good and bad aspects of such policies. On this use, justice is treated as a moral value. Second, considerations of distributive justice can help us determine whether certain climate policies are permissible, impermissible or obligatory. This is what I call the 'deontic' (from the Greek *deon*, meaning 'duty') use of distributive justice. On this use, justice is treated as a moral obligation, and we may speak of duties of justice as distinct from other types of duty (e.g. duties of beneficence). These two uses of justice are not entirely separable. Whether some policy is morally permissible, for example, will depend in part on whether that policy delivers morally valuable or disvaluable distributions of burdens and benefits. Nonetheless, these two uses of justice are distinct. To see why, consider a policy that involves some distributive injustice. Axiologically, this injustice is a bad thing. Deontically, however, the policy could be permissible in some scenarios and impermissible in others, because it is plausible to suppose that the permissibility of this policy will hinge on how it compares to other available policies, and this will differ across scenarios. For instance, in some cases there might not be a feasible policy that avoids distributive injustice altogether, and so it might be permissible to adopt the policy in question despite its (morally disvaluable) distribution. On the other hand, there may be cases in which there are policy options for securing distributively just outcomes, and in such cases a policy involving some degree of distributive injustice would be impermissible.

This indicates that a purely axiological use of justice is not enough to determine whether some climate policy ought to be pursued. To answer that question, we also need to compare the distributions likely to be entailed by competing policies while acknowledging that some of these will be more feasible than others (technically, economically and politically), and we should consider these policies as being pursued under conditions likely to hold in the future (Morrow and Svoboda 2016). While thinking about climate policy under idealized conditions might be useful for a variety of purposes, some policies might be infeasible or impossible to implement in the real world, such as extremely rapid emissions mitigation. As atmospheric greenhouse gas concentrations increase, we may lock ourselves into a future scenario in which some degree of distributive injustice is unavoidable, regardless of the policies pursued. In that case, it would be a mistake to suppose that any policy involving unjust distributions is impermissible, for that would entail that *no* policy is permissible in that context. Instead, in a bad situation like the one envisioned, a policy may be unjust in the axiological sense while being just in the deontic sense, and the latter because that policy involves less axiological injustice than any other option. I will discuss potential examples of this below, particularly in the case of hybrid climate policies that include SRM.

Most research on distributive justice and SRM has relied on the axiological use of justice, usually highlighting potentially disvaluable features of SRM deployment, such as disproportionately harming the global poor through precipitation change, shifting the costs and risks of SRM maintenance to future generations or undermining the moral solidarity needed for a long-term solution to climate change (Hourdequin 2012; Svoboda et al. 2011; Tuana et al. 2012). This is an important exercise, but it is not sufficient to tell us whether it is permissible to deploy SRM. To address that issue, we also need to know how an SRM policy compares to other feasible options. Now some might think that certain SRM policies are simply impermissible in and of themselves, regardless of how they compare to other options. For example, perhaps something about SRM deployment necessarily entails moral wrongdoing, such as its dramatic interference with natural processes (Jamieson 1996). But taking this view can quickly lead us into implausible territory. Most serious proponents of researching and testing SRM see it as a potential means to reduce risk associated with greenhouse gas emissions. If it turns out that, all things considered, some SRM policy likely would alleviate such risk, and supposing it would do so to a greater extent than other options not involving SRM, it may be a mistake to view SRM as impermissible, even if it violates some important moral norm, and even if violating that norm is ordinarily wrong. The problem is that anthropogenic emissions could create a future situation in which *no* feasible course of action manages to comply with such norms. This would certainly be a regrettable situation and one we ought to try avoiding if that is still possible. Unfortunately, we seem to be headed towards just such a scenario, and if we do find ourselves in that bad situation, the question remains: what should we do? In such a case, it is reasonable to compare the various alternatives and adopt the best (or least bad) option, using whatever standards are relevant—in the case of this chapter, standards of distributive justice. At the very least, given a scenario in which all options are morally bad in some sense, we would have moral reason to prefer the best (or least bad) of those options (Svoboda 2012).

Now perhaps we should view the situation just described as constituting a genuine moral dilemma, or a scenario in which all available courses of action involve moral wrongdoing (Gardiner 2010). Such a view is attractive because it captures the tragic nature of the scenario, but it is unattractive because it arguably undermines our moral reasons for preferring some course of action (e.g. the least bad one) over others. In a *genuine* dilemma, all options are impermissible and ought not to be pursued, hence the inescapability of wrongdoing. For this reason, framing a future climate scenario as a genuine moral dilemma has the unfortunate side effect of undermining moral action-guidance in such cases, including guidance on what concrete policies we ought to pursue (Svoboda 2015). Ethical theory is supposed to provide us with some guidance when it comes to thinking about how we ought to act, but it cannot do so in a genuine dilemma. While I lack space to argue explicitly for the view here, I think it sufficiently plausible to assume that, even in climate scenarios in which all courses of action carry moral disvalue and thus call for regret, there will be at least one course of action we are morally permitted to take, if only because that course is the last bad option available.

## WHAT SHOULD WE COMPARE?

I have suggested in the previous section that getting clear on whether SRM deployment is permissible in light of distributive justice requires comparing climate policies involving SRM to other options. This involves comparing the differential impacts of various policies insofar as they are relevant to the distributions of benefits and burdens. This requires us to think about what climate states are plausible to compare. Now one might question whether this is the most relevant issue—shouldn't we focus on climate *policies* rather than states, given that we have more control over the former? The reason for focusing on climate states is that distributive justice concerns states of affairs, namely how benefits and burdens are shared among relevant parties. Some climate states will be more just (or less unjust) than others, depending on their respective distributions. The ultimate question of this chapter is one of climate policy, and more specifically what types of policy are likely to minimize unjust outcomes, but we can't address that issue until we know something about the justice or injustice of the states of affairs those policies are likely to yield. I should note that, insofar as we are focused on states of affairs (rather than actions or policies), the relevant use of justice is axiological (rather than deontic).

There are many potential options for responding to climate change, all of which are likely to raise concerns about justice in the axiological sense. These include doing nothing (i.e. business-as-usual), various ways of mitigating anthropogenic emissions, adapting to changing climatic (and other environmental) conditions and climate engineering (including both CDR and SRM). Yet it is very important to remember that, with the exception of doing nothing, we are not bound to favour just one of these responses. Hybrid policies would involve two or more of the just-mentioned policy types. We may think of a hybrid policy as a portfolio of responses meant to complement one another. Such policies probably include the most attractive options from a justice perspective, both axiologically and deontically. None of the policy types just enumerated is a cure-all for climate change. Even very ambitious mitigation would not address the climate change to which past emissions have already committed the planet. But as Fragnière and Gardiner argue in this volume, it would be a mistake to suppose that these various policies are independent and exclusive of one another. For instance, coupling an ambitious mitigation plan with a plan to adapt to the expected changes in climate would be better from a justice perspective than mitigation alone, for the hybrid policy might offer helpful resources to those made more vulnerable by past emissions. There is also a reasonable case to be made for SRM if it is taken to be part of a hybrid policy. Many justice-related concerns about SRM lose much of their force when it is merely one part of a policy portfolio. I will turn now to considering the comparative merits and drawbacks of SRM in terms of distributive justice.

## Managing Climate Risks

SRM has the potential to avert or ameliorate various risks of harm associated with climate change. For example, by curbing global warming, SRM could keep sea-level rise within certain bounds, reducing the harm that vulnerable coastal populations might otherwise experience. The same holds for reducing other risks of warming-driven harm, such as the spread of diseases to new regions or an increase in the occurrence of more severe weather events. Although normally a moral good, *merely* reducing risks of harm is not itself a matter of distributive justice. Yet because climate risks tend to be more damaging to those with few resources for responding to them, such risks have a tendency to be distributively unjust by increasing the vulnerability of the global poor (Moellendorf 2015). This is why reducing risks of the above-mentioned harms is a matter of justice. If some SRM policy could ameliorate certain climate risks, it is plausible to expect it also to ameliorate the distributive injustice that tends to accompany those risks. For example, less-developed countries may have greater difficulty than more-developed countries in responding to a severe storm surge. Because anthropogenic climate change will elevate risks of such harm to less-developed countries, it will disproportionately burden parties within such countries, and this is plausibly viewed as an unjust burden. Insofar as SRM has the potential to reduce risks of this type, it has the potential to alleviate some of the injustices associated with climate change. This is an axiological justice-based consideration in favour of SRM.

It is true that SRM carries risks of its own, such as precipitation change in certain regions (Ferraro, Highwood, and Charlton-Perez 2014), which might impact agricultural productivity in potentially harmful ways. If such impacts disproportionately burden less-developed countries, then we have reason to view these impacts as unjust in the axiological sense. However, at least some of these risks could be lessened depending on how SRM is used. In the case of stratospheric aerosol injections, there is evidence that precipitation change would be responsive to both the latitude of deployment and the quantity of aerosols injected. For example, Southern Hemisphere deployment may carry a reduced risk of precipitation reduction in the Sahel compared to Northern Hemisphere deployment, and a smaller quantity of aerosols may have less impact on the hydrological cycle than a larger quantity (Haywood et al. 2013; Irvine, Ridgwell, and Lunt 2010).

Other justice-related concerns can be addressed to some degree by using SRM as only one part of a policy portfolio, along with long-term mitigation, adaptation and even CDR (Keith 2013). For example, there is a worry that deploying SRM could be distributively unjust to future generations, for it imposes on them the so-called termination problem, namely that a sudden cessation of SRM could result in extremely rapid global warming as global average surface temperature 'catches up' to the forcing of atmospheric green-house gases. But the concern is less acute if SRM is used only as a short-term complement to mitigation (and possibly to CDR as well). If atmospheric con-centrations of greenhouse gases decrease over time, then SRM can be drawn back as well, eventually being phased out entirely. While SRM is in effect, various parties would be at some risk due to the termination problem, and this may be unjust in the axiological sense. All else being equal, however, it is much better than deploying SRM in perpetuity, the latter of which would put many more parties at risk of unjust harm. In other words, here some form of SRM might be deontically just even if it is axiologically unjust.

A similar issue arises with ocean acidification, which is driven by increased concentrations of atmospheric carbon dioxide. A major drawback of SRM is that it would neither reduce nor curb carbon dioxide emissions and thus would allow ocean acidification to continue. This has the potential to create burdens for some parties—such as by damaging resources (e.g. coastal reefs and fisheries) on which coastal communities rely—while others benefit from SRM in the ways noted above. Once again, this problem can be ameliorated via some hybrid policy. Coupling SRM with mitigation and/or CDR could diminish the factors causing ocean acidification, and coupling SRM with cer-tain adaptive measures could reduce the burden that ocean acidification would otherwise bring. On this point, such hybrids are likely to yield states of affairs that are (in the axiological sense) more distributively just than an SRM-only policy, as the former have the tools to ameliorate the unjust burdens created by ocean acidification. This gives us some reason to suspect that such hybrid policies may be more just (in the deontic sense) than an SRM-only policy.

An additional option for assuaging the axiological injustice of SRM is to offer compensation to those who are unjustly burdened (Heyward 2014). Although there are challenges to crafting an SRM compensation scheme that is itself just—such as properly attributing particular impacts to SRM rather than natural variability in the climate and determining what parties are mor-ally responsible for paying such compensation (Svoboda and Irvine 2014)—this could go some distance in reducing the injustice of some distribution. I suggest this cautiously. Research on SRM compensation is just beginning, and so it is unclear how much of a contribution such compensation could make to alleviating SRM-induced axiological injustice.

None of the foregoing is to say that any hybrid policy including SRM is likely to yield a perfectly just (in the axiological sense) state of affairs. Even if SRM is part of the best option, it will still bring burdens (e.g. risks of harm), and those burdens and any benefits might not be distributed as they ought to be. Moreover, the non-SRM components of a hybrid policy might also bring unjust burdens, such as the economic costs of mitigation or adaptation. Now whether such costs would be axiologically unjust depends in part on what parties would be paying them. I do not think it unjust for more-developed countries who have greatly benefitted from past emissions to pay such costs (e.g. by subsidizing renewable energy or financing adaptation in less-developed countries), but the matter is otherwise if those burdens should fall to less-developed countries. Unfortunately, it might be the case that no feasible climate policy (hybrid or otherwise) can fully avoid all such injustices. But now it should be clear why the axiological/deontic distinction is both crucial and helpful, for it provides a way to acknowledge the real moral disvalue of certain distributions but without undermining our ability to act when all available options carry such disvalue. On the one hand, we can recognize that some state of affairs likely to be brought about by some policy includes morally bad features, such as burdening some less-developed country with the economic costs of mitigation. This is unjust in the axiological sense. On the other hand, we can simultaneously (and coherently) think that this same policy is morally permissible or even obligatory in light of our duties of justice, for it might be better (or less bad) from a justice perspective than the other options. In other words, pursuing some policy can be (deontically) just even if it is likely to carry some (axiological) injustice.

These examples indicate why, given a comparative approach to justice, it is important to consider the empirical conditions under which some climate policy is to be adopted, taking into account both how the policy in question is designed and how it is likely to play out in the actual world. The question is not whether SRM as such would be (deontically) just in some abstract sense. Rather, the question is whether some particular policy involving SRM would be (deontically) just given geophysical, political and social facts about the actual world. A policy that includes SRM but seriously strives to reduce risks of unjust burdens *might* be deontically just in some set of circumstances even if other SRM policies would not be deontically just in those same circumstances (Svoboda 2016). How this turns out would depend on the axiological question of what distributions of burdens and benefits are likely to be delivered by feasible policies, which are partly constrained by the possibilities afforded by the empirical conditions that happen to hold.

## Buying Time

By managing some climate risks and slowing planetary warming, SRM also has the potential to 'buy time' for achieving justice-relevant objectives. First, SRM might allow time for emissions mitigation (Wigley 2006). Even in the wake of the Paris Agreement at COP 21, it seems unlikely that sufficiently ambitious mitigation will occur quickly enough to avert dangerous climate change. SRM could be used to delay various (unjust) emissions-driven impacts, reducing the vulnerability of those under climate risk, while the world transitions to renewable sources of energy. Second, SRM could buy time for development that could greatly benefit the global poor. It should not be controversial to note that global economic benefits and burdens are not currently distributed in a just fashion, as wealth is concentrated in relatively few hands. This injustice could be alleviated to some degree through economic development, but this likely involves substantially increasing energy consumption in less-developed countries. A large-scale transition to renewable energy in the very near term does not currently appear feasible (technically, politically or economically) in less-developed countries, so such development requires increasing consumption of (relatively affordable) fossil fuels and their attendant emissions in order to combat energy poverty (see Long, this volume). Assuming that SRM would indeed be effective at managing much climate risk, increased reliance of fossil fuels in less-developed countries could be less harmful than it would be without SRM, all else being equal. Depending on how it is used, coupling SRM with a short-term increase in emissions concentrated in less-developed countries could be better from a distributive justice perspective than pursuing mitigation alone (Morrow and Svoboda 2016). Of course, there is a limit to how long this can go on without becoming a drain on distributive justice. Eventually, the unjust burdens of both growing emissions and SRM might outstrip the just benefits of poverty reduction and economic development. Nonetheless, pursued for a limited duration, SRM might offer a way for some countries to develop in the near term before transitioning to renewable energy on a large scale.

SRM might also be used to buy time for adaptation and CDR. Obviously, large-scale adaptation cannot be achieved immediately, especially if it requires massive infrastructure projects. Planning, financing and implementing such adaptation projects take time. Financing adaptation is, of course, a major issue for less-developed countries, some of which may lack the funds to pursue robust adaptation while also meeting the basic human needs of their citizens. By slowing the rate of warming, SRM could allow more time for such countries to secure necessary financing as well as to plan and implement specific adaptation measures. Delaying some climate impacts an extra decade or two could make a substantial difference in some cases, allowing time for substantial adaptation and thus reducing the unjust burdens that come into play.

Likewise, short-term SRM could also allow more time for research, development and deployment of CDR techniques. A major problem with CDR at present is its high cost (National Research Council 2015). Although the following is somewhat speculative, further research might yield cost-effective (or at any rate, less costly) CDR methods. It is possible that, with the extra time bought by temporary SRM, relatively affordable CDR techniques could be developed for large-scale use. Moreover, temporary SRM could also buy time for extensive implementation of CDR, effectively delaying some of the impacts of climate change while CDR is brought to scale. Without such extra time, unjust burdens might arise before CDR has any chance of averting them by drawing a significant amount of carbon dioxide out of the atmosphere. However, there are major concerns about CDR in general. Aside from high costs, there are also justice considerations about land use, such as using arable land for bioenergy with carbon capture and storage (BECCS), potentially driving up the cost of food or displacing vulnerable populations (Morrow and Svoboda 2016). It is important to note that I am not advocating any particular use of CDR here. My claim is only that SRM has the justice-relevant merit of potentially buying time for other measures. The climate policy that fares best in terms of axiological justice may or may not include a CDR component. That matter will hinge not just on features of the CDR technique(s) in question but also on the relevant empirical conditions and the features of other potential climate policies that are feasible under those conditions.

## CONCLUSION

I have argued in this chapter that, although SRM may impose distributive injustice, certain uses of SRM might nonetheless be distributively just. This may sound odd at first, but it becomes plausible if we distinguish axiological justice from deontic justice. SRM could have the morally disvaluable outcome of increasing the vulnerability of some parties to climate-related burdens, yet on the whole a policy involving SRM might be more just (or less unjust) than the alternatives, given SRM's potential to manage climate risk and buy time for mitigation, development, adaptation and, possibly, CDR. Accordingly, SRM might be permissible in light of our duties of justice, despite its potential to bring unjust burdens to some parties. To be clear, I am not advocating SRM deployment, but it is time for ethicists to begin broadening their consideration of SRM, attending not just to its potential ethical problems but also to its potential ethical merits.

# BIBLIOGRAPHY

Ferraro, Angus J., Eleanor J. Highwood, and Andrew J. Charlton-Perez. 2014. 'Weakened Tropical Circulation and Reduced Precipitation in Response to Geoengineering.' *Environmental Research Letters* 9 (1): doi:10.1088/1748-9326/9/1/014001.

Gardiner, Stephen M. 2010. 'Is 'Arming the Future' with Geoengineering Really the Lesser Evil? Some Doubts about the Ethics of Intentionally Manipulating the Climate System.' In *Climate Ethics*, edited by Stephen M. Gardiner, Simon Caney, Dale Jamieson, and Henry Shue. Oxford: Oxford University Press.

Haywood, Jim M., Andy Jones, Nicolas Bellouin, and David Stephenson. 2013. 'Asymmetric Forcing from Stratospheric Aerosols Impacts Sahelian Rainfall.' *Nature Climate Change* 3 (7): 660–65. doi:10.1038/nclimate1857.

Heyward, Clare. 2014. 'Benefiting from Climate Geoengineering and Corresponding Remedial Duties: The Case of Unforeseeable Harms.' *Journal of Applied Philosophy* 31 (4): 405–19.

Hourdequin, Marion. 2012. 'Geoengineering, Solidarity, and Moral Risk.' In *Engineering the Climate: The Ethics of Solar Radiation Management*, edited by Christopher Preston, 15–32. Lanham: Lexington Books.

Irvine, Peter J., A. Ridgwell, and D. J. Lunt. 2010. 'Assessing the Regional Disparities in Geoengineering Impacts.' *Geophysical Research Letters* 37 (September). doi:10.1029/2010gl044447.

Jamieson, Dale. 1996. 'Ethics and Intentional Climate Change.' *Climatic Change* 33 (3): 323–36.

Keith, David. 2013. *A Case for Climate Engineering*. Cambridge, Mass: The MIT Press.

Moellendorf, Darrel. 2015. 'Climate Change Justice.' *Philosophy Compass* 10 (3): 173–86.

Morrow, David, and Toby Svoboda. 2016. 'Geoengineering and Non-Ideal Theory.' *Public Affairs Quarterly*, 85–104.

National Research Council. 2015. 'Climate Intervention: Carbon Dioxide Removal and Reliable Sequestration.' National Academy of Science.

Svoboda, Toby. 2012. 'Is Aerosol Geoengineering Ethically Preferable to Other Climate Change Strategies?' *Ethics & the Environment* 17 (2): 111–35.

———. 2015. 'Geoengineering, Agent-Regret, and the Lesser of Two Evils Argument.' *Environmental Ethics* 37 (2): 207–20.

———. 2016. 'Aerosol Geoengineering Deployment and Fairness.' *Environmental Values* 25 (1): 51–68.

Svoboda, Toby, and Peter J. Irvine. 2014. 'Ethical and Technical Challenges in Compensating for Harm Due to Solar Radiation Management Geoengineering.' *Ethics, Policy & Environment* 17 (2): 157–74.

Svoboda, Toby, Klaus Keller, Marlos Goes, and Nancy Tuana. 2011. 'Sulfate Aerosol Geoengineering: The Question of Justice.' *Public Affairs Quarterly* 25 (3): 157–80.

Tuana, Nancy, Ryan L. Sriver, Toby Svoboda, Roman Olson, Peter J. Irvine, Jacob Haqq-Misra, and Klaus Keller. 2012. 'Towards Integrated Ethical and Scientific Analysis of Geoengineering: A Research Agenda.' *Ethics, Policy & Environment* 15 (2): 136–57. doi:10.1080/21550085.2012.685557.

Wigley, T. M. L. 2006. 'A Combined Mitigation/geoengineering Approach to Climate Stabilization.' *Science* 314 (5798): 452–54. doi:10.1126/science.1131728.

*Chapter 2*

# Why Geoengineering Is Not "Plan B"

## Augustin Fragnière and Stephen M. Gardiner

Geoengineering—roughly the 'intentional large-scale manipulation of the environment' (Keith 2000: 247)—to combat climate change is often introduced as 'Plan B': an alternative solution in case 'Plan A,' reducing emissions, fails. This framing is typically deployed as part of an argument that research and development is necessary in case robust conventional mitigation is not forthcoming or proves insufficient to prevent dangerous climate impacts. Since coming to prominence with the release of the Royal Society report in 2009 (Shepherd et al. 2009: v), the Plan B framing has proved popular with scientists, in policy circles and in the news media (Nerlich and Jaspal 2012; Luokkanen, Huttunen, and Hilden 2014). Though sometimes used to describe geoengineering as a whole, it is associated particularly strongly with stratospheric sulphate injection (SSI) techniques. Consequently, these will be our focus here.

In introducing this volume, Christopher Preston emphasizes the need for a "second-generation" ethical assessment of geoengineering that compares its upsides and downsides with those of mitigation and other options. We argue that the Plan B framing is particularly ill-suited to this task, because it oversimplifies a complex issue in a misleading and deceptive way. For instance, it highlights extreme positions, presents SSI as an alternative independent from mainstream policies, ignores the multiplicity of options available and neglects threats of morally indecent SSI in a context of ongoing political inertia. Such problems increase the risk of injustice. We are particularly concerned about the way the Plan B framing risks conveying an implicit hyper-optimism about SSI and obscures the need for ethical standards. One upshot of our analysis is that rather than a *comparative* assessment of mitigation and geoengineering, we should encourage a more *integrative* approach.

## FRAMING GEOENGINEERING AS PLAN B

**Frames**

Frames are "interpretive story lines that set a specific train of thought in motion, communicating why an issue might be a problem, who or what might be responsible for it, and what should be done about it" (Nisbet 2009: 15). Typically, they are expressed through the choices of words, labels, metaphors and examples used to talk about an issue. Such choices involve selecting what one takes to be the *salient* features of a given situation—the ones worthy of attention—and thereby excluding other (*non-salient*) features. As a result, framings of geoengineering have significant effects on our understanding of its aims and prospects, and our judgements about its acceptability (Scott 2012: 152–53).

Though framing is to some extent unavoidable, framing decisions raise important normative issues. Most notably, framing typically involves value judgements, yet those judgements are often implicit in, left undefended by, and made less visible through the framing device. Consequently, frames often become strategic devices when arguing for or against particular policies. For instance, Corner and Pidgeon report that describing geoengineering schemes by means of natural analogies—for example, comparing SSI to the effect of volcanic eruptions or casting direct air capture techniques as "artificial trees"—increases public support for them (Corner and Pidgeon 2014).

Despite its short intellectual history, geoengineering has been framed in numerous ways. In an analysis of metaphors from 91 news articles, Brigitte Nerlich and Rusi Jaspal found three broad recurring themes (Nerlich and Jaspal 2012). The first understands geoengineering as a *techno-fix* (e.g. "dimmer switch", "global thermostat") and is linked to the overarching metaphor "the planet is a machine". The second treats geoengineering as a *medical fix* (e.g. "chemotherapy") and is connected to the general metaphor "the planet is a body or patient". The third theme casts geoengineering as an *insurance policy* and includes the Plan B metaphor. This theme is associated with metaphors of risk reduction, management and control, and with the more general motivation of avoiding climate catastrophe.[1] Notably, the insurance framing of geoengineering encourages an argument by analogy: just as it is prudent to have an insurance policy, so it is said to be *prudent* and *wise* to pursue SSI, at least as far as developing an extensive research programe.

**The Insurance "Family"**

The insurance theme is typically understood very broadly,[2] so as to encompass a whole family of metaphors, including not only Plan B but also "back-up plan", "emergency measure", "lesser evil" and "last resort" (Luokkanen,

Huttunen, and Hilden 2014; Kreuter 2015). Though these various metaphors are often run together, in our view there are important differences between them. While we will not attempt (and indeed are not particularly interested in) a rigid classification, we do want to suggest that *sliding between* the metaphors has counterproductive effects on how people understand SSI, especially in the public sphere.

One general issue is that the metaphors typically differ in the *kind of defence* they suggest SSI offers against the failure of mitigation. For instance, compare the Plan B framing to conventional insurance. A standard insurance policy, such as fire insurance, does not aim to prevent an initial loss, but rather to *compensate* the victim financially once the loss has occurred. By contrast, when SSI is offered as Plan B, its aim is to *prevent* losses from occurring in the first place, or at least to reduce their magnitude, and through nonfinancial means.

This suggests that one important framing effect of running together Plan B and insurance proper is the misleading implicit suggestion that SSI might largely "make up for" climate-related damages. Notably, not only does SSI plausibly aim only at reducing negative impacts to some extent, leaving many actual impacts unaddressed, but it also brings on serious new risks of its own (e.g., of side effects or abuse). It is then risky and limited insurance, and in ways that strain the analogy. For instance, the offer of *risky insurance* may not fit how we usually think of insurance. This increase the risk of injustice.

Another general issue concerns how the various metaphors within the insurance family represent the *attractiveness* of SSI. Importantly, the Plan B language *implicitly promotes* SSI right to the top of the list of *insurance* (and other) strategies—as the next option after Plan A—over other, more obvious insurance options. For instance, arguably the closest equivalent to a conventional insurance policy against climate change would be something more like a global reconstruction fund or liability regime than SSI. Worryingly, understanding SSI as "Plan B insurance" in climate policy risks *suppressing or* "crowding out" such options as salient alternatives, and so undermines effective assessment and encourages injustice

In contrast to insurance proper, sometimes people speak of rival prevention measures as "insurance" in an extended sense, as a "back-up plan". Sometimes such references are at least partly humorous, and the humour involves the equivocation between compensation and prevention. For example, an action hero might refer to her Colt 45 as an "insurance policy", where the humour lies in the fact that she is foreswearing genuine (compensatory) "insurance" for a more radical, risky and aggressive form of prevention. Still, the extended sense need not be ironic. For instance, the Dutch sea defence is sometimes referred to as "insurance" even though it aims to prevent the impacts of sea-level rise rather than compensate for them.

One difference between the back-up plan and Plan B framings is that back-up plans are often employed only after several other approaches have failed. Consequently, the back-up plan is not necessarily the second most attractive option: it is often much less desirable relatively speaking than a plan B and may be much lower down on the desirability list (e.g. Plan Y or Z). Sliding between the back-up plan and Plan B framing obscures this difference in desirability.

Notably, the Plan B metaphor also typically suggests an *alternative* course of action that is *at least reasonably attractive* in a more absolute sense. Though in some sense suboptimal, a Plan B is more benign than an option one would take only as an "emergency measure", "lesser evil" or "last resort".[3] Whereas each of these suggests serious problems with the approach, in the sense that there is something grave, even desperate, about the option under consideration, Plan B usually does not convey the same (indeed, any) sense of misgiving or urgency. Plausibly, the idea is that even if Plan B is not able to prevent all losses, it is decently effective in preventing many or the most serious, and at least *reasonably approximates* what is achievable through Plan A.[4]

Some proponents of geoengineering emphasize this feature of the Plan B framing by insisting that SSI be regarded merely as a "second-best" option. For example, in resisting the lesser evil framing, Darrel Moellendorf maintains:

> It is useful to *distinguish* between a lesser evil choice and a second-best choice. One difference is that being in the situation of having to choose the lesser evil is never desirable. But because the second-best choice is better than all the others save the best, *choosing the second-best might not be particularly unattractive.* (Moellendorf 2014: 198; emphasis added)

He goes on to characterize SSI as the second best and Plan B, concluding:

> Preparing a Plan B often is the responsible approach, especially if there are good reasons to worry that Plan A will be unsuccessful. (2014: 202)[5]

Though our arguments have broader relevance, in the following we focus on this "second-best" interpretation of SSI as Plan B and argue that it is misleading and deceptive.

## Presuppositions

Our analysis is structured around the idea that the second-best/Plan B framing of SSI generally involves several important presuppositions:

1. *Distinctness*: A and B are clearly distinct plans.
2. *Independence*: Plan B can be carried out independently from Plan A.
3. *Exclusiveness*: There are (or have been) only two salient plans.
4. *Attractiveness*: Plan B presents a reasonably attractive solution to the initial problem.
5. *Relative feasibility*: Plan B is relatively feasible compared to Plan A, in the sense that it is less subject to the forces responsible for undermining Plan A.

In what follows, we consider each in turn.

## DISTINCTNESS

Let us begin with two background issues. According to distinctness, A and B are (a) clearly distinct and (b) plans. Yet both claims are contentious and misleading.

### Classification

To begin with, there are general issues of classification. Suppose, as is typical, that Plan A is equated with mitigation and Plan B with geoengineering. Unfortunately, it is difficult to differentiate geoengineering techniques from other policy measures, and attempts to do so raise complex scientific and ethical questions. For instance, geoengineering techniques are often divided into two forms: carbon dioxide removal (CDR) and solar radiation management (SRM). Yet the distinction between mitigation and CDR is controversial. For example, forestry schemes aimed at enhancing the uptake of atmospheric carbon dioxide by trees have traditionally been discussed under the label of *mitigation* by the UNFCCC and the IPCC, but are considered as CDR in the most prominent reports on geoengineering (Shepherd et al. 2009; Committee on Geoengineering Climate 2015). Similarly, there are issues about separating out adaptation and SRM. SRM encompasses a diverse range of techniques, including sulphate injection and painting roofs white to reflect more sunlight. Yet roof whitening is sometimes thought of as adaptation.

Such difficulties lead some to propose alternative classification schemes (Heyward 2013; Jamieson 2014; cf. Gardiner 2016). However, the key issue for our purposes is that framing geoengineering as Plan B presupposes some classification scheme or the other. Our approach is to sidestep this issue by focusing on just one paradigmatic case of geoengineering, SSI. Yet, as we shall see, this raises further issues for the Plan B/second-best framing.

## Plans Versus Technologies

The second background issue is that it is not clear that we should accept the framing of geoengineering as such, or SSI in particular, as a distinct *plan*. Arguably, considered by themselves, technologies are not plans. For instance, according to the *Oxford English Dictionary*'s primary definition, a plan is "an organized (and usually detailed) proposal according to which something is to be done; a scheme of action; a strategy". Consequently, a "plan" describes a reasonably well-thought-out programe of action more than a mere technology or technique.[6] One might even argue that labelling a technology a "plan" involves a *category mistake*: a logical error of classification in which an item is placed in a category in which it does not belong (e.g. describing the abstract number 1 as blue).

Plausibly, SSI and geoengineering techniques more generally are better seen not as plans in themselves but as tools whose development and implementation may or may not find their place in much more complex and comprehensive programs of actions that do count as plans. This approach is not just plausible in its own right, but also seems the most relevant to climate policy.[7] Consequently, in our view, geoengineering techniques should be considered as potential parts of more general schemes of action, rather than being framed as separate "plans."

Notably, rather than encouraging a merely *comparative* evaluation of mitigation and geoengineering, which characterizes them as separate options, this account points towards an *integrated* ethical assessment— "uniting in one system several constituents previously regarded as separate" (OED)—where SSI and other technologies are assessed as components of broader schemes of action.[8] One upshot is that, while issues of classification may remain of theoretical interest, they are not crucial to the main task at hand. Whichever broad classification of technologies one employs, the central issue is the scientific and ethical assessment of particular policy measures and mixtures thereof proposed as general competing strategies of action. Consequently, these background issues lead us away from a discussion of the distinctness of technologies towards an assessment of the independence of plans.

## INDEPENDENCE

The "geoengineering as Plan B" framing suggests that we are faced with two primary policy options: the first best (Plan A) is conventional emissions reductions; the second best (Plan B) is geoengineering, understood as SSI. At first glance, the most natural reading is that these present two mutually exclusive and alternative plans—emissions reductions *only* and geoengineering *only*—that can be carried out independently. At a bare minimum, since Plan B is to *replace* Plan A if Plan A fails, Plan B must not presuppose Plan A.

Unfortunately, this framing is seriously misleading.

## Highlights Extremes

First, the natural reading highlights the wrong views and thereby *lends credibility to extreme positions*. Most importantly, the position that we should pursue "geoengineering only" is exceedingly rare and highly controversial, especially among scientists.[9] Consequently, the Plan B framing misleadingly highlights as the salient "second-best" option for policy an extreme position that turns out to be both marginal and roundly criticized by most geoengineering proponents. As well as being unfair to more mainstream advocates, this is a dangerous form of climate (mis)communication in the public sphere.

## Misdescribes the Debate

A second problem is that the natural reading misdescribes what is at issue. Most geoengineering advocates refuse to see SSI as *any kind of significant alternative to* or substitute for emissions reductions, especially in the medium to long term. Instead, they argue that SSI is at best a "stop gap" measure to "buy time" for the necessary emissions reductions to occur. Consequently, they propose their so-called Plan B only to facilitate Plan A by allowing longer for its central goals to be realized, *not as a genuine alternative* to an emissions reduction strategy.

Indeed, many SSI advocates would make the stronger claim that some version of "Plan A" is really included as part of Plan B, as a *necessary condition for its acceptability*. In particular, they would defend the pursuit of SSI *only* as part of a policy that eliminates emissions over the next century or so, and some would defend SSI only if it were accompanied by serious emissions reductions in the short term (Wigley 2006; Caldeira 2013; also see Horton and Keith, and Long, this volume).

## Neglects Ethics

A third problem with the natural reading is that it *obscures* the strong ethical concerns about SSI that typically stand behind the more mainstream position and are central to the wider debate. Among other things, this obscuring *conceals a broad ethical convergence* of writers on geoengineering and is one way in which the Plan B framing encourages an unhelpful "for and against" mentality (Gardiner 2013).

Most notably, there is widespread agreement that SSI without mitigation poses particularly acute problems of international and intergenerational justice (Svoboda et al. 2011). For instance, as greenhouse gas (GHG) concentrations increase, "SSI only" would commit future generations to the use of ever-increasing amounts of sulphate aerosols to counteract the effects, unjustly imposing escalating risks on them and aggravating distributive injustices [e.g. perhaps through an increasing disruption of precipitation patterns over time (Committee on Geoengineering Climate 2015b: 48)]. Similarly, many believe that committing future generations to an *endless* technical management of the global climate system is itself unjust. According to this view, any ethical geoengineering scheme must include the possibility of being discontinued at some point. However, this "cessation requirement" can obviously not be met with ever-increasing GHG emissions and therefore rules out SSI without mitigation (Preston 2016).

We conclude that ethically responsible forms of SSI are not independent of other policy measures in the way the Plan B framing suggests. They cannot, and ought not, be implemented alone. Most notably, SSI does not seem to be a new or trump card that can be held in reserve to be played *in place of* other measures if those measures alone appear to fail. Instead, this alleged Plan B presupposes the success of "Plan A", at least eventually and probably also in the short to medium term. Moreover, the central issues are ethical as much as scientific or technical.

## EXCLUSIVENESS

The third presupposition of the Plan B framing of SSI is exclusiveness: there are (or have been) only two salient plans. Here, we argue not only that there are many more options than the framing suggests but also that SSI faces serious competition for the ranking of second-best, both historically and in the current policy setting.

### Multiplicity of Options

The first problem with exclusiveness involves the multiplicity of alternatives. First, there are many important policy options beyond mitigation and geoengineering (e.g. global reconstruction funds, economic retrenchment, population measures). Second, even within the category of "geoengineering", many different kinds of technologies might be considered (e.g. marine cloud brightening, direct air capture, BECCS, space mirrors). Third, there are also multiple possible realizations of each specific kind of technology. For instance, one might practice SSI at different levels (e.g. to offset different global temperatures), to realize distinct objectives (e.g. preserving precipitation patterns rather than suppressing temperature rise) or with competing regional implications (e.g. ensuring moderate temperature in the tropics, maintaining the Indian monsoon). Fourth, there are numerous ways to combine particular technologies with other policy measures, such as mitigation and adaptation, and multiple forms of these measures too.

As a result of this extreme multiplicity, it is seriously misleading to characterize the salient alternatives as "mitigation" (Plan A) versus "geoengineering (in general)" or even "SSI (specifically)" (Plan B). Instead, we should take an integrative approach to the relevant options. So, if we were to employ the language of plans at all, it might be better to speak of, for example, market incentives for clean energy, conventional regulation of power plants and large industry as Plan A, these plus moderate adaptation as Plan B, all these plus carbon capture and storage as Plan C and so on.

## Historical Inaccuracy

The second problem with the idea that there are (or have been) only two salient plans is that it seems historically inaccurate. Though characterizations of the evolution of international climate policy are likely to be contentious, most plausible versions would not describe SSI as part of the historical Plan B. To illustrate, consider two simplistic examples.

First, one might attempt a crude history based on broad policy types. For example, Dale Jamieson recalls that in the early days of international climate policy, "prevention"—measures aimed at avoiding climate change—was the preferred option, followed by "mitigation" and "adaptation" (Jamieson 2014: 201). Arguably, then, historically speaking, our best pick, the real Plan A,[10] was a voluntary and progressive shift to renewable energies, starting in the early nineties, after James Hansen told the U.S. Congress that 'It is time to stop waffling so much and say that the evidence is pretty strong that the greenhouse effect is here' (Shabecoff 1988). When it became clear that this preventive approach would be insufficient, attention turned to mitigation and adaptation.[11] On this crude story, one might describe the evolution as follows:

- *Plan A:* Prevention (early 1990s)
- *Plan B:* Mitigation (e.g. Kyoto)
- *Plan C:* Mitigation plus significant adaptation funding (e.g. Bali, Copenhagen)
- *Plan D:* Mitigation plus serious adaptation funding plus loss and damage funding (e.g. Durban, Paris)

Notably, this history renders the first plan to include SSI no closer than Plan E.

In our view, it is better to understand the evolution of international climate policy in a way that pays more attention to the basic political strategy rather than broad policy types. In particular, if we see a plan as an organized and fairly detailed scheme of action, we might see previous strategies for launching substantive climate action as failed plans. For example, consider a second possible characterization of the policy evolution:

- *Plan A:* Voluntary emissions stabilization (*covering the period up to 2000*)
  At the Rio Earth Summit in 1992, developed countries agreed to stabilize their emissions at 1990 levels by 2000.
- *Plan B:* Binding target approach (*covering the period up to 2012*)
  Faced with the failure of the voluntary approach, countries negotiated the Kyoto Protocol, where developed nations committed themselves to cutting their GHG emissions by 5% on average, relative to 1990, between 2008 and 2012.
- *Plan C:* Dual-track period (*covering the period up to 2020*)
  Negotiations in Copenhagen in 2009 failed to develop a robust second commitment period for Kyoto, and a distinct, more inclusive and "bottom up" strategy emerged based in the brief and hastily assembled Copenhagen Accord; though both "tracks" technically remained in place, the ambition is low and the focus shifted to developing a new approach for a post-2020 agreement.
- *Plan D:* Pledge approach (*covering the period up to 2030*)
  The "bottom up" strategy was subsequently developed in Cancun and Durban for the post-2020 period and formalized in Paris (2015) and Marrakesh (2016).

Notably, even on this better (though still simplistic) history, any plan that includes SSI again counts as *Plan E* or worse. Thus, exclusiveness—the claim that there are (or have been) only two salient plans—appears seriously misleading. There are and have been many more "plans", and those that include SSI come much later historically speaking than the Plan B rhetoric implies.

## ATTRACTIVENESS

This leads us to the next presupposition of the Plan B metaphor: *attractiveness*. Here we suggest that there are strong reasons to resist presenting SSI as "a reasonably attractive solution" to climate change, especially in the sense of constituting the second best.

## Moral Context

The first worry is that the moral context of our appraisal of geoengineering matters, and the history suggests that this is one of repeated moral failure, without which SSI would be unnecessary (Gardiner 2011, 2013). Therefore, in context, the Plan B framing (as opposed to, say, a Plan E, F or Z framing) paints a misleading picture of our situation.

First, it *sugarcoats a disturbing reality*. On the one hand, it obscures important facts. For instance, it fails to register the extent of past failure, presents SSI as "second best" when it is arguably way further down the list, and proceeds as if we could wipe the slate clean (forgetting intermediate failures). On the other hand, it draws our attention away from the morally salient fact that we appear to be asking ourselves a paradoxical question: 'what are we ethically obliged to do given that we are not doing (and not going to do) what we are ethically obliged to do?'[12]

Second, "SSI as Plan B" appears *morally and politically complacent* with respect to the challenge we face. For one thing, the second-best language obscures the importance of considering and confronting the deep and ongoing roots of political inertia, and especially how these might shape which policy measures are truly available, and so limit the prospects for ethically defensible SSI (see below). For another, it obscures the fact that if the threat of severe climate change emerges because of our moral failure, we may, as a matter of justice, owe the victims more than a risky and uncertain way out (e.g. compensation, reconciliation).

At this point, SSI advocates may respond that, no matter what happened in the past, the best options are now *de facto* unavailable and current circumstances oblige us to think outside the box of mainstream climate policy, past and present. In other words, though historically SSI might count as Plan E, for us here and now it is in effect our (new) Plan B *relative to* the currently available best option, which though historically Plan D has become *our current* Plan A.

## Competition

In our view, even if this response were persuasive, there would still be value in preserving the honesty of a wider (e.g. Plan E, F or Z) framing. Still, it is also worth pointing out that the Plan B narrative is a little too quick in suggesting that there are only two options left (Plan D and SSI), and thereby obscures other possibilities that are still on the table. In short, it is far from clear that Plan D is the last desirable plan that does not include SSI.

First, according to major authorities, the official international goal of keeping global temperature rise below 2°C is still within reach without recourse to SSI. For instance, the IPCC claims that there are multiple mitigation pathways that are likely to bring about that result (IPCC 2014: 20),[13] while the Royal Society states that 'decarbonisation at the magnitude and rate required ... *remains technically possible*' (Shepherd 2009; Baatz and Ott, this volume). 'Moreover, though Paris' enthusiasts believe that their "bottom up" Plan D is the best hope for achieving these goals, we should not simply assume that other approaches to mitigation (e.g. a global carbon tax, global constitutional reform) could not work or are less desirable than plans that include SSI (cf. Gardiner 2014).

Second, even if more radical methods may be required, SSI is not the only candidate for inclusion in a relative Plan B. Other policy measures (e.g. global reconstruction funds, consumption restrictions, population incentives, etc.) would need to be part of any sensible integrated assessment. Arguably, simply *framing* SSI as second best promotes it without argument, while submerging these more stringent and less politically popular measures.

## Implicit Utopianism?

Sometimes this competition from rival plans is obscured because the Plan B framing encourages a kind of hyper-optimism about SSI that amounts to utopianism. On occasion, some advocates presuppose ethically ideal forms of SSI in their arguments, such as those that would benefit everyone or maximally favour the world's poor, when it is questionable whether such interventions are feasible or at all likely to be socially and politically available, especially on the timescales envisioned. In other words, some arguments for plans that include SSI may rest more on the bare logical possibility of ethically ideal forms of SSI than on any closely accessible reality.

This worry gains credence when one considers the seriousness and wide range of candidate presumptions against SSI interventions, including (but not limited to) the current poor state of scientific preparation, the questionability of our ability to close that gap sufficiently in the time available, the high risks involved, concerns about control and domination, the expansion of the political to include the basic physical structure of the planet, the threat to natural values and the deterioration in our relationship to nature (Gardiner 2016). Such presumptions suggest that plans that include SSI are likely to be ranked lower than many alternatives.

Similarly, even though it seems probable that there are good arguments for factoring in some forms of geoengineering at some point, this need not involve selecting the most risky and ethically dubious techniques first. For instance, it seems plausible that, though some plan (say Plan E) may include CDR technologies, plans that include SSI ought to be pushed further down the list. Thus, for example, a plan including full-blown SSI coupled with serious CDR, mitigation and adaptation measures might be better considered Plan S than Plan B.

## New Threats

A fourth, and vitally important, worry exacerbates such concerns: SSI brings with it new risks, especially in the context of ongoing moral failure. For example, one such threat is that of parochial forms of geoengineering, such as short-term geoengineering "fixes" which defer the worst impacts of climate change beyond the lifetimes of the current generation (e.g. 50–100 years), but at the cost of *making matters much worse* for future people. This worry gives us a strong reason to resist framing SSI as merely second-best policy that, addresses climate problems in a reasonably attractive way that approximates other approaches, and especially "Plan A".

## Decency

The fifth worry builds on the others. Framing plans that include SSI as Plan B suggests a level of attractiveness that threatens to dissipate the further one descends down the desirability list. Indeed, even "Plan Z" may suggest a level of endorsement that should not be conceded without argument. In particular, it is easy to subconsciously assume that anything that counts as a serious Plan B or Plan Z *does not violate reasonable standards of decency*. Yet this assumption is questionable. Unfortunately, there is nothing about SSI as such—simply injecting sulphates into the stratosphere—that ensures this requirement is satisfied. Notably, it does not do so *by definition*. For instance, in the past, massive injections of sulphates from volcanoes blocked out enough sunlight to have serious implications (e.g. the 1815 eruption of Mount Tambora caused the "Year without a Summer", with severe impacts on global agriculture). Less dramatically, one can easily imagine unscrupulous, or just heavily biased, controllers of SSI measures using them to inflict harm on or dominate particular groups, including not merely their rivals but also vulnerable and unpopular minorities.

In general, the claim that SSI is minimally attractive, at least in the sense of not violating reasonable standards of decency, is insecure and requires defence. Arguably, this is obscured not just by the Plan B framing, but more generally by all the simple plan framings down to Plan Z.

One upshot is that providing a defence of any plan that includes SSI will require identifying relevant ethical standards. For one thing, *any responsible framing must signal the live threat of morally indecent forms of SSI*. Importantly, pursuit of SSI appears to involve a calculated gamble, especially in a setting of ongoing political inertia where there are serious risks of injustice.

Consequently, one can expect reasonable disagreement not just about whether SSI should be characterized as "second best" or Plan B but also about whether it passes any reasonable decency threshold of desirability, as even Plan Z might be taken to imply. For another thing, regrettably, it is necessary to consider other criteria of attractiveness—such as the morally indecent but still justifiable—and the issues they raise. (On both, see Gardiner unpublished.)

## RELATIVE FEASIBILITY

A last presupposition often (though not always) associated with the Plan B metaphor is *relative feasibility*: Plan B is less subject to the forces responsible for undermining Plan A, at least to the extent of not being undermined by the very same obstacles to the same or greater extent. By contrast, our central concern is that plans that include SSI are in fact subject to feasibility con-straints similar to those undermining mitigation.[14] This concern is especially pressing under some explanations for past climate failure,which suggest that plans that include SSI face the same obstacles.

### Institutional Barriers

First, consider institutional explanations. Olaf Corry argues that scaling up CDR so that it is effective would need global cooperation of the kind required by mitigation. He concludes: 'Plan B in this case appears more difficult than Plan A and would logically fall on the same political ground as mitigation' (Corry 2014: 5). Similarly, he argues that, though SRM methods (in particular SSI) do not require the same coordination for implementation, they would necessitate a global and long-term governance system, and so stand in need of an agreement that might be very difficult to reach (Corry 2014).

### Resisting Justice

Second, there are moralized explanations. One worry is that our inaction in the face of climate change and our recent interest for geoengineering share the same root. For instance, Gardiner argues that both stem from "the perfect moral storm," a nexus of three challenging features of climate change (its global and intergenerational dimensions as well as the lack of clear theoreti-cal understanding of its ethical upshots) that renders us vulnerable to moral corruption (Gardiner 2011). Most notably, Gardiner suggests that, just like mitigation but perhaps to an even greater extent, many forms of climate engineering require complex and morally demanding processes of justifica-tion to be deemed politically legitimate, where these include meeting serious requirements of global justice and community. Yet resistance to such require-ments is a major reason for past climate failures. Consequently, morally supe-rior (e.g. intergenerationally just) forms of SSI are very likely to be blocked by the very same social and political forces that defeated earlier unsuccessful plans (e.g. Plans A–P), leaving only more morally compromised forms as live options. Among other things, this suggests that *if one could make ethically decent forms of SSI more feasible, this may also facilitate more desirable approaches, and so render SSI itself much less necessary.* Again, the Plan B framing tends to obscure this important question of integrative assessment.

## CONCLUSION

This chapter argues against the common Plan B framing of SSI. In general, it claims that the framing encourages distortions of our ethical judgement by unnecessarily narrowing the variety of options available to future cli-mate policy and underestimating the relevance of past moral failures. More specifically, it identifies five presuppositions of the Plan B framing (distinct-ness, independence, exclusiveness, attractiveness and relative feasibility) and argues that each is seriously problematic in the case of SSI. Most notably, the Plan B framing: (a) highlights extreme positions; (b) presents SSI as an alternative to mainstream policies rather than presupposing them; (c) ignores the multiplicity of options, suppressing relevant alternatives; (d) risks utopia-nism; (e) neglects threats of morally indecent SSI and (f) is insensitive to the roots of ongoing political inertia. For such reasons, we conclude that the plan B language is particularly unhelpful when it comes to comparing geoengi-neering to other means to tackle climate change. One lesson is that rather than a *comparative* assessment of mitigation and geoengineering—which tends to depict SSI as a standalone solution—we should encourage a more *integrative* assessment that situates SSI within the wider context of climate policy as a potential part of more general schemes of action. Another lesson is that ethics is central to this task.

## ACKNOWLEDGEMENTS

Earlier versions of this paper were presented at Goethe University (Frankfurt), Purdue University, and the University of Leeds. We thank the participants. For particularly helpful comments, we are grateful to Catriona McKinnon, Christopher Preston and to our colleagues in the UW research group on geo-engineering, especially Thomas Ackerman, Alex Lenferna, Dustin Schmidt and Rick Russotto. Augustin Fragnière has benefited from research support from the Swiss National Science Foundation (Grant P300P1_161110). The views expressed are solely the responsibility of the authors.

## NOTES

1. Apparently, the "insurance policy" metaphor originates in a 1977 article by Freeman Dyson (Scott 2012).

2. Some writers use "Plan B" and "insurance policy" interchangeably (Nerlich and Jaspal 2012; Scott 2012).

3. Cf. "emergency planetary device" (Scott 2012); "lesser evil" (cf. Gardiner 2010 2011).

4. For example Catriona Mackinnon reminds us that it is sometimes connected with the more specific metaphor "safety net".

5. One particularly troubling slide between insurance metaphors is that from a risky and troubling course of action ("emergency measure", "last resort") to a merely suboptimal (but otherwise reasonably attractive) Plan B or "second best".

6. For current purposes, a minimal and relatively uncontroversial characterization seems sufficient. For a more elaborate conception, see Bratman (1987).

7. "Plan" can be understood "more weakly" as "a method or way of proceeding" (OED). Still, even this is more than a technology (e.g. I might have a gun but not a plan; I may not even intend to use it).

8. Cf. the scientific notion of "integrated assessment" (IPCC 2014, 124)

9. Though a few appear to suggest that SSI could replace emissions reductions (e.g. perhaps Levitt and Dubner 2009, 105), the more common extreme position is that SRM might enable us to *postpone* the needed shift towards renewable energies 'while we wait for truly efficient and affordable green-energy technologies to come on line' (Lomborg 2010).

10. Interestingly, an early official document about climate change, the President's Science Advisory Committee's report of 1965, does not even mention mitigation as a potential solution but emphasizes SRM instead. Therefore, perhaps the true "Plan A" was: "wait and see (but ultimately consider SRM)".

11. As Jamieson observes, subsequent science revealed prevention was not really possible even then; still, historically speaking, it was the initial plan.

12. See especially Wayne's Folly (Gardiner 2013).

13. However, many IPCC pathways include so-called "negative emissions" technologies (Anderson 2015).

14. SSI is also currently relatively less technically feasibility than mainstream mitigation and adaptation techniques.

## BIBLIOGRAPHY

Anderson, Kevin. 2015. 'Duality in Climate Science.' *Nature Geoscience* 8 (12): 898–900.

Bratman, Michael E. 1987. 'Plans and Practical Reasoning.' In *Intention, Plans, and Practical Reason*, edited by Michael E. Bratman, 28–49. Harvard University Press.

Caldeira, Ken. 2013. 'We Need Some Symptomatic Relief.' *Earth Island Journal*, April, 1–2.

Committee on Geoengineering Climate. 2015a. 'Climate Intervention: Carbon Dioxide Removal and Reliable Sequestration'. National Research Council.

Committee on Geoengineering Climate. 2015b. 'Climate Intervention: Reflecting Sunlight to Cool Earth.' National Research Council.

Corner, Adam, and Nick Pidgeon. 2014. 'Like Artificial Trees? The Effect of Framing by Natural Analogy on Public Perceptions of Geoengineering.' *Climatic Change* 130 (3): 425–438.

Corry, Olaf. 2014. 'Questioning the plan-B Framing of Climate Engineering: Political Feasibility and Emergency Measures.' *Presented at the CEC Conference, Berlin.*

Gardiner, Stephen M. 2010. 'Is 'Arming the Future' with Geoengineering Really the Lesser Evil? Some Doubts about the Ethics of Intentionally Manipulating the Climate System.' In *Climate Ethics: Essential Readings*, edited by Stephen M. Gardiner, Simon Caney, Dale Jamieson, and Henry Shue, 284–312. New York: Oxford University Press

———. 2011. *A Perfect Moral Storm: The Ethical Tragedy of Climate Change*. New York: Oxford University Press.

———.2013. 'Geoengineering and Moral Schizophrenia.' *In Climate Change Geoengineering: Philosophical Perspectives, Legal Issues, and Governance Frameworks*, edited by Wil Burns and Andrew Strauss, 11–38. Cambridge MA: Cambridge University Press.

_____. 2014. 'A Call for a Global Constitutional Convention focused on Future Generations', *Ethics and International Affairs* 28.3: 299–315.

———. 2016. 'Geoengineering: Ethical Questions for Deliberate Climate Manipulators.' In *The Oxford Handbook on Environmental Ethics*, edited by Stephen Gardiner and Allen Thompson. Oxford: Oxford University Press.

———. Unpublished. 'If a Climate Catastrophe is Possible, is Everything Permitted?' Paper presented at University of Melbourne, 2014.

Heyward, Clare. 2013. 'Situating and Abandoning Geoengineering: A Typology of Five Responses to Dangerous Climate Change.' *PS: Political Science & Politics* 46 (1): 23–27.

IPCC. 2014. *Climate Change 2014: Synthesis Report.* Edited by R. K. Pachauri and L. A. Meyer. Geneva, Switzerland.

Jamieson, Dale. 2014. *Reason in a Dark Time*. New York: Oxford University Press.

Keith, David. 2000. 'Geoengineering: History and Prospect.' *Annual Review of Energy and the Environment* 245–84.

Kreuter, Judith. 2015. 'Technofix, Plan B or Ultima Ratio?' *Institute for Science, Innovation and Society, Occasional Paper* 1–51.

Levitt, Steven D., and Stephen J. Dubner. 2009. *SuperFreakonomics*. New York: Harper Collins.

Lomborg, Bjorn. 2010. 'Geoengineering: A Quick, Clean Fix?' *Time*, November 14.

Luokkanen, M., S. Huttunen, and M. Hilden. 2014. 'Geoengineering, News Media and Metaphors: Framing the Controversial.' *Public Understanding of Science* 23 (8): 966–81.

Moellendorf, Darrel. 2014. *The Moral Challenge of Dangerous Climate Change: Values, Poverty, and Policy*. New York: Cambridge University Press.

Nerlich, Brigitte, and Rusi Jaspal. 2012. 'Metaphors We Die By? Geoengineering, Metaphors, and the Argument From Catastrophe.' *Metaphor and Symbol* 27 (2): 131–47.

Nisbet, Matthew C. 2009. 'Communicating Climate Change: Why Frames Matter for Public Engagement.' *Environment* 51 (2): 12–23.

Preston, Christopher J. 2016. 'Climate Engineering and the Cessation Requirement: The Ethics of a Life-Cycle.' *Environmental Values* 25 (1): 1–28.

Scott, Dane. 2012. 'Insurance Policy or Technological Fix? The Ethical Implications of Framing Solar Radiation Management.' In *Engineering the Climate: The Ethics of Solar Radiation Management*, edited by Christopher J. Preston, 151–68. Lanham: Lexington Books.

Shabecoff, Philip. 1988. 'Global Warming Has Begun, Expert Tells Senate.' *The New York Times*, June 24.

Shepherd, John et al. 2009. 'Geoengineering the Climate: Science, Governance and Uncertainty'. The Royal Society, London.

Svoboda, Toby, Klaus Keller, Marlos Goes, and Nancy Tuana. 2011. 'Sulfate Aerosol Geoengineering: The Question of Justice.' *Public Affairs Quarterly* 25 (3): 157–80.

Wigley, T. M. L. 2006. 'A Combined Mitigation/Geoengineering Approach to Climate Stabilization.' *Science* 314 (5798): 452–54.

*Chapter 3*

# Justice, Recognition and Climate Change

## Marion Hourdequin

For decades, much of the debate surrounding climate ethics and climate justice has focused on emissions reductions. Should there be a cap on global greenhouse gas emissions? Where should the cap be set? And how should the emissions reductions needed to meet that cap be distributed among nations?

These are important—in fact, critical—questions. However, they focus on just one dimension of justice, having to do with how the burdens of mitigating climate change are distributed. Issues of distributive justice have played a similarly central role in discussions of climate adaptation. From the perspective of distributive justice, we can ask how the costs of adaptation should be divided among (or within) nations. For example, should wealthy, high-emitting countries such as the United States provide adaptation assistance to less-developed countries? If so, how much?

Again, these are critical questions. However, they raise further questions about *process*: Who decides what is fair and just in distributing climate burdens and benefits? How are various voices expressed and incorporated into climate decisions? These latter questions fall under the umbrella of procedural justice, which focuses on the processes by which climate governance mechanisms are discussed, developed and implemented. A key element of procedural justice is participatory justice—based on the idea that people should have fair opportunities to participate in and shape the institutions, policies and procedures that affect them. When protestors demonstrate outside the official UN climate negotiations or when small island states bind together to establish a coalition that represents their interests and perspectives, they are seeking not only just outcomes but also just processes that incorporate under-represented voices in climate policy and planning.

Attention to participatory justice in environmental decision-making has expanded significantly in recent decades. In the United States, the National

Environmental Policy Act (1969) formalized procedures for public engagement in federal environmental decisions and increased transparency in these decisions. Similar laws and policies exist in many other nations and at state and local levels. Additionally, environmental decision-making often incorporates collaborative processes involving multiple stakeholders. Lastly, new models of scientific research have been developed that engage stakeholders throughout the research process (Lemos and Morehouse 2005: 61). These approaches challenge linear models of science and policy, where scientists provide the knowledge and policymakers then use it to make decisions (Beck 2011, Lemos and Morehouse 2005, Stirling 2008).

Interactive research models, collaboration and increased transparency in environmental decisions all reflect greater attention to public engagement and represent important steps towards participatory justice. Yet not all areas of climate policy incorporate robust forms of engagement or take account of genuine diversity in cultural perspectives and values. The aim of this chapter is to argue that the concept of *recognition* provides an important lens through which to evaluate and improve participatory processes in three domains: climate mitigation, climate adaptation and climate engineering. In developing the analysis, the chapter shows how each of these domains raises challenges for inclusive participation, and it draws on the idea of *participatory parity* (Fraser 2000) to articulate an ideal towards which participatory processes should aim. The ideal of participatory parity stresses the importance of engaging all constituents as peers with equal standing in deliberative processes. Ultimately, the analysis reveals that although participatory parity is lacking in all three domains, recognitional concerns are particularly acute in relation to global-scale geoengineering research and planning.

As discussed below, recognition is a dimension of justice that is closely linked to both distributive and participatory justice. Participatory justice cannot be achieved in the absence of recognition, because without recognition, the participation of some individuals or groups is hindered: these participants lack the opportunity to fully express their points of view, or their perspectives are not fully taken up and considered, or both (Schlosberg 2007, Figueroa 2011, Whyte 2011). What's more, failures in participatory justice often contribute to failures in distributive justice. This is because participation plays a key role in identifying what goods need to be distributed fairly and creates greater accountability in decisions that determine distributive outcomes. Without robust participation that treats all parties as equal partners in deliberation, distributive decisions may reflect culturally biased assumptions about the importance of some goods, such as economic opportunities, as the expense of others, such as the maintenance of traditional lifeways (Tsosie 2007). Thus, the development of institutions and policies that incorporate recognition are needed to support both procedural and distributive justice, and recognition is a critical component of climate justice as a whole.

## RECOGNITION'S ROLE IN JUSTICE

The concept of recognition is rooted in the idea of mutual respect as foundational for human life, interaction and community. Paddy McQueen (2015) describes recognition as 'the act of acknowledging or respecting another being' and argues that genuine autonomy for individuals and groups depends on forms of dialogue and interaction that affirm the value of others' distinct perspectives. This notion of recognition can be translated to the political arena in a formulation of recognition justice offered by Kyle Powys Whyte (2011: 200):

> Recognition justice requires that policies and programmes must meet the standard of fairly considering and representing the cultures, values, and situations of all affected parties.

At its core, recognition emphasizes the importance of respect and mutual acknowledgement in establishing just processes and outcomes. This, in turn, requires respect and acknowledgement of difference. Recognition therefore calls for receptivity and openness rather than imposition and presupposition. From an institutional perspective, recognition focuses on the ways in which the vulnerable and marginalized garner lesser status in the moral community, and seeks to address 'malrecognition as a cultural and institutional form of injustice' (Schlosberg 2007: 16).

Nancy Fraser's idea of participatory parity provides an important way of understanding recognition's importance for participatory justice. Fraser argues that 'it is unjust that some individuals and groups are denied the status of full partners in social interaction simply as a consequence of institutionalized patterns of cultural value ... which disparage their distinctive characteristics or the distinctive characteristics assigned to them' (Fraser and Honneth 2003: 29). To counter this injustice, participatory parity requires that institutions and participatory processes provide equal standing and respect for all participants (Fraser and Honneth 2003: 36).

For climate policy, the design of participatory processes should reflect the breadth of climate change's reach. Although the scope and scale of the climate problem make it difficult to design participatory processes in which every individual has a direct say, to honour the spirit of participatory parity requires that all stakeholders be represented in climate policy dialogues and that participatory processes consider fairly the perspectives of minority groups, vulnerable populations, indigenous peoples and subsistence-based cultures.

Participatory parity requires access to certain basic goods, and for this reason, it is intertwined with distributive justice (Fraser and Honneth 2003). Inequalities that block participatory parity are unjust: lack of access to education, employment or a basic level of financial security impedes people's ability to engage as peers in social decisions (Fraser and Honneth 2003: 36). When applied to collectives, the distributive condition on participatory parity demands that participant groups have access to the resources—such as time, knowledge, technology, education and money—needed to act as equal partners in policy processes.

Access to key resources is needed for participatory parity, but so are social norms that enable participation. Thus, it is critical to dismantle 'institutionalized value patterns that deny some people the status of full partners in interaction' (Fraser and Honneth 2003: 36). For example, if dominant gender norms encourage women to be demure and agreeable and to avoid challenging authority, then these norms will undermine women's capacity to engage as peers in decision-making processes. Recognition requires the revision or elimination of such disabling norms. At the collective level, recognition would question norms that privilege certain cultural orientations—such as those that are cosmopolitan, economically oriented, future focused and highly mobile—over others, such as those that are more strongly place based.

Often, the ways in which recognition and participatory parity are compromised in decision-making processes go unnoticed. When decision processes provide formal opportunities for input from all affected parties, it is easy to think that participatory justice has been achieved. However, the concepts of recognition and participatory parity provide lenses through which deficiencies in participatory justice can be more easily identified and addressed.

To take just one example from outside the climate arena, the work of Danielle Endres (2012) shows how the participatory processes involved in the evaluation of Yucca Mountain, Nevada, as a possible nuclear waste repository reflect deficiencies in recognition and participatory parity. Here, the perspectives of the Shoshone and Paiute tribes—who have cultural and spiritual connections with Yucca Mountain—were formally included, yet marginalized. Federal officials were well prepared to consider and address concerns regarding health and environmental risks. However, the indigenous tribes' core objection—that a waste site in Yucca Mountain would desecrate and destroy an important part of their homeland, regardless of whether environmental and health risks were well managed—simply did not compute in the Department of Energy's (DOE) calculus, which emphasized quantitative risks (Endres 2012). According to Endres's analysis, the DOE implicitly privileged certain technocratic values; thus, participation processes produced a fundamental asymmetry between the U.S. government and the tribes, such that the Shoshone and Paiute concerns lacked full status in the debate.

One important lesson from this case is that certain concerns may be invisible to those who establish participatory and decision-making processes. Thus, even if well intentioned, these processes may marginalize, exclude or devalue certain individuals, groups, values or points of view. In this case, federal officials took seriously risks associated with radioactive leakage and associated health concerns; however, they did not develop a process well equipped to consider spiritual risks, or risks to identity, cultural heritage and sense of place. This likely resulted because the risks of greatest concern to the dominant culture focused on environmental pollution and human (physical) health, and not on the issues of concern to the tribes, and because the government's quantitative risk framework could not easily accommodate the tribes' cultural and spiritual values. In this case, the tribes' concerns were not easily quantified and measured; in other cases, quantitative risk analysis may be helpful in addressing the concerns of indigenous peoples, but require attention to diverse lifeways in order to be effectively employed.

## RECOGNITION AND CLIMATE CHANGE

Even in cases involving relatively few stakeholders and local or regional scales, recognition can be hard to achieve. Climate change poses special challenges for recognition, however, because it involves both immediate and long-term timescales along with spatial scales from local to global and affects every inhabitant of the planet. Although international climate negotiations involve representatives from many different nations and groups across the world, representation does not guarantee recognition.

Taking recognition seriously would encourage a deeper dialogue about the principles of distributive justice and about what climate policy aims to distribute. It might prompt more careful thought about how climate change interacts with diverse cultures and ways of life, such that climate losses and vulnerabilities would not be reduced to economic losses and vulnerabilities (Preston 2015, McShane 2015). Additionally, it would require greater engagement with the perspectives and needs of those who lack significant political, economic and cultural power. Although the need for recognition cuts across the three domains of mitigation, adaptation and geoengineering, the concerns take different forms in each case. For that reason, I consider each domain separately before turning to some detailed recommendations in an emerging area of concern, governance of research and possible deployment of global-scale solar radiation management. Considering recognition in relation to mitigation, adaptation and geoengineering not only illuminates distinct concerns in each domain but can also reveal common themes and key interactions. Such interactions are important, because failures or successes of justice in one domain may affect those in others.

## Mitigation

The risks and costs of misrecognition are likely to be greatest where there are significant asymmetries in power, considerable background injustices and important yet divergent interests at stake. All of these conditions exist in relation to climate change. Nevertheless, widespread international consensus has emerged on the need to reduce net greenhouse gas emissions in order to mitigate climate change. Thus, the greatest concerns for recognition in mitigation arise not so much from the question of *whether* to mitigate, but *how* to do it. When national and international targets translate into actions on the ground, how does that affect various communities and groups, and to what extent are their views taken into account?

To take just one example, as coal is phased out as an energy source, what opportunities are being developed to retrain miners with livelihoods tied to this industry? Or to take another, do international carbon markets that incentivize development projects to enhance carbon sinks—such as tree planting or alternative agricultural techniques—adequately consider the perspectives of local people? What forms of control do local people have over these projects, and how do they affect social and cultural dynamics?

In one African case study documented by Betsy Beymer-Ferris and Thomas Bassett (2012), the interests and livelihoods of local people were devalued in Tanzania's Rufiji Delta, as the Tanzanian government and the World Wildlife Foundation (WWF) collaborated to restore mangrove forests as part of the international Reduced Emissions from Deforestation and Degradation (REDD+) programme. Although many of the delta's mangrove forests ostensibly operated under joint management by local people and government agencies, in practice, local people had limited control. As part of the REDD+ project, the lead government agency—the Forestry and Beekeeping Division (FBD) of Tanzania's Ministry of Natural Resources and Tourism—established plans to relocate rice farmers out of the delta in order to conserve and restore mangroves in the area. The WWF–FBD plan relied on little input from local people, and Beymer-Ferris and Bassett argue that it employed a problematic environmental history that failed to acknowledge more than a century of rice cultivation in the delta on a shifting mosaic of agricultural lands. Instead, the plan constructed a conservation narrative that framed long-standing subsistence land uses as illegal and destructive. This is particularly troubling, since 'REDD+ sees decentralization of forest resource management as the key to empowering local communities' —yet in this case, the local Warufiji people had 'very limited representation with accountability and reduced access to significant material resources' (Beymer-Ferris and Bassett 2012: 340). This case illustrates both the way in which international mitigation efforts may shift burdens onto vulnerable populations and how even well-intentioned initiatives need scrutiny to ensure recognition and inclusion of local people.

In sum, recognition requires greater attention to how mitigation is achieved on the ground and how mitigation efforts affect diverse groups, with diverse values and lifeways. Explicit attention to recognition would highlight the ways in which the consensus on the need to mitigate can obscure important questions about the specific strategies used to achieve it.

## Adaptation

Turning to adaptation, the case for recognition comes further into focus. Here, we can clearly see the importance of scale and the variety of approaches needed for adaptation. Whereas carbon dioxide concentrations in the atmosphere are often summed up in a single number, adaptation calls to mind the diverse ways in which climate change impacts different parts of the planet. Coastal adaptation requires different approaches than inland adaptation; adaptation to drought will look different from adaptation to more intense storms. However, physical or environmental contexts alone can't capture the full diversity of adaptation needs; cultural contexts and relationships to place are crucial as well (Adger et al. 2009). This is where recognition can play a critical role in challenging dominant assumptions about what adaptation requires and in questioning the adequacy of expert-driven adaptation policies that fail to engage local communities. Without recognition, adaptation can compound or reinforce existing vulnerabilities and further exclude marginalized voices in climate policy.

In conceptual and empirical work, geographer Neil Adger and colleagues (see, e.g. Adger et al. 2006, 2009, 2011) highlight how adaptation planning can overlook diverse cultural interests and values, and may 'consolidate or exacerbate current vulnerabilities rather than reduce them' (Adger, Paavola and Huq 2006: 4). Such failures have multiple sources. They include:

1. Assuming parochial conceptions of value. For example, approaches to adaptation that focus only on meeting basic needs such as food and shelter without considering other dimensions of life quality such as attachments to place, religious and cultural traditions, and livelihoods will miss critical dimensions of adaptation.
2. Relying on analytical methods and decision tools that further reinforce parochial conceptions of value. For example, conventional cost–benefit

analysis and many forms of risk assessment treat all interests as fungible. Such approaches may implicitly assume that the loss of one's home in one location can be compensated by relocation to another, though this assumption may fail to hold for those whose identities are bound to place.
3. Excluding diverse perspectives—particularly those of marginalized or vulnerable groups—from the design of methods, models and metrics that assist in identifying adaptation needs, from the interpretation of the results of these models and metrics and from the planning of appropriate responses.
4. Overlooking the ways in which adaptation measures at one scale influence, interact with and constrain adaptation at other scales.

Each of these problems could be remedied through recognition and participatory parity, and the scalability of adaptation makes inclusive participation particularly achievable in this domain.

A key first step is to acknowledge that in climate decisions relying on extensive scientific research and modelling, asymmetries in knowledge create asymmetries in power, and models themselves may encode value assumptions that are not fully shared. While global climate models used to predict broad-scale effects of climate change and determine appropriate mitigation targets share these limitations, the more fine-grained, regional and local-scale models that inform adaptation can be more easily tailored to the concerns of affected people within their scope. Thus, in the case of adaptation, interactive research approaches are especially apt, as participants can help to define the relevant parameters for regional models and adaptation strategies (see Armitage et al. 2011, Lemos and Morehouse 2005). Interactive research and planning can contribute to the recognition of vulnerable groups and is consistent with the statement of the 2009 Indigenous Peoples' Global Summit on Climate Change, which appealed to the United Nations Framework Convention on Climate Change (UNFCCC) to develop both 'structures and mechanisms for and with the full and effective participation of Indigenous peoples' (Figueroa 2011, Galloway McLean et al. 2009). The background injustices faced by most indigenous communities make these steps particularly pressing, but the need for recognition extends to all those whose perspectives, values and livelihoods may be overlooked.

Although climate adaptation involves multiscale planning, funding and coordination, and adaptation measures in one area can impact those in another, the scalability of adaptation planning provides a ripe opportunity for the development of institutions that embrace recognition and participatory parity as key organizing principles. Because adaptation can be tailored to particular locations and contexts, it allows for a multiplicity of responses and approaches, making it easier to incorporate and respond to diverse cultural values and perspectives.

## Climate Engineering

The last domain of climate policy—climate engineering—is the newest, and the least institutionalized. Although the idea of actively manipulating the climate to counteract global warming has a history extending back many decades, only recently has it entered the mainstream and been taken up by major scientific organizations, including the Royal Society of London (2009) and the U.S. National Academy of Sciences (NAS) (National Research Council 2015). Climate engineering strategies are generally divided into two categories: carbon dioxide removal (CDR) and solar radiation management (SRM). CDR includes approaches such as carbon capture and storage, whereas SRM proposals range from painting surfaces white to injecting sulphate aerosols into the earth's upper atmosphere to reflect sunlight.

I focus here on SRM, which raises some particularly difficult justice issues. While certain forms of solar radiation management—such as painting roofs white—would be decentralized and carry fewer side effects, other SRM techniques raise significant concerns. For example, the leading strategy for SRM—releasing sulphate aerosols into the stratosphere—would likely have unintended environmental consequences. It could deplete stratospheric ozone, exacerbating the ozone hole, and disrupt Asian and African monsoons, which are critical to agriculture (Royal Society 2009; see also Robock, Oman, and Stenchikov 2008). Sulphate aerosol SRM would also increase acid deposition, whiten the skies and affect the amount of sunlight available for solar energy (Robock 2008).

There are at least four reasons why global-scale SRM, such as proposals to inject sulphate aerosols into the stratosphere, require special attention to participatory justice and recognition:

1. *Scope and scale:* SRM climate intervention strategies are typically global in scope, scale and effects. Thus, they may have significant consequences or side effects without consent of those affected. Ideally, participatory justice should reflect a match between the scope of effects and the scope of the participating public. For a technology that affects more than 7 billion, forms of representation that provide recognition for diverse groups and distinct perspectives are crucial.
2. *Risk and uncertainty:* SRM poses significantly greater risks than standard forms of mitigation, such as reduced burning of fossil fuels, and these risks are not well understood. From the perspective of participatory justice, more substantive participation should be sought for responses that introduce greater risk and uncertainty, because the nature and magnitude of the impacts on various individual groups are not fully understood and because people may have divergent views regarding acceptable levels of risk.

3. *Shift from past practice*: Although humans have been influencing climate for over a century, SRM represents a break with past practice because it involves an *intentional* effort to control global climate. This raises novel ethical concerns about which there has been limited discussion, and inclusive participatory processes are needed to consider concerns that might otherwise be overlooked. Although ethical approaches that emphasize consequences, such as cost–benefit analysis, may not distinguish between intentional and unintentional climate change, from the perspective of other value systems, this distinction may be critical.

4. *Lack of agreement/lack of process for resolving disagreement:* Whereas there is a consensus about the need to mitigate climate change through greenhouse gas emissions reductions, no similar consensus exists regarding the importance or acceptability of large-scale climate engineering. In fact, the climate engineering debate has been highly polarized thus far, and conversations within the Intergovernmental Panel on Climate Change (IPCC) and UNFCCC about SRM are just beginning. The first IPCC report to include a discussion of climate engineering was issued in 2013, and the UNFCCC has yet to tackle governance of SRM in earnest. Though various principles have been proposed (see Rayner et al. 2013), there is no existing international policy framework governing SRM research and planning, and both technical research on the feasibility of SRM and research exploring the social, cultural and ethical dimensions of SRM are occurring in a relatively *ad hoc* and uncoordinated way. If SRM becomes another area of climate policy in which the wealthy and powerful nations dominate, the risks to trust, cooperation and international solidarity could be significant (cf. Hourdequin 2012). Global-scale geoengineering research and planning should be guided by broad and inclusive deliberative processes, and a key first step is to establish institutions that enable engagement and participation (see Long, this volume).

In general, certain kinds of activities and proposals warrant greater participation than others. Elsewhere, I have argued that increased participation is needed in decisions involving high risk, major shifts from past practice, uncertain outcomes, ambiguous policy direction, or significant disagreement (Hourdequin et al. 2012).[1] As indicated above, all of these conditions obtain for SRM, with the addition of SRM's significant scope and scale.

## PARTICIPATORY JUSTICE AND RECOGNITION: CRUCIAL STEPS FOR SRM RESEARCH AND PLANNING

Given these characteristics, the stakes in global-scale solar radiation management research and planning are extremely high. For mitigation and adaptation, failures of recognition undermine both participatory and distributive justice, but in these arenas, the failures are often more diffuse and cumulative. In contrast, failures of recognition for SRM—a highly visible, global technology with the potential to be controlled by a select few—could generate a dangerous cascade of anger and mistrust. Because the need for global participation is so clear, failures to take recognition seriously in this domain would not only deprive people of autonomy and respect, but would also convey a flagrant disregard for the possibility of global cooperation and participatory parity in responding to climate change. Moving ahead with SRM—even if well intentioned—without careful attention to participation and recognition would reinscribe the paternalistic attitudes that have historically characterized relationships between the powerful and the vulnerable and overlook critical dimensions of SRM's potential impacts.

Recognition is thus especially critical for global-scale SRM, yet also especially challenging, precisely because this technology would affect the entire planet. The silver lining is that research on SRM is still in its early stages and inclusive governance strategies can be developed from the ground up.

To achieve participatory justice for SRM requires returning to the fundamental goal of addressing recognition by 'replacing institutionalized value patterns that impede parity of participation with ones that enable or foster it' (Fraser 2000; 115). In addition, it requires that participants have access to adequate resources needed for full participation (Fraser 2000). How can this be achieved? I close the chapter with three suggestions.

First, discussions of SRM climate engineering should avoid dichotomous framings that limit ethical discourse and the scope of decision space. Too often, geoengineering is framed as a critical emergency measure that warrants the suspension of careful ethical analysis and bracketing a wide range of ethical concerns (see Fragnière and Gardiner, this volume). To those who suggest that global-scale climate engineering would problematically alter human relationships with the natural world and reinforce a dangerous hubris (Hamilton 2013), proponents suggest that the time for such debate has passed; we need hard-headed consequentialist thinking to move forward. This particular debate has been occurring among scholars from wealthy, developed nations—and even here we see certain positions being quickly marginalized. If recognition is to be achieved, participants in climate engineering debates need to be open to multiple framings and to perspectives that may be unfamiliar or counterintuitive. Such receptivity is crucial for recognition and has the potential to generate responses and approaches as yet unenvisioned. Institutionally, this openness needs to be created through the active construction of mechanisms that enable participation. As noted below, this will require the investment of resources and careful attention to the barriers that impede participatory parity.

Second, the governance of SRM research and development should keep in mind the following question, 'Are the actions being undertaken ones that others can reasonably accept?' Kyle Powys-Whyte (2012) has argued that with respect to indigenous peoples, free, prior and informed consent should be a condition of research on SRM from the very outset and that indigenous people themselves need to have a role in establishing the consent process itself. Whyte sets a high bar, but at the core of his arguments are notions of partnership and participatory parity. Although consent may be an ideal way to ensure partnership in decision-making, recognition and participatory parity provide helpful conceptual resources, because both can be understood along a continuum, whereas consent is typically understood as binary. It is hard to see how we might secure the consent of all affected parties in the case of global-scale SRM, but we can certainly move towards greater recognition. Together, the ideas of partnership, consent, recognition and participatory parity indicate that the initial question—regarding what others could reasonably accept—cannot be answered in the abstract. Scientists, policymakers and others engaged in SRM research and planning should not assume that their activities and plans would be acceptable to others without partnering directly with affected groups, and they need to be open to the possibility that inclusive participatory processes could result in the rejection of SRM as an acceptable climate response or confine its use to a particularly stringent set of conditions.

Lastly, it is critical to recall that recognition seeks both to address the cultural, social and institutional roots of distributive injustice and to transform formal opportunities for engagement into genuine participatory parity (Schlosberg 2007; 14–16). For global-scale SRM, initial research directions and priorities will determine what knowledge becomes available as decisions are made regarding further research and possible deployment. Without collaborative, interactive research from the early stages, the models and strategies for SRM are likely to reflect only a small slice of the many concerns associated with this technology. Participatory research that involves early engagement and an iterative process of stakeholder engagement is particularly needed (see, e.g. Carr et al. 2013, Corner, Pidgeon, and Parkhill 2012, Lemos and Morehouse 2005, Stirling 2008, Wilsdon and Willis 2004).

A key component of such iterative and engaged research involves sustained interaction, where stakeholders help to define research questions and directions, then assist in reassessing and refining those questions and directions as new knowledge emerges (Lemos and Morehouse 2005). For SRM, this will require globally distributed research that includes the active contributions of those in less-developed countries, rather than research concentrated in wealthy, industrialized nations like the United States (cf. Carr et al. 2013; Preston 2012; SRMGI/AAS 2013). It is here that the institutional and distributive dimensions of recognition enter as key concerns, because achieving this goal of distributed research, located in and engaging with diverse communities of stakeholders from different nations and cultures, will require the establishment of new models for generating and distributing scientific knowledge. For example, it may require investments in training, equipment and other resources to empower the development of SRM research in less-developed nations, with the involvement of concerned publics there. It will also require better integration of natural science research with research in the social sciences and humanities.

Precisely because SRM research *is* in its early stages, it offers genuine opportunity to advance participatory justice and institutionalize inclusive models for engagement. Such models are needed in all domains of climate policy, and progress on participatory justice in one domain has the potential to strengthen it in others. Conversely, failures of recognition and participatory justice in one domain can endanger it elsewhere, and this is of special concern for global SRM. Whereas failures of participatory justice in adaptation may be localized (though widespread), failures of participatory justice for sulphate aerosol SRM have global reach. It is not possible for each nation or people to choose an SRM strategy appropriate to its particular needs. Instead, decisions about SRM research and deployment are planetary-scale choices, and they are decisions we need to make together, as best we can. Without participatory justice for SRM, we risk endangering the trust and social capital needed to address climate change as a whole.

## NOTE

1. This earlier work also identifies decisions with outcomes that are irreversible or difficult to reverse as demanding greater participation, but I leave the discussion of reversibility for another occasion.

## BIBLIOGRAPHY

Adger, W. Neil, Jouni Paavola, Saleemul Huq, and M. J. Mace, eds. 2006. *Fairness in Adaptation to Climate Change*. Cambridge, MA: MIT Press.

Adger, W. Neil, Jouni Paavola, and Saleemul Huq. 2006. 'Toward Justice in Adaptation to Climate Change,' in *Fairness in Adaptation to Climate Change*, edited by W. Neil Adger, Jouni Paavola, Saleelmul Huq, and M. J. Mace, 1–19. Cambridge, MA: MIT Press.

Adger, W. Neil, Suraje Dessai, Marisa Goulden, Mike Hulme, Irene Lorenzoni, Donald R. Nelson, Lars Otto Naess, Johanna Wolf, and Anita Wreford. 2009. 'Are there Social Limits to Adaptation to Climate Change?' *Climatic Change* 93 (3–4): 335–54.

Adger, W. Neil, Jon Barnett, F. S. Chapin III, and Heidi Ellemor. 2011. 'This Must be the Place: Underrepresentation of Identity and Meaning in Climate Change Decision-making.' *Global Environmental Politics* 11 (2): 1–25.

Armitage, Derek, Fikret Berkes, Aaron Dale, Erik Kocho-Schellenberg, and Eva Patton. 2011. 'Co-management and the Co-production of Knowledge: Learning to Adapt in Canada's Arctic.' *Global Environmental Change* 21 (3): 995–1004.

Beck, Silke. 2011. 'Moving Beyond the Linear Model of Expertise? IPCC and the Test of Adaptation.' *Regional Environmental Change* 11 (2): 297–306.

Beymer-Farris, Betsy A., and Thomas J. Bassett. 2012. 'The REDD Menace: Resurgent Protectionism in Tanzania's Mangrove Forests.' *Global Environmental Change* 22 (2): 332–41.

Carr, Wylie A., Christopher J. Preston, Laurie Yung, Bronislaw Szerszynski, David W. Keith, and Ashley M. Mercer. 2013. 'Public Engagement on Solar Radiation Management and Why it Needs to Happen Now.' *Climatic Change* 121 (3): 567–77.

Corner Adam, Nick Pidgeon, and Karen Parkhill. 2012. 'Perceptions of Geoengineering: Public Attitudes, Stakeholder Perspectives & the Challenge of 'Upstream' Engagement.' *WIRES Climate Change* 3 (5): 451–66.

Endres, Danielle. 2012. 'Sacred Land or National Sacrifice Zone: The Role of Values in the Yucca Mountain Participation Process.' *Environmental Communication: A Journal of Nature and Culture* 6 (3): 328–45.

Figueroa, Robert Melchior. 2011. 'Indigenous Peoples and Cultural Losses.' In *The Oxford Handbook of Climate Change and Society,* edited by John S. Dryzek, Richard B. Norgaard, and David Schlosberg, 232–50. New York: Oxford University Press.

Fraser, Nancy. 2000. 'Rethinking Recognition.' *New Left Review* 3: 107–20.

Fraser, Nancy and Axel Honneth. 2003. *Redistribution or Recognition: A Political-Philosophical Exchange.* London: Verso.

Galloway McLean, K., A. Ramos-Castillo, T. Gross, S. Johnston, M. Vierros, and R. Noa. 2009. Darwin: United Nations University-Traditional Knowledge Initiative.

Hamilton, Clive. 2013. *Earthmasters: The Dawn of the Age of Climate Engineering.* New Haven: Yale University Press.

Heyward, Clare. 2013. 'Situating and Abandoning Geoengineering: A Typology of Five Responses to Dangerous Climate Change.' *PS: Political Science & Politics* 46 (1): 23–27.

Hourdequin, Marion. 2012. 'Geoengineering, Solidarity, and Moral Risk.' In *Engineering the Climate: The Ethics of Solar Radiation Management,* edited by Christopher Preston, 15–32. Lanham, MD: Lexington Books.

Hourdequin, Marion, Peter Landres, Mark J. Hanson, and David R. Craig. 2012. 'Ethical Implications of Democratic Theory for US Public Participation in Environmental Impact Assessment.' *Environmental Impact Assessment Review* 35: 37–44.

Jackson, Robert B., and James Salzman. 2010. 'Pursuing Geoengineering for Atmospheric Restoration.' *Issues in Science and Technology* 26: 67–76.

Jamieson, Dale. 2014. *Reason in a Dark Time: Why the Struggle Against Climate Change Failed—And What It Means for Our Future.* New York: Oxford University Press.

Lemos, Maria Carmen, and Barbara J. Morehouse. 2005. 'The Co-production of Science and Policy in Integrated Climate Assessments.' *Global Environmental Change* 15 (1): 57–68.

McShane, Katie. 2015. 'Values and Harms in Loss and Damage.' Conference paper presented at the Second Workshop on Ethics and Adaptation, University at Buffalo, NY.

McQueen, Paddy. 2015. 'Social and Political Recognition.' *Internet Encyclopedia of Philosophy*. http://www.iep.utm.edu/recog_sp/.

National Research Council. 2015. *Climate Intervention: Reflecting Sunlight to Cool Earth*. Washington, DC: The National Academies Press. doi: 10.17226/18988.

Preston, Christopher. 2012. 'Solar Radiation Management and Vulnerable Populations: The Moral Deficit and its Prospects.' In *Engineering the Climate: The Ethics of Solar Radiation Management*, edited by Christopher Preston, 77–93. Lanham, MD: Lexington Books.

Preston, Christopher J. 2015. 'Challenges and Opportunities for Understanding Non-Economic Loss and Damage.' Conference paper presented at the Second Workshop on Ethics and Adaptation, University at Buffalo, NY.

Rayner, Steve, Clare Heyward, Tim Kruger, Nick Pidgeon, Catherine Redgwell, and Julian Savulescu. 2013. 'The Oxford Principles.' *Climatic Change* 121 (3): 499–512.

Robock, Alan. 2008. '20 Reasons Why Geoengineering May Be a Bad Idea.' *Bulletin of the Atomic Scientists* 64 (2): 14–18.

Robock, Alan, Luke, Oman, and Georgiy L. Stenchikov. 2008. 'Regional Climate Responses to Geoengineering with Tropical and Arctic $SO_2$ Injections.' *Journal of Geophysical Research* 113: D16101–D16115.

Royal Society. 2009. *Geoengineering the Climate: Science, Governance, and Uncertainty*. London: The Royal Society.

Schlosberg, David. 2007. *Defining Environmental Justice: Theories, Movements, and Nature*. New York: Oxford.

Solar Radiation Management Governance Initiative/African Academy of Sciences (SRMGI/AAS). 2013. *Governance of Research on solar geoengineering: African Perspectives* (Consolidated Report). http://www.srmgi.org/files/2013/10/AAS-SRMGI-Africa-Report-Final-for-Release.pdf.

Stirling Andy. 2008. 'Opening Up and Closing Down: Power, Participation and Pluralism in the Social Appraisal of Technology.' *Science, Technology, and Human Values* 33: 262–94.

Tsosie, Rebecca A. 2007. 'Indigenous People and Environmental Justice: The Impact of Climate Change.' *University of Colorado Law Review* 78: 1625–77.

Whyte, Kyle Powys. 2011. 'The Recognition Dimensions of Environmental Justice in Indian Country.' *Environmental Justice* 4 (4): 199–205.

Whyte, Kyle Powys. 2012. 'Indigenous Peoples, Solar Radiation Management, and Consent.' In *Engineering the Climate: The Ethics of Solar Radiation Management*, edited by Christopher Preston, 65–76. Lanham, MD: Lexington Books.

Wilsdon James, and Rebecca Willis. 2004. *See-through Science: Why Public Engagement Needs to Move Upstream*. London: Demos.

*Chapter 4*

# Do We Have a Residual Obligation to Engineer the Climate, as a Matter of Justice?

Patrik Baard and Per Wikman-Svahn

Given the slow progress of mitigation, it seems increasingly likely that climate change will cause much suffering. This evokes the issue of what to do to reduce that suffering or how to compensate for it having emerged. Joshua Horton and David Keith (Chapter 6, this volume) argue that solar geoengineering[1] should be an option because it can reduce much of the suffering caused by climate change. Solar geoengineering is often seen as a 'Plan b' should other policies, such as mitigation, fail. In this sense it is regarded as an option that is activated in addition to our primary obligations towards mitigation and adaptation. Could solar geoengineering reasonably be seen as a *residual obligation*?

The concept of a residual obligation and its significance was first discussed in detail by Bernard Williams (1973), who pointed out that if an agent has two, or more, moral demands but can fulfil only one but not both, then the agent is not 'off the hook' regarding the obligation that the agent has not chosen to fulfil. Fulfilling one obligation does not cancel out the moral import of the other. Rather, 'the item that was not acted upon may, for instance, persist as regret' (Williams 1973: 179).[2] This regret may then be expressed in different ways that remedy the omitted duty. In other words, the fact that an agent has not fulfilled her *primary obligations* does not absolve that agent of the remaining obligations; the agent still has *residual obligations*.[3]

For example, imagine that we have promised to meet a friend at a certain time and place, but observe an accident along the way to the meeting. Then, our obligation to fulfil our promise to meet our friend is overridden by the obligation to help out at the accident (Hansson and Peterson 2001). This, however, does not cancel out our initial obligation to our friend; instead, it creates additional residual obligations. In the example, our residual obligation could be to reach out to our friend as soon as our acute help at the accident is no longer needed. We thereby assure our friend that, having experienced this moral dilemma, we still recognized the moral weight of the original commitment.

Applying the notion of primary and residual obligations to climate change, we will here assume that both mitigation and adaptation are primary obligations of countries. We believe this to be a reasonable assumption, and it seems to be implied by the United Nations Framework Convention on Climate Change (UNFCCC), in which countries that have signed the convention agree both to achieve the 'stabilization of greenhouse gas concentrations in the atmosphere at a level that would prevent dangerous anthropogenic interference with the climate system' (United Nations 1992, Article 1) and to take national and regional 'measures to facilitate adequate adaptation to climate change' (United Nations 1992, Article 4).

Many states have obligations to reduce climate change, as a matter of justice (Shue 2014).[4] The impacts of climate change do, of course, vary across the world, and to expect each nation to take on their own adaptation burdens would in many cases assign high costs to developing states harmed by climate change (Moellendorf 2014: 186). Moreover, and more relevant as a matter of justice, for developing states to take on burdens to adapt could be considered unjust, as it often entails that those with the greatest responsibility for contributing to climate change would be exempt from helping to mitigate the conditions of those most vulnerable, who have often contributed the least to the problem. As an alternative, those most vulnerable may have a legitimate claim to resources for enhancing their adaptive capacities by appealing to different moral principles.[5]

However, it seems increasingly likely that mitigation will be insufficient to avoid dangerous climate change and that adaptation is also unlikely to be successful, given the psychological, social and institutional barriers to adaptation (Stafford Smith et al. 2011), as well as systemic social and ecological limitations of adaptation (Dow et al. 2013). In this chapter we examine the idea that a failure of the primary obligations of mitigation and adaptation does not let countries 'off the hook'—instead, it creates residual obligations. But what are these residual obligations? Do they include a moral obligation to engineer the climate?

The aim of this chapter is to critically examine the thesis that we have a residual obligation of solar geoengineering. We start by looking at financial compensation for climate damages, a proposal that is increasingly being discussed in international climate policy. Financial compensation is a paradigmatic example of a possible residual obligation that arises out of failure to fulfil primary obligations of mitigation and adaptation. We then turn to the more controversial proposal of solar geoengineering and compare and contrast it with financial compensation. We find that solar geoengineering has some attractive features compared to financial compensation, but we argue that solar geoengineering cannot reasonably be considered a residual obligation. Finally, instead of promoting solar geoengineering as a residual obligation, we propose that more emphasis ought to be given to other types of residual obligations as a response to the challenges of climate change.

## FINANCIAL COMPENSATION

The need for mechanisms to ensure that financial compensation[6] is provided for damages due to climate change has been discussed at the international level since at least 1991, when the Republic of Vanuatu, on behalf of the Alliance of Small Island States, proposed that an international fund be created to help cover the cost of damages due to climate change (Roberts and Huq 2015: 149). In 2013 the UNFCCC established the Warsaw International Mechanism for Loss and Damage (in short, the Loss and Damage Mechanism) for compensating vulnerable agents for substantial losses caused by climate change (Huq et al. 2013). The purpose of the Loss and Damage Mechanism is, in part, to determine the approximate cost of these losses as part of an effort 'to address residual losses and damages not avoided by mitigation and adaptation' (Roberts and Huq 2015: 152).

Even if the details of the framework has differed throughout the years, the compensation for losses incurred due to climate change has been proposed to come in two forms: first, money is allocated to decrease avoidable losses and damages by assisting with adaptation, and second, compensation is provided for unavoidable losses and damages (e.g. through the establishment of contingency funds and insurance systems) (Huq, Roberts and Fenton 2013: 948, Roberts and Huq 2015: 150). When we use the term *financial compensation*, we will here mean the latter, which is a central part of what the Loss and Damage Mechanism was originally designed to address.

Scholarly discussion of ethical issues regarding financial compensation for climate damages has so far been sparse (Thompson and Otto 2015, Wallimann-Helmer 2015). Here we will point only to three aspects of financial compensation, which are relevant for our further discussion of solar geoengineering.

*The aim of financial compensation is to compensate for harms that have already occurred.* The Loss and Damage Mechanism has in part meant to secure compensation for losses that have already occurred, or losses and damages that are unavoidable, and which are attributable to climate change. That is, compensation is allocated towards rectifying harms that would not have occurred if it had not been for climatic changes. Consequently, those most responsible for climate change, and thus for contributing to the resulting harms, have a duty to compensate for the incurred losses. Financial compensation in this case, then, can be ethically interpreted as the restoration of justice after a moral violation (Thompson and Otto 2015).

*There are damages that are very hard to compensate for by money.* Climate change has some irreversible effects that are very difficult to rectify in terms of financial compensation. Climate impacts that are very difficult (if not impossible) to resolve include extinction of species and countries that may disappear due to sea-level rise (Kelman 2015). Such, and other, impacts are difficult, or even impossible, to quantify in monetary terms (cf. Wallimann-Helmer 2015). Compensation in these cases will likely do very little to rectify a wrong and may not meet the demands of fair remedy (Wallimann-Helmer 2015: 477). Irreversible consequences may differ greatly in nature, with each calling for different solutions for restoration (again, if restoration is even possible). Moreover, there are potential institutional and practical difficulties in distributing the compensation in a just way, and some individuals are likely to benefit more than others from financial compensation.

*Agency and attribution for financial compensation is not easily determined.* In situations when someone is harmed, and the harm can be attributed to an identified agent, it is generally easy to determine who should be responsible for financial compensation and who should be the recipient of that compensation. However, as has convincingly been argued by Dale Jamieson (1992), this is far from the typical case with climate change. Rather than a specific individual agent doing something harmful to an identifiable individual, such as Smith stealing a bike from Jones, moral responsibility for climate change is geographically and temporally dispersed. In the case of Smith and Jones, it is easy to suggest that Smith has an obligation to compensate Jones for the stolen bike. In the case of climate change, however, the agents and victims are much more indeterminate and compensating vulnerable agents becomes a matter of assessing whether a specific harm would not have emerged given that appropriate adaptation measures had been in place. Consequently, it is difficult to draw definitive moral conclusions from this form of counterfactual reasoning.

In conclusion, financial compensation for climate damages is difficult to put into practice, given that such resources cannot be used for irreparable and irreversible damages, and since it can be a very arduous task to identify (or at least narrow down) the relevant agents and their corresponding obligations. Several of the mentioned problems with financial compensation could be reduced by avoiding the harm in the first place. But as argued above, even extensive mitigation of greenhouse gases and implementing of adaptation measures will likely not suffice to avoid all harm. Might solar geoengineering be a better alternative to reduce the residual harm?

## SOLAR GEOENGINEERING

The Intergovernmental Panel on Climate Change (IPCC) defines geoengineering as 'methods and technologies that aim to deliberately alter the climate system in order to alleviate impacts of climate change' (Boucher et al. 2013: 627). Solar geoengineering involves directly changing the radiative balance of Earth, for example by injection of sulphur particles into the stratosphere, deploying mirrors into space, or whitening clouds or the ocean (Boucher et al. 2013). We will here discuss three aspects of solar geoengineering and contrast these with financial compensation.

*The aim of deploying solar geoengineering is to prevent or reduce harm from climate change.* Emissions of greenhouse gases entails a time lag before harmful climate changes occur, and solar geoengineering could therefore perhaps be seen as another form of 'compensation' for insufficient mitigation, but which occurs *before* the harm. Everything being equal, avoiding a harm is preferable to suffering the harm even with (imperfect) financial compensation. The aim of solar geoengineering could therefore be seen as more ambitious compared to financial compensation.

*Solar geoengineering cannot perfectly compensate for increasing concentrations of greenhouse gases.* While solar geoengineering could potentially reduce or reverse global warming, it cannot in general restore the climate that would have been without increased concentrations of greenhouse gases in the atmosphere (Robock et al. 2008). One reason for this is that the climatic effects of increased concentrations of greenhouse gases in the atmosphere are different than the climatic effects of solar geoengineering (Boucher et al. 2013). Solar geoengineering will likely mean that some geographical areas will benefit more than others (Robock et al. 2008). All this means that solar geoengineering cannot perfectly compensate anthropogenic climate change. However, financial compensation is also rarely perfect, especially regarding irreversible and irreparable harm, and since some people will likely benefit more than others from financial compensation.

*The local effects of solar geoengineering will in many cases be uncertain.* Climate model simulations suggest that the regional climatic effects of solar geoengineering can be very diverse and uncertain (Kravitz et al. 2011). The level of understanding of solar geoengineering is still low (Boucher et al. 2013), and given the considerable difficulties in modelling the regional and local effects of clouds and aerosols, it seems unlikely that accurate prediction of the regional effects of solar geoengineering will be possible in the foreseeable future. A case can therefore be made that the problems of attribution is even more difficult for solar geoengineering than for climate change, as it introduces additional sources of uncertainty (in addition to the natural variability and anthropogenic emissions of greenhouse gases and aerosols).

Comparing harms from climate change with or without solar geoengineering will therefore be even more difficult and uncertain than focusing only on financial compensation, thus further complicating the problem of determining who carries the responsibilities and corresponding obligations.[7]

In conclusion, the main advantage of solar geoengineering compared to financial compensation is that solar geoengineering could potentially avoid harms before they occur. However, solar geoengineering cannot perfectly compensate for increased concentrations of greenhouse gases, and the local and regional effects will in many cases be very uncertain, which poses a problem for assigning responsibility and entitlements. But the most serious problem for seeing solar geoengineering as a residual obligation is that it also introduces new risks, which we discuss in the next section.

## IS SOLAR GEOENGINEERING A PERMISSIBLE RESIDUAL OBLIGATION?

One of the most commonly discussed problems of solar geoengineering is that it introduces negative side effects (cf. Shepherd et al. 2009). The potential for negative side effects is particularly problematic from a justice perspective as individuals will by necessity be exposed to risks that are causally related to solar geoengineering. Note that this might be a problem from a justice perspective even though many of the same type of risks might be caused by other sources, including anthropogenic climate change or natural variability.

In addition, solar geoengineering also creates completely new types of risks, including risks of much greater magnitude. Bostrom and Cirkovic (2011) argue that the category of *global catastrophic risks* merits special attention as they affect a large percentage of the human population and/or the ecosystem of the planet. The global catastrophic risk of solar geoengineering that has been most discussed is that a rapid termination of solar geoengineering (known as the 'termination effect') would lead to abrupt climate change (Jones et al. 2013, Matthews and Caldeira 2007). Such an effect would be catastrophic for many ecosystems and would put severe stress on both agricultural and socio-economic development.[8] This particular global catastrophic risk is causally connected to solar geoengineering as it does not exist if solar geoengineering is not deployed. Another global catastrophic risk of solar geoengineering is that it could potentially cause a worldwide Ice Age or even a "snowball earth", which could be even more devastating for life on Earth than a global nuclear war (Keith 2013: 110–11).

In order to confidently say that we have an *obligation* to engineer the climate, we must be able to justify this claim from a reasonable ethical perspective. While a utilitarian calculation could at least in theory potentially justify exposing people to new risks from solar geoengineering,[9] duty-based ethical views are based on a completely different understanding of when it is permissible to expose others to risk (Cranor 2007). When performing an act that may expose someone to a possible, but not certain, harm, different aspects of the act need to be considered, such as whether or not those exposed to the possible harm provided their consent (cf. Hermansson 2005). Since such consent—from a global population, which also includes future generations—in this case is difficult to obtain, the main problem with considering solar geoengineering as a residual obligation from a duty-based perspective is that it exposes other persons to risks. But furthermore, not only does it expose others to risk, but it also seems as an inadequate manner to restitute the wrongs of unmitigated climate change, where mitigation is a primary duty. Therefore, the use of solar geoengineering as a form of compensation for a previous wrongdoing, or even to reduce some of the effects of climate change, is hard to see as an *obligation* from a duty-based ethical perspective.

The difficulties of considering solar geoengineering as an obligation perhaps become more clear to us from this hypothetical example. Imagine a chemical plant has released toxins into the environment as a side effect of its operations over an extended period of time. The toxins are responsible for both human health problems and damage to ecosystems. The owners of the chemical plant propose that they could fix the problems by releasing genetically modified bacteria into the environment. Model simulations and laboratory experiments show that the bacteria consume and neutralize the environmental toxin, and confirm the predicted success of their resolution. However, scientists are not completely certain that the release of the bacteria into the environment would not lead to other unintended side effects, including human health problems and ecosystem damages. Furthermore, it is projected that the new bacteria will likely spread over wide geographical areas not yet directly affected by the original environmental toxin.[10] In this example, it seems strange to claim that the owners of the chemical plant have an obligation to release the bacteria into the environment. Instead, more plausibly, they have many other residual obligations that come first, including financial compensation and other less-risky ways of restoring the polluted land.

If some agents were to initiate solar geoengineering in order to benefit a specific group of individuals, for example the individuals that will be most harmed by anthropogenic climate change, then they will necessarily also impose additional risks to his group, as well as to other groups (because of the risks causally related to solar geoengineering discussed above). Implementing solar geoengineering would therefore result in additional obligations due to the extra harm (or risk of harm) inflicted. Since these harms have to be compensated for in turn, this would create additional problems (see, e.g. Heyward 2014, Svoboda and Irvine 2014), and geoengineering could therefore create a long stretch of additional residual obligations. This is an important disadvantage of solar geoengineering as a form of rectifying past harms, as compared to financial compensation, which does not carry the same burden. Financial compensation is in this sense much more straightforward since distributing a benefit to one individual does not at the same time mean that another individual is exposed to a risk, and certainly not global catastrophic risks.

In conclusion, while solar geoengineering has some advantages compared to financial compensation, it also has some disadvantages. Not only does solar geoengineering pose several great risks and create local uncertainties, but also it cannot compensate fully for increasing emissions of greenhouse gases. It would thus seem to be even more risky than letting emissions proceed unmitigated and is an inadequate alternative as a residual obligation for omitted primary obligations of mitigation and adaptation. The main problem with considering solar geoengineering as a residual obligation from a duty-based perspective is that it exposes other persons to risks, where the primary obligation is to provide safety for those very same persons. For these reasons, it is doubtful that solar geoengineering would be a morally permissible residual obligation. Instead of promoting solar geoengineering as a residual obligation, we argue that more emphasis ought to be given to other, more reasonable residual obligations. We suggest some of these alternatives in the next section.

## ALTERNATIVE RESIDUAL OBLIGATIONS

Sven Ove Hansson and Martin Peterson have proposed the following typology of residual obligations that are applicable in relation to technologies that give rise to risks affecting individual persons: (1) obligations to compensate, (2) obligations to communicate, (3) obligations to improve, (4) obligations to search for knowledge and (5) attitudinal obligations (Hansson and Peterson 2001, Peterson and Hansson 2004). We have already discussed the first type of residual obligation (financial compensation) and will here propose other residual obligations that might be relevant to the problem of climate change.

*Obligations to communicate:* Obligations to communicate may involve informing the harmed agents as to why an initial obligation has not been fulfilled, including stakeholders, and carries with it the corresponding obligation to listen to their concerns. There could thus be obligations to inform potentially harmed agents about the risks of climate change. The obligation to communicate may also entail apologies. Official recognition in the form of a public statement is one way of acknowledging that a wrong has been committed and fulfilling this type of obligation (cf. Thompson and Otto 2015).

An obligation to communicate may also mean a strengthening of dialogue with stakeholders. Of course, when it comes to negotiations on the burdens of climate change, this could be expected to involve not only the current global community but also future generations, which present some serious challenges.

*Obligations to improve*: Reducing emissions by aggressively increasing the development of low-carbon emission technology and taxing or banning high-carbon emissions are both potential policies that could improve the current situation and reduce the risk of exposure due to climate change. Such improvements could also include the implementation of carbon dioxide removal technologies, the development of early warning systems for tipping points as well as the establishment of more effective warning systems for extreme weather events. If an agent has violated a primary obligation once, moral self-improvement may be expected of this agent to ensure that similar violations will not happen again (Hansson and Peterson 2001). With respect to climate change, this could mean that agents guilty of producing high emissions (i.e. higher than their justified entitlements) have an obligation to reduce their emissions in the future.

*Obligations to search for knowledge:* The obligation to search for further knowledge is often instrumental for determining other potential residual obligations (Hansson and Peterson 2001: 161). It is, for instance, necessary to evaluate what damages climate change has resulted in when determining the appropriate amount of financial compensation. In addition, further research on damages could also be a means to fulfil obligations to improve (see above). Furthermore, the search for knowledge could be especially relevant to the problem of adaptation. If a group of agents have duties to another group of agents to enhance their adaptive capacities, and, through research, it is determined that this will not be possible, the result might be that the initial group of agents has other residual obligations. Such obligations could include the obligation to search for knowledge regarding geoengineering options.

*Attitudinal obligations:* An agent who harms another agent in order to avoid a greater harm, but who feels no remorse or any sense of a residual obligation, could be deemed 'morally defective' (Peterson and Hansson 2004: 272). Somewhat analogous to this case would be the lack of remorse some agents have for exposing future generations to great harm. This could have implications for the discount rate that is often discussed in climate change debates, representing to what extent the interests of future generations should be taken into account when making decisions at the present time.[11] The lack of remorse for exposing future generations to great harms could signal that the other agent's interests are not adequately taken into consideration. But climate change is not only of concern to future generations. For instance, climate change is already contributing to increases in extreme weather events (e.g. increased precipitation in some parts of the world and severe heat waves in others). Attitudinal obligations would here entail taking into account the distress that people in these areas experience as a result of these changes in weather patterns and expressing regret over past actions that have contributed to such events (such as the rapid development of coal mining and the overuse of other fossil fuels).

Given the risk that even mitigation and adaptation policies will not be successful, the need for alternative, ethically justifiable, additional measures is becoming all the more urgent. Solar geoengineering has an advantage over financial compensation in that it could potentially avoid some harm *ex ante* by reducing the effects of anthropogenic climate change. However, it is difficult to determine who will benefit from solar geoengineering and who will be made worse off, making it inadequate as an alternative to restitute omitted initial obligations. Furthermore, solar geoengineering exposes individuals to new risks, including global catastrophic risks. We argued from a duty-based ethical view that solar geoengineering is not a permissible residual obligation and propose that a wider range of alternative residual obligations should be more seriously considered in climate policy.

# NOTES

1. When we use the term "solar geoengineering" we refer to *solar radiation management*, as defined by the IPCC (Boucher et al. 2013).
2. Such conflicts between obligations is also what motivated W. D. Ross (1930) to discuss *prima facie* obligations (cf. Hansson and Petersson 2001, 159).
3. Such an interpretation may be permitted given enough confidence in the principle of "ought implies can" (cf. Williams 1973, 182). Given that two moral demands exist but can be performed only at the expense of each other, choosing one of them would imply that the other is not demanded, provided that it cannot be performed. However, as noticed by Williams, the reasoning would equally hold in cases where A and B are empirically incompatible, such as between a moral demand and, as he puts it, "some gross inclination" (Williams 1973, 183). Succumbing to the "gross inclination" may render meeting the moral demand impossible; thus, it is not obligatory since it cannot be performed. This is a very permissive notion of obligations and of the principle of ought implies can.
4. The discussion of different principles, such as polluter pays, ability to pay, beneficiary pays or equal per-capita views, are assumedly familiar to the reader of this anthology and will not be portrayed here.
5. See Duus-Otterström and Jagers (2012) for a typology of adaptation duties.
6. It should be noted that loss and damage has had several, somewhat different and broader, forms than discussed here, not only limited to financial compensation. Regardless of the details of the loss and damage framework in practice, loss and

damage is primarily viewed as a form of compensation intended to restitute a moral wrong (cf. Thompson and Otto 2015; cf. Wallimann-Helmer 2015). This chapter is primarily concerned with issues of principle and justice, and whether geo-engineering is permissible as a matter of justice if compared to different forms of compensation for moral wrongs (in this case, financial).

7. The agency aspect of solar geoengineering might at first glance seem straightforward, as the agents responsible for deploying solar geoengineering might be relatively easy to identify (although an eventual deployment might plausibly be the result of a long international process). However, agency in this trivial sense is very similar for financial compensation, so this cannot be used as an advantage of solar geoengineering compared to financial compensation.

8. Baum et al. (2013) envisions a "double catastrophe" scenario where geoengineering is started and then terminated due to some other global catastrophe (e.g. a pandemic or global nuclear war) that eliminates society's ability to continue geoengineering, resulting in abrupt global warming that strikes at an already weak society causing a risk of complete human extinction.

9. Some studies based on cost–benefit analysis methods show extremely large expected benefits of solar geoengineering (e.g. Bickel 2013; Moreno-Cruz and Keith 2013). However, these results might not be robust under different assumptions of climate damages and inclusion of global catastrophic risks (cf. Goes et al, 2011). Moreover, the very same integrated assessment models that are typically used to calculate the positive and negative consequences of solar geoengineering have been criticized for being deeply flawed (e.g. Ackerman et al. 2009; Pindyck 2013). It should also be noted that the cost–benefit analysis cannot in general be taken to be a proxy for utilitarianism. The ethical theory of utilitarianism says that an act is right only if it maximizes the good, while the cost–benefit analysis is based on much simplified assumptions (Hansson 2007).

10. This example is somewhat analogous to Gavin Schmidt's "rocking the boat" example (Schmidt 2006). That is this is a case where an agent does something overly complicated and dangerous to counteract risks, when there are less-risky alternatives available.

11. See Jamieson (2014, ch. 4) for an overview.

## BIBLIOGRAPHY

Ackerman, Frank, Stephen J. DeCanio, Richard B. Howarth and Kristen Sheeran. 2009. 'Limitations of Integrated Assessment Models of Climate Change.' *Climatic Change* 95: 297–315. doi:10.1007/s10584-009-9570-x

Baum, Seth D., Timothy M. Maher Jr., and Jacob Haqq-Misra. 2013. 'Double Catastrophe: Intermittent Stratospheric Geoengineering Induced by Societal Collapse.' *Environment Systems & Decisions* 33: 168–80.

Bickel, J. Eric. 2013. 'Climate Engineering and Climate Tipping-Point Scenarios.' *Environment Systems & Decisions* 33: 152–67. doi:10.1007/s10669-013-9435-8.

Boucher, Olivier, David Randall, Paulo Artaxo, Christopher Bretherton, Graham Feingold, Piers Forster, Veli-Matti Kerminen, Yutaka Kondo, Hong Liao, Ulrike Lohmann, Philip Rasch, S.K. Satheesh, Steven Sherwood, Bjorn Stevens, and Xiao-Ye Zhang 2013. 'Clouds and Aerosols.' In *Climate Change 2013: The Physical Science Basis. Contribution of Working Group I to the Fifth Assessment Report of the Intergovernmental Panel on Climate Change,* edited by Thomas F. Stocker, Dahe Qin, Gian-Kasper Plattner, Melinda M. B. Tignor, Simon K. Allen, Judith Boschung, Alexander Nauels, Yu Xia, Vincent Bex and Pauline M. Midgley. Cambridge, MA: Cambridge University Press.

Bostrom, Nick, and Milan M. Cirkovic. 2011. *Global Catastrophic Risks.* Oxford: Oxford University Press.

Cranor, Carl F. 2007. 'Toward a Non-Consequentialist Theory of Acceptable Risks.' In *Risk: philosophical perspectives,* edited by Tim Lewens, 36–53. New York: Routledge.

Dow, Kirstin, Frans Berkhout, Benjamin L. Preston, Richard J. T. Klein, Guy Midgley and M. Rebecca Shaw. 2013. 'Limits to Adaptation.' *Nature Climate Change* 3: 305–307. doi:10.1038/nclimate1847.

Duus-Otterström, Göran and Sven C. Jagers. 2012. 'Identifying Burdens of Coping with Climate Change: A Typology of the Duties of Climate Justice.' *Global Environmental Change* 22: 746–753.

Goes, Marlos, Nancy Tuana and Klaus Keller. 2011. 'The Economics (or Lack Thereof) of Aerosol Geoengineering.' *Climatic Change* 109: 719–44.

Hansson, Sven Ove. 2007. 'Philosophical Problems in Cost–Benefit Analysis.' *Economics and Philosophy* 23: 163–83.

Hansson, Sven Ove and Martin Peterson. 2001. 'Rights, Risks, and Residual Obligations.' *Risk Decision & Policy* 6: 157–66.

Hermansson, Helene. 2005. 'Consistent Risk Management: Three Models Outlined.' *Journal of Risk Research* 8: 557–68.

Heyward, Clare. 2014. 'Benefiting from Climate Geoengineering and Corresponding Remedial Duties: The Case of Unforeseeable Harms.' *Journal of Applied Philosophy* 31: 405–29.

Huq, Saleemul, Erin Roberts and Adrian Fenton. 2013. 'Loss and Damage.' *Nature Climate Change* 3: 947–49. doi: 10.1038/nclimate2026.

Jamieson, Dale. 1992. 'Ethics, Public Policy, and Global Warming.' *Science, Technology & Human Values* 17: 139–53.

Jamieson, Dale. 2014. *Reason in a Dark Time: Why the Struggle Against Climate Change Failed—And What it Means for our Future.* Oxford: Oxford University Press.

Jones, Andy, Jim M. Haywood, Kari Alterskjær, Olivier Boucher, Jason N. S. Cole, Charles L. Curry, Peter J. Irvine, Duoying Ji, Ben Kravitz, Jón Egill Kristjánsson, John C. Moore, Ulrike Niemeier, Alan Robock, Hauke Schmidt, Balwinder Sing, Simone Tilmes, Shingo Watanabe, and Jin-Ho Yoon. 2013. 'The Impact of Abrupt Suspension of Solar Radiation Management (Termination Effect) in Experiment G2 of the Geoengineering Model Intercomparison Project (GeoMIP).' *Journal of Geophysical Research Atmosphere* 118: 9743–52.

Keith, Davod. 2013. *A Case for Climate Engineering.* Massachusetts: The MIT Press.

Kelman, Ilan. 2015. 'Difficult Decisions: Migration from Small Island Developing States under Climate Change.' *Earth's Future* 3: 133–42. doi: 10.1002/2014EF000278.

Kravitz, Ben, Alan Robock, Olivier Boucher, Hauke Schmidt, Karl E. Taylor, Georgiy Stenchikov, and Michael Schulz. 2011. 'The Geoengineering Model Intercomparison Project (GeoMIP).' *Atmospheric Science Letters* 12: 162–67.

Matthews, H. Damon and Ken Caldeira. 2007. 'Transient Climate–Carbon Simulations of Planetary Geoengineering.' *Proceedings of the National Academy of Sciences* 104: 9949–54. doi: 10.1073/pnas.0700419104.

Moellendorf, Darrel. 2014. *The Moral Challenge of Dangerous Climate Change: Values, Poverty, and Policy*. Cambridge, MA: Cambridge University Press.

Moreno-Cruz, Juan B., and David W. Keith. 2013. 'Climate Policy under Uncertainty: A Case for Geoengineering.' *Climatic Change* 121: 431–44.

Peterson, Martin and Sven Ove Hansson. 2004. 'On the Application of Rights-based Moral Theories to Siting Controversies.' *Journal of Risk Research* 7: 269–75. doi: 10.1080/1366987042000171933.

Pindyck, Robert S. 2013. 'Climate Change Policy: What Do the Models Tell Us?' *Journal of Economic Literature* 51: 860–72. doi:10.1257/jel.51.3.860.

Roberts, Erin and Saleemul Huq. 2015. 'Coming Full Circle: The History of Loss and Damage under the UNFCCC.' *International Journal of Global Warming* 8: 141–57. doi: 10.1504/IJGW.2015.071964.

Robock, Alan, Luke Oman and Georgiy L. Stenchikov. 2008. 'Regional Climate Responses to Geoengineering with Tropical and Arctic $SO_2$ Injections.' *Journal of Geophysical Research* 113. doi: 10.1029/2008JD010050.

Ross, William David. 1930. *The Right and the Good*. Oxford: Oxford University Press.

Schmidt, Gaving. 2006. 'Geoengineering in Vogue.' *Real Climate*, June 28. Accessed January 12, 2016. http://www.realclimate.org/index.php/archives/2006/06/geo-engineering-in-vogue/.

Shepherd, John, Ken Caldeira, Peter Cox, Joanna Haigh, David Keith, Brian Launder, Georgina Mace, Gordon MacKerron, John Pyle, Steve Rayner, Catherine Redgwell, and Andrew Watson. 2009. *Geoengineering the Climate: Science, Governance and Uncertainty*. London: The Royal Society.

Shue, Henry. 2014. *Climate Justice: Vulnerability and Protection*. Oxford: Oxford University Press.

Stafford Smith, Mark, Lisa Horrocks, Alex Harvey and Clive Hamilton. 2011. 'Rethinking Adaptation for a 4°C world.' *Philosophical Transactions. Series A, Mathematical, Physical, and Engineering Sciences* 369: 196–216. Accessed January 12, 2016. doi:10.1098/rsta.2010.0277.

Svoboda, Toby, and Peter Irvine. 2014. 'Ethical and Technical Challenges in Compensating for Harm Due to Solar Radiation Management Geoengineering.' *Ethics, Policy & Environment* 17: 157–74. Accessed January 12, 2016. doi: 10.1080/21550085.2014.927962.

Thompson, Allen, and Friederike E. L Otto. 2015. 'Ethical and Normative Implications of Weather Event Attribution for Policy Discussions Concerning Loss and Damage.' *Climatic Change* 133: 439–51. Accessed January 12, 2016. doi: 10.1007/s10584-015-1433-z.

United Nations. 1992. United Nations Framework Convention on Climate Change. Accessed November 3, 2015. http://unfccc.int/files/essential_background/background_publications_htmlpdf/application/pdf/conveng.pdf.

Wallimann-Helmer, Ivo. 2015. 'Justice for Climate Loss and Damage.' *Climate Change* 133: 469–80. Accessed January 12, 2016. doi: 10.1007/s10584-015–1441-z.

Williams, Bernard. 1973. 'Ethical Consistency' In *Problems of the Self: Philosophical Essays 1956-1972*, 166–86. Cambridge, MA: Cambridge University Press.

*Chapter 5*

# Paying It Forward

## *Geoengineering and Compensation for the Further Future*

### Allen Habib and Frank Jankunis

Since Henry Shue's seminal work on climate change and intergenerational justice (Shue 1993, 1992), philosophers and other theorists have largely agreed on both the diagnosis of and the general solution to the problem of harm to future generations from climate change. The problem is typically understood in terms of compensatory justice: earlier generations, by their greenhouse gas emissions, cause loss and damage to later generations because of climate change. These damages are unjust and thus merit compensation. The solution is also typically straightforward: contemporary generations can compensate future ones by increasing their 'savings', that is, by passing a larger amount of capital to the future than they would have otherwise (Caney 2009, Faber 2007; Mackinnon 2013, *inter alia*).

Saving and bequeathing capital to our heirs is the standard way that we propel value into the future. This 'capital transfer' strategy for paying the future is seen in action everywhere. Rich nations, for example, often put aside capital funds expressly to furnish future generations with that capital.

The Alberta Heritage Trust Fund, established by the Government of Alberta in 1976 with non-renewable resource revenue, is a Canadian example of the intergenerational capital transfer strategy. Legislation creating the Heritage Trust Fund describes its mission as 'to provide prudent stewardship of the savings from Alberta's non-renewable resources by providing the greatest financial returns on those savings for current and future generations of Albertans' (Alberta Queen's Printer 1976).

Internationally, perhaps the most familiar example is Norway's Government Pension Fund. Like the Alberta Heritage Trust Fund, Norway's fund establishes saving oil revenue for future generations as a target:

The purpose of the Government Pension Fund is to facilitate government savings to finance rising public pension expenditures, and support long-term considerations in the spending of government petroleum revenues. A sound long-term management of the Fund contributes to intergenerational equity, by allowing both current and future generations to benefit from the petroleum revenues. (Ministry of Finance, n.d.)

We argue below that the capital transfer approach faces serious difficulties as a method of compensation for future loss and damage from anthropogenic climate change, especially for the further future, and that some geoengineering schemes may avoid these difficulties, and so hold some promise as compensatory mechanisms for anthropogenic climate change.

Before we rehearse the problems with the capital transfer approach, we should first note a few framework assumptions. The most important one is this: We will be concerned here largely with compensation to those generations in the middle to distant future, that is, generations at least 100 years in the future. Mirroring climate science's primary focus on modelling to the year 2100, contemporary debates about compensation for the harms of climate change have largely ignored the question of middle to distant generations and focused instead on compensation to immediate successor generations. But this inattention is unwarranted. While issues of proximate generations are pressing, later generations will also suffer the effects of anthropogenic climate change. "A large fraction of anthropogenic climate change resulting from $CO_2$ emissions," the IPCC writes, "is irreversible on a multi-century to millennial timescale, except in the case of a large net removal of $CO_2$ from the atmosphere over a sustained period" (IPCC 2014: 73–4).

It remains, however, unclear precisely what harms, and what extent of harm, middle to distant generations will suffer on account of anthropogenic climate change. This is because it is unclear both what the exact effects of the present generation's emitting activities will be on distant generations and how harmful these effects will be to them. Some effects, such as long-term droughts, may span across many generations, while other effects, such as the collapse of the West Antarctic Ice Sheet, whose decline NASA said appears inevitable (NASA 2014), may emerge anew for distant generations (Collins et al. 2013). However, it's reasonable to assume that, at least for the next couple of centuries, generations of people will suffer harms and losses due to anthropogenic change in the climate as we and our immediate successors do and expect to suffer.

Distant future generations are theoretically interesting because, as we will see, they pose difficulties for capital transfer that earlier ones do not. Also, later generations play importantly different roles, morally speaking, in the transfer of capital into the future. One effect of this focus on the more distant future is that questions of the distribution of contemporary responsibility for climate change, and concomitant debates about the proper distribution of the burden of compensation, are made secondary. At century lengths, the most natural level of analysis is generational, or perhaps more accurately multi-generational, and so questions about intragenerational responsibility for emissions and their effects are less salient. This is not to say such problems don't arise for the distant cases, merely that questions about how much a generation owes in total will precede questions about how that bill should be divided.

Now we can begin to address the issue of intergenerational capital transfer as compensation for future damage. First, we should specify what type of capital we are concerned with. Since there is no reason to favour or bar any particular type of capital from serving to pay this debt *a priori*, we will consider five standard sorts of capital economists generally speak of: financial, manufactured, social, natural and human capital.

To begin with the last, human capital, by which we mean the capital value of extant humanity's efforts—their skills, knowledge and labour—is not itself projectable into the future. Its products are, but they will be covered by the other categories. So human capital is not the sort of thing that we can pay the future as compensation.

Secondly, financial capital, meaning here exclusively the instruments of finance, that is, money, certificates, bonds and the like, is also incapable of paying this form of debt. Considered entirely on its own, financial capital cannot transfer actual value from an earlier to a later generation. To see this, consider what would happen if we suddenly discovered a treasure trove of ancient money, in the form of seashells, say, from an earlier generation chastened by its pollution of the world. Would we take it that they had paid us some of the debt they owed us for fouling the world? Obviously not, and similarly with generations distant from now, contemplating buried gold (or what have you) from us. And this is not merely because the generations in the example don't share a currency. If George Washington's generation had buried a pile of notes in an attempt to pay of some debt of theirs to the future, the current U.S. government wouldn't upon their discovery have any extra money in the budget. If we could solve the problem this way, it would suffice to write out a cheque to the future, or rather a series of cheques, for whatever sum we project will cover our best estimates of our debts to each succeeding generation.

The above is not intended to deny that financial capital can be used to transfer value into the future at all. Rather, financial capital is a standard vehicle of intergenerational transfer. But it accomplishes this transfer in conjunction with other forms of tangible capital, capital with 'use value', as opposed to merely exchange value. When governments put 'money' in a savings fund, as in the projects mentioned above, what they really do is carve off some money and earmark it for investing in various actual projects to realize returns, financial and otherwise, from those investments. These returns are then reinvested, and the process can then iterate into the (distant) future. So financial capital alone can't be projected into the distant future.

What financial capital generally helps to produce is social and manufactured capital. Manufactured capital is durable materials and objects, from pencils to dykes to hydroelectric grids. Social capital is institutional and intellectual capital, organizations, systems, methods, communities, processes and human wisdom of all sorts.

These two categories, social and manufactured capital, are the most promising for paying an intergenerational debt. They are durable over the appropriate span of time (in some instances, at least) and they are valuable in a way that can transcend temporal distance in a way that money cannot. Future generations can use our bridges, go to our universities or bake our recipes, and derive value from doing so.

But both sorts of capital have problems when serving as intergenerational payments. That's because both sorts suffer from what we might call decay; that is, they tend to lose their value over time. This is as a result of two processes, ageing and obsolescence. Manufactured capital of all sorts (with some rare exceptions) loses its value as it ages, because ageing deteriorates material, as a general rule. Things fall apart, entropy increases; that is the nature of the world.

But manufactured capital also becomes obsolete and in ways that can be hard to predict from our point of view now. This is an independent process from ageing, although it does take some time. Anyone with any familiarity with contemporary computer equipment knows how obsolescence can destroy the value of a machine long before it breaks down from age. We can't pay our debt to the future in computer parts, for these reasons, even if we made them to last a thousand years. We cannot reasonably be expected to reliably accommodate unpredictable shifts in values between the present and middle to distant future generations.

Social capital also ages, although not in the same way as machinery and housing. Institutions become hidebound and tired, things go out of fashion and people forget and neglect the old ways for other reasons as well. More troublesome for this category is obsolescence. Progress in the arts and sciences means much of earlier learning and intellectual effort loses its value as it is superseded by new knowledge. This effect worsens over time, so that in many disciplines, like medicine, earlier theories and beliefs don't even have pedagogical value now.

So in both cases, it seems that the value of the transferred capital decays over time. Of course, this isn't a universal claim about the nature of all capital, nor even a claim about every member of these two sorts. Obviously some tokens of capital decay less quickly than others, and some, like fundamental mathematical theories and art, can endure for (we assume) the entire run of the species. But it does pose a *prima facie* problem for the capital transfer approach to intergenerational compensation. What can we make or build, what can we discover or learn, that to those a hundred years or more ahead of us would be useful enough and that we could know would be useful enough, to acquit us of the debt?

Even if we think we can manufacture or invent things of sufficient value to people belonging to the middle to distant future, though, there's a deeper problem: These sorts of capital in general require extensive effort on the part of intervening generations to deliver goods through time. Debtor generations have no right to demand such effort on the part of intermediary generations. Moreover, such a demand dilutes the value of the compensation by diluting the value of the compensatory goods and thus the degree to which the earlier generations can be said to have compensated middle to distant futures for the harm they suffer from anthropogenic climate change.

For manufactured capital, the intervening effort is largely a matter of maintenance and repair: bridges need shoring up, roads need resurfacing, and so on. Obviously, the longer the time of service for an object, the more maintenance and repair will be needed. Over a sufficiently long amount of time, the amount of maintenance and repair work will equal or surpass the initial effort of producing the object. And for really long-lived things, like roads and bridges, the maintenance budget will eventually dwarf the initial production outlay. As such, it will be harder for the builders to be able to claim very much credit for the road, for use as payment of an intergenerational debt.

To make this point we don't have to solve the riddle of the ship of Theseus, where every board of the ship was replaced over the course of its travels, since we aren't concerned with the ontology of the objects, but rather with their value and its source. We don't have to know if this is *the same* highway the county built in the nineteenth century; for our purposes it's enough to say that after many years of resurfacing and maintenance, this road is no longer a gift from those builders to the present, but rather a joint effort on the part of many generations, in the same way that a family estate handed down through many generations isn't a gift from the founder to the present heir.

Social capital also requires effort to maintain. Institutions have to be run, folkways have to be practised, languages have to be studied. We can keep some formal elements (records, recipes, etc.) of social capital alive for generations without too much effort (although libraries have to be staffed and maintained). But to be of any use we generally have to invest much time and effort tending to social capital and the institutions and organizations it embodies. So again, as time goes on, the original expenditure is dwarfed by the contributions of later generations, and as such it isn't promising as pay-ment for intergenerational debt.

We don't intend by this to mean that originators and founders of social and manufactured capital have no credit to take for the delivery of that capital to the hands of later generations. Nor that the fact that they must share this credit with other, intervening generations eliminates the value they produced. Rather we only mean to say that the amount of value that a generation can claim credit *for a given piece of social or manufactured capital* decreases as the relative amount of effort they put into it decreases, and so it decreases over time as more and more maintenance and repair is added to the total for that bit of capital.

We said earlier that originating generations have no right to the mainte-nance work of intervening generations. It might be objected that some do, particularly when the intervening generations either participate in the activi-ties that produce the damage or benefit from those activities on the part of the originating generation. Such are the circumstances of those generations immediately after ours concerning climate change, on the plausible assump-tion that they will continue to contribute to climate change through things like greenhouse gas emissions. If they themselves emit, or if they benefit from our emissions, then they owe the future the same sort of debt we do, and their maintenance might be a form of payment in that instance. While this is true, it's also true that many intervening generations likely won't be so implicated. If it takes us one generation to wean ourselves off of hydrocarbons, but the effects of climate change last for 20, then 18 generations will have to par-ticipate in the effort to deliver capital from 1 to 20 without themselves being liable for compensation.

So it seems that the capital transfer method is in a bind when it comes to compensating the future. Much of the capital becomes obsolete, and those things that can project into the future decay. And the maintenance and repair necessary to forestall that decay and make such capital useful in the future comes from generations other than the one owing the debt. This means that both the capital itself and the share of the capital the originators can claim as compensatory decay over time.

Of course, it is open to the supporter of capital transfer to accept all of the above and claim that the method is still capable of being of some use despite the decay of capital. This is perfectly possible, and we don't mean to rule out any role for capital transfer across longer spans of time. Rather we only want to point out that its efficacy decreases over time and that at about the 100-year mark it starts to look poor as a strategy for value transfer.

Finally, there is natural capital, or the capital value of the natural world, measured in 'ecosystem services' (Costanza et al. 1997) or some similar met-ric. It seems reasonable to suppose at least that future generations will value the natural world as we do, although this view might be merely chauvinistic of present tastes. But even if we assume this, there's still a problem with using natural capital to pay an intergenerational debt.

As we mentioned above at the outset, the method of capital transfer requires that a paying generation 'save' or amass and transfer more than they would have otherwise. This baseline condition recognizes that successor generations are owed something of our stock as our heirs, and we calculate extra payment (such as intergenerational compensation) starting above the (already owed) baseline.

The problem is that the baseline for the natural world seems very high—in other words, it seems that we take it that subsequent generations are owed very much, if not all, of the natural world already, leaving us little room to conserve to pay our debt. As evidence of this, consider Brian Barry's argument in his seminal 1983 piece 'Intergenerational Justice in Energy Policy' for intergenerational equality as regards natural resources:

> The basic argument for an equal claim on natural resources is that none of the usual justifications for an unequal claim—special relationships arising in virtue of past service, promises, etc.,—applies here. From an atemporal perspective, no one generation has a better or worse claim than any other to enjoy the earth's resources. In the absence of any powerful argument to the contrary, there would seem to be a strong presumption in favour of arranging things so that, as far as possible, each generation faces the same range of opportunities with respect to natural resources. I must confess that I can see no further positive argument to be made at this point. All I can do is counter what may be arguments on the other side. Is there any way in which the present generation can claim that they are entitled to a larger share of the goods supplied by nature than its successors? If not, then equal shares is the only solution compatible with justice (Barry 1983: 20).

If this argument, echoed by others (cf. Holland 1998), is correct, then every generation is owed the full measure of natural resources, as if they were the first generation, with a world unspoilt by previous occupants. Generalized to all of nature, and the reasons above certainly seem extendable to the nonresource parts of nature, this baseline leaves us no room at all to pay in natural capital. And even if we eschew the extreme position, and (*pace* Beckerman 1995) take a weaker form of baseline demand, like Daley and Cobb (Daley and Cobb 1989), there is still not enough room to pay much in this manner.

Moreover, it seems as if the effects of climate change on natural systems will, in some meaningful sense, despoil much, if not all, of nature (McKibben 1989), at least against the standard of untouched pristineness that the Barry position implies. The problem we face is one of despoiling the natural world and seeking to compensate the future for that pollution—on its face that's hardly compatible with paying the debt in the coin of pristine nature.

In this last vein, in all of the above we assume, for the sake of the case, that the actual implementation of the capital transfer could be made compatible with our other goals and in particular with the goal of remedying the problem of climate change. But this assumption isn't obvious. There are many forms of both manufactured and social capital the production of which will cause a net increase in greenhouse gas emissions, which also counts against them as possible forms of compensation for the damage caused by climate change.

So manufactured, social, financial and natural capital all face serious hurdles in being transferred over time to pay a debt of compensation. But we propose that some other techniques entirely, in particular some forms of geoengineering, can do this sort of job. How exactly can geoengineering serve as a possible method of intergenerational compensation? Before we address the technical aspect, let's first clear up a conceptual issue. Generally, theorists in the area (Caney, Gardiner, Faber, etc.) have defined compensation to mean only steps taken to pay for damage already committed after other steps have failed to avert it. If we take this approach, then geoengineering is barred by definition from counting as compensation, since it would be classified either as mitigation or as adaptation (cf. Boucher et. al. 2014, Heyward 2013).

While there is some merit in carving things up this way, we don't have to, and indeed, the law and legal philosophers typically don't. Both in theory and in practice, the 'remediation' of a harm or the cause of a harm counts as a form of compensation (cf. Goodin 1989). In fact, what is generally assumed is that remediation as a form of compensation is preferable to capital transfer, that paying money for damage is second best to remediating the damage. This preference is shared by climate compensation commentators, who often add the compensation category as an afterthought, or 'for completeness' (cf. Heyward 2013: 25).

And rights views, like Caney's (Caney 2009, 2010), make it out that compensation, meaning here money for damage as opposed to remediation, is what is owed as a result of a violation of rights, from which we can infer that it is a second choice to actions (like adaptation and mitigation) that seek to avoid rights violations in the first place (cf. Caney 2010: 171–72).

But regardless, even if we don't classify it as compensation, if we can make out that geoengineering has the potential to deliver value to later generations, then those are reasons in its favour as an approach to the problem of distant future damage, something which has not, so far as we have found, yet been elaborated.

As it is used, the term 'geoengineering' covers a number of different approaches and techniques, with quite a lot of variation between them, in terms of both mechanism and effect. None are ruled out in principle, though some of them, particularly methods of solar radiation management, appear, at least as presently conceived, to require maintenance against decay in a similarly problematic way to social and manufactured capital. For example, as is well known, solar radiation management by injection of sulphate aerosols into the stratosphere is effective, to the extent that it is effective, for only a few years at a time. The decay of such injections would clearly burden future generations indefinitely with their maintenance (Svoboda 2012).

The sort of geoengineering that we think will best serve our purposes here, again at least as presently conceived, approaches the issue by lowering the total amount of greenhouse gas in the atmosphere (relatively) permanently. This is generally known as carbon dioxide removal. Specific proposals range from enhanced rock weathering to ocean fertilization to direct air capture (Royal Society 2009), and the technologies that may be involved are coming to be known as negative emissions technologies (NET) (Caldecott et al. 2015; Lomax et al. 2015). What's significant for our purposes about carbon dioxide removal approaches is that the removal of greenhouse gases is permanent and doesn't 'decay' in the same way that capital does over time. On the assumption that there is an appreciably positive relationship between greenhouse gas load and damage in the future, lessening greenhouse gas load lessens such damages. And the amount of reduction (so long as the gas doesn't re-enter the atmosphere during the time period in question) lessens damages for all future generations, although perhaps not all to the same amount, given the complex nature of the actual relationship between climate and atmospheric greenhouse gas concentrations.

Carbon dioxide removal strategies are not perfect. Compensation seldom is perfect. But carbon dioxide removal has an advantage over capital transfer as a method of compensating the distant future for climate change. Unlike capital, which decays and must be maintained by intervening generations, reductions in greenhouse gas load are relatively stable and do their work indefinitely. The nature of the value delivered is different, of course. Rather than capital on the positive side of the ledger, carbon dioxide removal gives the future relief from damage, on the negative side. But as we noted above, this is generally taken to be a superior form of compensation, with capital transfer being the remedy of last resort, or an addendum to the remediation for other sorts of damages.

It might be objected that if the lessening of the overall greenhouse gas load is what is doing the compensating (or addressing, or whatever), then geoengineering as compensation to the middle to distant future for past emissions is not importantly different than simple mitigation. If by emitting less we can lower the overall future greenhouse gas load by the same amount as by removal, then there's no reason to favour carbon dioxide removal particularly, or geoengineering more generally, over mitigation simpliciter.

We have two responses to this criticism. The first is that it presupposes a purely consequentialist framework for assessing the relative merits of actions.

Geoengineering is on a par with mitigation, goes the objection, because all we care about is the eventual outcome of the different actions, measured in damage relief. But if we broaden our moral horizons to include deontic principles, like the compensatory principle we invoke here, or others such as the Polluter Pays Principle (OECD 1972), we can see that a remedial action for a transgression can have a very different moral character than the mere cessation of harm. Deontic principles like these mandate that some acts are matters of our moral duty, given how we have acted in the past. Such acts then have extra reasons for their commission, reasons beyond their consequential outcomes.

For example, if I foul your well with my run-off, then my coming over to clean it out and help you make it safe again is, as an action, a very different sort of thing from my merely ceasing to let my water run onto your property. In the first case, I seek to atone for what I have done, which is my duty, having caused the initial harm. In the second I simply stop doing what I ought not do. And the difference persists even if, by leaving the well alone for a stretch of time after the pollution stops, it would run itself clean again; that is, if the long-run results of the two actions were the same in terms of damage relief.

The second response is to remind us that mitigation has a ceiling (or perhaps, more accurately, a floor) of effectiveness. Once emissions get to zero, there is no further good that sort of action can do. But even if we were to get to zero tomorrow, there would still be future damage to compensate for, from the greenhouse gas load already emitted. And unlike the running well example, we don't think that the problem will remedy itself if left alone. As mentioned above, even if the present generation were to emit no greenhouse gases for tomorrow, anthropogenic climate change for generations will still occur and be harmful. How middle to distant generations will be affected gives us reasons to take geoengineering, particularly, as things stand, carbon dioxide removal technologies, seriously from a moral point of view. This is in addition to our moral obligation not to continue to contribute to greenhouse gas levels that we can plausibly believe will be harmful to near, middle and distant future generations. Just as there might be reasons for me to come clean your well even after I have stopped fouling it, so there are reasons to further investigate geoengineering with an eye to its potential as a compensatory mechanism for harm from anthropogenic climate change even in the best case scenario of a full-fledged and successful mitigation programme.

## BIBLIOGRAPHY

Alberta Queen's Printer. 1976. 'Alberta Heritage Savings Trust Fund Act.' http://www.qp.alberta.ca/1266.cfm?page=A23.cfm&leg_type=Acts&isbncln=97807797 26646&display=html.

Barry, Brian. 1983. 'Intergenerational Justice In Energy Policy'. In *Energy and the Future*, edited by Douglas Maclean and Peter G. Brown, 15–30. Totowa: Rowman and Littlefield.

Beckerman, Wilfred. 1995. 'How Would you Like your 'Sustainability', Sir? Weak or Strong? A Reply to my Critics', *Environmental Values* 4 (2): 169–79.

Boucher, Olivier, Piers M. Forster, Nicolas Gruber, Minh Ha-Duong, Mark G. Lawrence, Timothy M. Lenton, Achim Maas, and Naomi E. Vaughan. 2014. 'Rethinking Climate Engineering Categorization in the Context of Climate Change Mitigation and Adaptation.' *Wiley Interdisciplinary Reviews: Climate Change* 5 (1): 23–35.

Caldecott, Ben, Guy Lomax, and Mark Workman. 2015. *Stranded Carbon Assets and Negative Emissions Technologies*. Working Paper, University of Oxford's Smith School of Enterprise and the Environment. http://www.smithschool.ox.ac.uk/research-programmes/stranded-assets/Stranded%20Carbon%20Assets%20and%20NETs%20-%2006.02.15.pdf.

Caney, Simon. 2005. 'Cosmopolitan Justice, Responsibility, and Global Climate Change.' *Leiden Journal of International Law* 18 (4): 747–75.

Caney, Simon. 2009. 'Climate Change and the Future: Discounting for Time, Wealth, and Risk.' *Journal of Social Philosophy* 40 (2): 163–86.

Caney, Simon. 2009. 'Justice and the Distribution of Greenhouse Gas Emissions.' *Journal of Global Ethics* 5 (2): 125–46.

Caney, Simon. 2010. 'Climate Change, Human Rights, and Moral Thresholds.' In *Climate Ethics: Essential Readings*, edited by Stephen Gardiner, Simon Caney, Dale Jamieson, and Henry Shue, 163–77. New York: Oxford University Press.

Caney, Simon. 2012. 'Just Emissions.' *Philosophy & Public Affairs* 40 (4): 255–300.

Collins, M., R. Knutti, J. Arblaster, J.-L. Dufresne, T. Fichefet, P. Friedlingstein, X. Gao, W. J. Gutowski, T. Johns, G. Krinner, M. Shongwe, C. Tebaldi, A. J. Weaver and M. Wehner. 2013. 'Long-term Climate Change: Projections, Commitments and Irreversibility.' In: *Climate Change 2013: The Physical Science Basis. Contribution of Working Group I to the Fifth Assessment Report of the Intergovernmental Panel on Climate Change*, edited by T. F. Stocker, D. Qin, G.-K. Plattner, M. Tignor, S. K. Allen, J. Boschung, A. Nauels, Y. Xia, V. Bex and P. M. Midgley. Cambridge and New York: Cambridge University Press.

Costanza, Robert, Ralph d'Arge, Rudolf de Groot, Stephen Farber, Monica Grasso, Bruce Hannon, Karin Limburg, Shahid Naeem, Robert V. O'Neill, Jose Paruelo, Robert G. Raskin, Paul Sutton, Marjan van den Belt. 1997. 'The Value of the World's Ecosystem Services and Natural Capital.' *Nature* 387 (15): 253–60.

Daly, Herman and John Cobb, Jr. 1989. *For the Common Good: Redirecting the Economy Toward Community, the Environment, and a Sustainable Future*. London: Boston: Beacon Press.

Den Elzen, Michel, and R. Dellink. 2009. 'Sharing the Burden of Adaptation Financing: Translating Ethical Principles into Practical Policy.' *IOP Conference Series: Earth and Environmental Science* 6 (11): 112021.

Farber, Daniel A. 2007. 'Basic Compensation for Victims of Climate Change.' *University of Pennsylvania Law Review* 155 (6): 1605–56.

Gardiner, Stephen M. 2006. 'A Perfect Moral Storm: Climate Change, Intergenerational Ethics and the Problem of Moral Corruption.' *Environmental Values* 15: 397–413.

Gardiner, Stephen M. 2010. 'Is 'Arming the Future' With Geoengineering Really the Lesser Evil? Some Doubts About the Ethics of Intentionally Manipulating the Climate System.' In *Climate Ethics: Essential Readings*, edited by Stephen Gardiner, Simon Caney, Dale Jamieson, and Henry Shue, 284–314. New York: Oxford University Press.

Gardiner, Stephen M. 2011. *A Perfect Moral Storm: The Ethical Tragedy of Climate Change*. Oxford University Press.

Gardiner, Stephen M. 2013. 'Why Geoengineering is Not a 'global public good', and Why it is Ethically Misleading to Frame it as One.' *Climatic Change* 121 (3): 513–25.

Goodin, Robert E. 1989. 'Theories of Compensation.' *Oxford Journal of Legal Studies* 9 (1): 56–75.

Hayward, Tim. 2007. 'Human Rights Versus Emissions Rights: Climate Justice and the Equitable Distribution of Ecological Space.' *Ethics & International Affairs* 21 (4): 431–50.

Heyward, Clare. 2013. 'Situating and Abandoning Geoengineering: a Typology of Five Responses to Dangerous Climate Change.' *PS: Political Science & Politics* 46 (1): 23–27.

Holland, A. 1999. 'Sustainability: Should we Start from Here?' In *Fairness and Futurity: Essays on Environmental Sustainability and Social Justice*, edited by Andrew Dobson. Oxford: Oxford University Press.

IPCC. 2014. *Climate Change 2014: Synthesis Report. Contribution of Working Groups I, II and III to the Fifth Assessment Report of the Intergovernmental Panel on Climate Change*, edited by Core Writing Team, R. K. Pachauri and L. A. Meyer. Geneva: IPCC.

Jamieson, Dale. 1996. 'Ethics and Intentional Climate Change.' *Climatic Change* 33 (3): 323–36.

Keith, David W., Minh Ha-Duong, and Joshuah K. Stolaroff. 2006. 'Climate Strategy with $CO_2$ Capture from the Air.' *Climatic Change* 74 (1–3): 17–45.

Keith, David W. 2000. 'Geoengineering the Climate: History and Prospect.' *Annual Review of Energy and the Environment* 25 (1): 245–284.

Kriegler, Elmar, Ottmar Edenhofer, Lena Reuster, Gunnar Luderer, and David Klein. 2013. 'Is Atmospheric Carbon Dioxide Removal a Game Changer for Climate Change Mitigation?' *Climatic Change* 118 (1): 45–57.

Lomax, Guy, Mark Workman, Timothy Lenton, and Nilay Shah. 2015. 'Reframing the Policy Approach to Greenhouse Gas Removal Technologies.' *Energy Policy* 78: 125–36.

Lomax, Guy, Timothy M. Lenton, Adepeju Adeosun, and Mark Workman. 2015. 'Investing in Negative Emissions.' *Nature Climate Change* 5 (6): 498–500.

McKibben, Bill. 1989. *The End of Nature*. New York: Random House.

Meadowcroft, James. 2013. 'Exploring Negative Territory: Carbon Dioxide Removal and Climate Policy Initiatives.' *Climatic Change* 118 (1): 137.

McKinnon, Catriona. 2012. *Climate Change and Future Justice: Precaution, Compensation and Triage*. New York: Routledge.

Ministry of Finance. Norway. https://www.regjeringen.no/en/topics/the-economy/the-government-pension-fund/id1441/.

NASA. 2014. 'Decline of West Antarctic Glaciers Appears Irreversible.' http://earthobservatory.nasa.gov/IOTD/view.php?id=83672.

OECD. 1972. 'Recommendation of the Council on Guiding Principles Concerning International Economic Aspects of Environmental Policies.' http://acts.oecd.org/Instruments/ShowInstrumentView.aspx?InstrumentID=4&InstrumentPID=255&Lang=en&Book=False.

Page, Edward. 1999. 'Intergenerational Justice and Climate Change.' *Political Studies* 47 (1): 53–66.

Royal Society. 2009. *Geoengineering the Climate: Science, Governance and Uncertainty.* https://royalsociety.org/~/media/Royal_Society_Content/policy/publications/2009/8693.pdf.

Ryaboshapko, A. G., and A. P. Revokatova. 2015. 'A Potential Role of the Negative Emission of Carbon Dioxide in Solving the Climate Problem.' *Russian Meteorology and Hydrology* 40 (7): 443–55.

Shue, Henry. 1993. 'Subsistence Emissions and Luxury Emissions.' *Law & Policy* 15 (1): 39–60.

Shue, Henry. 1992. 'The Unavoidability of Justice.' *The International Politics of the Environment: Actors, Interests, and Institutions*, edited by Andrew Hurrell and Benedict Kingsbury, 373–97. Oxford: Oxford University Press.

Svoboda, Toby, and Peter Irvine. 2014. 'Ethical and Technical Challenges in Compensating for Harm due to Solar Radiation Management Geoengineering.' *Ethics, Policy & Environment* 17 (2): 157–74.

Svoboda, Toby. 2012. 'Is Aerosol Geoengineering Ethically Preferable to Other Climate Change Strategies?' *Ethics & the Environment* 17 (2): 111–35.

Wallimann-Helmer, Ivo. 2015. 'Justice for Climate Loss and Damage.' *Climatic Change* 133 (3): 469–80.

*Part II*

# GEOENGINEERING JUSTICE IN PRACTICE

*Chapter 6*

# Solar Geoengineering and Obligations to the Global Poor

Joshua Horton and David Keith

One of the very few things that nearly all participants in the climate change debate agree on is that the effects of climate change will disproportionately affect the poor, for the simple reason that poorer people will have fewer resources available to them to manage climate risks and adapt to unavoidable changes compared to their wealthier neighbours. This simple fact applies both to disadvantaged people in every country and more broadly to the developing world in relation to rich, industrialized nations. Some concrete examples help illustrate this particularly tragic aspect of climate change.

More frequent and more intense heat waves will harm the poor more than the rich both because the rich are more protected by technology such as air conditioning and because the regions most prone to future extreme heat events are generally less wealthy. The poor have less reliable access to water, which will only be exacerbated by the growth in the number and severity of droughts. Climate change will reduce yields of many staple crops, with disproportionate impacts on the global poor whose economies rely more on agriculture and whose existence is more marginal to begin with. The disadvantaged are more likely to depend on local ecosystems for their subsistence and livelihoods, so that climate-induced ecosystem stresses will prove particularly harmful to the least well off. The loss of coral reefs, for example, will be especially damaging for poor coastal communities who rely on reefs for food and income as well as protection from increasingly destructive storm surges. Rising sea levels are also likely to affect the poor most of all, since they can least afford to relocate.

From a moral perspective, this asymmetry of impacts is particularly troubling since the emissions that give rise to climate change come from energy use that disproportionately benefits the rich. The rich have got richer doing things that will hurt the poor most of all.

Distributive concerns arise at two separate levels of analysis. First, *within* countries, climate change entails rich people making gains at the expense of poor people, who must bear the brunt of its consequences. This is as true within developing countries as it is within developed countries, since the disadvantaged in each will be relatively less capable of dealing effectively with climate stresses. Second, *among* countries, climate change entails rich nations making gains at the expense of poor nations, who similarly must bear the brunt of global warming. Individuals and collectives are distinct moral entities, each operating in recognizable ethical spheres that, while interconnected, are characterized by separate assumptions, expectations and internal logics (Cohen and Sabel 2006). In what follows, we proceed from an international, global perspective, although many of our arguments and conclusions may be equally applicable to individuals within societies.

Intuition tells us that the requirements of justice are violated when an activity benefits wealthy countries at the expense of poorer ones. In such cases, there would seem to be an obligation to, at a minimum, take steps to reduce harms falling on the most vulnerable nations. Additional obligations may exist as well, such as halting the activity in question or compensating states that have suffered harms.

We develop and defend in this chapter the central thesis that taking principles of global distributive justice seriously entails a moral obligation to conduct research on solar geoengineering. In the first section, we make a case grounded in temporal considerations that justice requires a thorough investigation of solar geoengineering, also known as solar radiation management (SRM), as a potential tool of climate policy to complement mitigation and adaptation. SRM is a set of technologies that would reflect a small fraction of incoming sunlight back to space, thereby cooling the planet. The most commonly discussed type of SRM would involve scattering reflective aerosols in the upper atmosphere to reduce warming on a global scale. Following this we consider and critique two justice-based arguments against research into SRM: (1) that solar geoengineering would hurt the global poor disproportionately and (2) that solar geoengineering would represent an abdication of historical responsibility on the part of the global North. We conclude by situating these arguments in the context of the broader debate about geoengineering, contending that opposition to research on SRM threatens to violate principles of justice by effectively condemning developing countries to suffer the consequences of activities of which they have not been the primary beneficiaries.

## DIFFERENT CLIMATE CHANGE POLICIES, DIFFERENT DISTRIBUTIONS OF BENEFITS AND HARMS

The ethical concerns arising from solar geoengineering are best understood in the context of the range of responses to growing climate risks. We consider four kinds of responses to limit climate risks: *mitigation* entails reducing emissions of carbon dioxide and other greenhouse gases (GHGs); *carbon removal* technologies remove carbon dioxide from the atmosphere; *adaptation* involves implementing social and technological changes that reduce the damage from a given amount of climate change; and finally, *solar geoengineering* would partially and temporarily offset some of the climate changes caused by a given level of accumulated GHGs.

The ethical implications of these responses turn on the particular distribution of benefits and harms associated with each. We focus on two dimensions over which benefits and harms are unequally distributed: time and wealth. For simplicity, we consider two time periods, the *near term*, or roughly the next half-century, and the *long term*, more than half a century out. Climate change is a slow-motion problem. In what follows, we also assume that our world is one of limited resources, so that money spent on one policy today entails the opportunity cost of what investing in another policy might have paid tomorrow.

Now let us consider how the four responses vary in their impacts across time and wealth. Because of inertia in the climate system and in the world's energy infrastructure, the benefits of any mitigation policy—say a commitment to a vastly faster transition to low-carbon energy—are necessarily slow. Cutting emissions does surprisingly little to reduce climate risks in the near term.

Suppose emissions are cut to zero in 50 years—an extraordinarily rapid energy system transition. Taking global surface temperatures as a proxy for climate risks, such a transition would reduce the growth of risks, but risks would still grow. And rapid emission cuts would impose significant economic costs that may, for example, appear as increased energy prices. While there would also be side benefits in the form of reduced air pollution, there is broad consensus that emission cuts impose costs, and, all else being equal, these costs will be felt more by the poor for whom energy is a larger fraction of expenses. So in the near term, mitigation has significant costs compared to only modest benefits, and a disproportionate share of the costs may fall on the poor.

Mitigation looks very different in the long term. From a more distant perspective, the benefits appear larger since it is mainly after the next half-century when climate risks that otherwise would have become manifest will be avoided due to emission cuts in the present. Furthermore, future benefits from present mitigation will accrue to rich and poor alike. At the same time, since most of the costs of mitigation are borne in the near term, future costs would be small. Thus, while the net short-term effects of mitigation would be harmful and may be concentrated on the poor, the long-term effects would generally be beneficial and universal.

The distribution of benefits and harms associated with carbon removal is very similar to that which characterizes mitigation (Keith 2009). Indeed, until net emissions are near zero, the distinction between mitigation and carbon removal is moot: both have local costs and reduce net emissions. The one exception relates to the ability of carbon removal technologies to generate 'negative emissions'—in the long term, carbon removal methods would enable society to draw down legacy emissions and thereby further reduce climate risk and/or reduce the amount of any solar geoengineering deployed. However, mitigation and carbon removal are sufficiently similar that, for purposes of the present discussion, we will not address carbon removal further.

Unlike mitigation, adaptation will provide substantial benefits in the short term. These benefits, however, are local in nature in that they reduce damages from climate impacts in a way that is spatially restricted. For example, a seawall protects only those located behind it from the encroaching sea. One consequence of the local scale of adaptation benefits is that the strongest incentives for action apply to local actors. All things being equal, the poor will therefore have fewer resources to devote to those adaptation measures that would benefit them. This situation is further aggravated by the costly nature of many adaptation measures. Because the benefits of adaptation are both local and expensive, the only way that all the world's poor will share in them equally is if global redistribution of wealth is perfect so that everyone can equally afford to adopt this response. This is theoretically possible, and for many it is the morally preferred outcome, but the persistence of inequality over millennia argues that it is unlikely to obtain.

If there is a trade-off between funds spent on adaptation and mitigation today, as might be the case if there were a de facto fixed amount of resources available for all climate response measures, then the opportunity cost of investing in adaptation would be the benefits of emission cuts that would have improved the welfare of future generations. Compared to mitigation, then, adaptation directly benefits the present at some expense to the future, but its theoretical potential to help the poor most of all is undermined by the practical consequences of its costly, local character.

Similar to adaptation, solar geoengineering might also provide benefits in the short term, but these benefits would differ from those provided by adaptation in two fundamental ways. First, the advantages conferred by solar geoengineering would be global in scale by virtue of SRM's inherently global nature, in contrast to the local-scale benefits typical of adaptation. This means that local actors pursuing local interests through the use of SRM might, if the intervention was properly designed, benefit the rest of the world (especially the global poor) as a virtual by-product of their otherwise self-interested use of solar geoengineering. Second, assuming for the moment that adaptation provides the same reduction in climate risk as SRM, the cost of providing a given level of climate protection would likely be much lower for SRM than for adaptation, since SRM implementation is estimated to be relatively inexpensive (at least in direct cost terms) (McClellan, Keith, and Apt 2012). Since a given unit of climate protection would benefit the poor disproportionately, the cost differential between adaptation and SRM imparts a comparatively greater redistributive potential to the latter response option.

At the same time, differences in the nature of the radiative forcings produced by greenhouse warming compared to solar geoengineering mean that SRM cannot perfectly compensate for the effects of elevated GHG levels; in other words, solar geoengineering is incapable of wholly undoing climate change. Solar geoengineering would also entail potentially negative side effects such as uneven regional changes in temperature and precipitation (although such effects could probably be minimized or possibly even negated through optimization—see below). Moreover, as with adaptation, the opportunity cost of mitigation foregone in favour of SRM would be greater climate risk in the long term. Overall, therefore, compared to mitigation, SRM would likely provide net benefits in the near term that would help the poor most of all, at the cost of emission cuts today that would otherwise benefit everyone in the future. Unlike adaptation, however, the functionally redistributive benefits of SRM would be relatively cheap to provide and could in principle be supplied globally by agents acting primarily in their own interest.

We assumed above that adaptation and SRM are perfect local substitutes, but in reality they are not. Limits exist to the ability of adaptation measures to reduce climate risks. Coastal defences may be adequate to protect against storm surges, and people may be relocated away from areas vulnerable to sea-level rise, but other climate harms, such as those related to unavoidable temperature increases, will not be amenable to adaptation measures. Some staple crops such as maize, rice and wheat, for example, are subject to temperature thresholds above which yields fall dramatically. Similarly, coral bleaching above fixed thresholds will be irreversible on human timescales, depriving coastal communities of critical natural resources.

By contrast, if SRM were proven effective in reducing the global mean temperature, as the available evidence strongly suggests it would be, both the direct effects of increased temperature such as threats to public health and the indirect effects such as agricultural losses and more destructive storms could be at least partially offset by use of the technology.[1] And SRM appears capable of reducing some major present-day risks that cannot be addressed nearly as effectively by adaptation. For instance, there is new evidence that increased temperatures have direct impacts on human physical and intellectual productivity as well as on mortality and that even in wealthy countries which have technology to lessen these effects (such as air conditioning), the economic value of these impacts can be roughly as large as all other climate impacts combined (Park 2016). Given that these impacts are regressive in that they harm the poor more than the rich, and given that the one thing SRM is best able to achieve appears to be an approximately globally uniform reduction in temperatures, there is now an additional reason to expect that SRM would benefit the poor even more than the rich.

Based on these arguments demonstrating both that adaptation and solar geoengineering are capable of benefitting today's poor in ways that mitigation cannot and that the benefits from SRM compared to adaptation are cheaper, more global in scale and effect, and more reliant on the realistic assumption of self-interested behaviour, we conclude that a prima facie moral obligation exists to investigate the potential of SRM to help the developing world. An obligation to investigate is not the same as an obligation to use. SRM technology is subject to a range of significant uncertainties, and if research into SRM were to demonstrate a potential for harmful side effects or unresolvable uncertainties with serious risks for people or the natural environment, SRM should at the least be critically reassessed and may ultimately warrant abandonment. Yet such research has yet to be performed, and without an adequate evidence base, the *a priori* dismissal of SRM as one potential tool of climate policy is at best imprudent, and at worst immoral.

## ARGUMENTS AGAINST RESEARCH

From this perspective, the fact that many critics of SRM research base their opposition on self-described concerns about global distributive justice is paradoxical. There are at least two types of argument against research into SRM formulated in terms of global distributive justice.

### 'Solar Geoengineering Would Hurt the Global Poor'

The first argument contends that, just as impacts from climate change will disproportionately affect developing countries, so too the harms likely to result from solar geoengineering would affect the global South most of all. Christopher Preston refers to this exacerbated global gap as a 'moral deficit' (Preston 2012: 79). Arguably, this view derives in large measure from a widely publicized 2008 article by Alan Robock and colleagues, who reported that solar geoengineering could potentially disrupt Asian and African summer monsoons (Robock 2008). Martin Bunzl, for example, raises the possibility that 'SRM itself may do harm by making some *worse off than they would be with global warming alone*. In support of this inference, Robock et al. have a model that suggests that sub-Saharan Africa would have less cloud cover after geoengineering and thus be hotter and drier than it would be with climate change alone' (italics in original) (Bunzl 2011: 71). Building on this, Toby Svoboda and colleagues catalogue possible reductions in precipitation caused by sulphate aerosol geoengineering (SAG) in Africa, South America and Southeast Asia, leading them to conclude that solar geoengineering 'has the potential to increase benefits for some by increasing harms for others. For this reason, … SAG faces an obstacle in meeting the requirements of … theories of distributive justice' (Svoboda et al. 2011: 165). We might call this the Hurts the Global Poor argument.

A substantial part of this argument rests on an empirical claim either that solar geoengineering will be inherently harmful to parts of the world where poverty is greatest or that a specific implementation of solar geoengineering would be harmful. We first address the strongest empirical claim before discussing the implications arising from the range of ways in which solar geoengineering might be implemented.

Scientific analysis of SRM remains at a very early stage. Yet preliminary work already indicates that use of SRM could reduce the most important aspects of climate change, including changes in temperature, precipitation and extreme events. Specifically, research shows that if relatively small SRM interventions were conducted, *all* regions of the world, encompassing global North *and* South, would be better off in the sense that the most salient climate risks would be reduced (Moreno-Cruz et al. 2011, Ricke et al. 2013). Ben Kravitz et al., for instance, show that when a moderate amount of SRM is used, and both temperature and precipitation values are taken into account, all regions are brought closer to preindustrial conditions than they would be without SRM (Kravitz et al. 2014). Under this admittedly idealized scenario, using SRM in effect shifts the Pareto curve outward, so that no region is harmed in absolute terms. Since in relative terms developing countries stand to gain more from reductions in climate change than developed countries, the world's poorest and most vulnerable people would likely benefit disproportionately under this scenario. This study is the only multi-model study that examines all regions systematically, and, at a minimum, it casts substantial doubt on the types of claims we cite above which tend to focus on a single model, variable or region. The assertion that SRM hurts the poor requires demonstrating that those regions where damages from SRM are largest correlate with poverty. We are unaware of any such study for even a single experimental model run of SRM, let alone for a representative ensemble of SRM methods and models.

Note that to the extent that specific harms such as reduced rainfall did fall on developing countries as a result of solar geoengineering, it is possible that these would be offset by the gains attributable to other avoided damages from climate change. Quantifying the costs and benefits of SRM is undoubtedly a problematic proposition, and practical efforts to do so would certainly fall short of the ideal (Davies 2010). In addition, any utilitarian assessment would need to ensure robust procedural and substantive protections so as not to violate fundamental principles of justice (Rawls 1999). But given these not inconsiderable caveats, the available evidence indicates that developing countries could enjoy absolute gains in welfare over the short term as a result of SRM, while also making relative welfare gains compared to industrialized countries.

Now let us turn to the question of how specific implementations of SRM might harm the poor. While it is true that SRM may *hurt* the developing world disproportionately, it is equally true that SRM may *help* the developing world disproportionately, at least in the near term. Indeed, a multitude of global distributive outcomes might result from the use of SRM. Which outcome obtains in practice, that is which particular distribution of harms and benefits materializes, would depend entirely on *how* SRM is used. In other words, the short-term distributive impact of solar geoengineering is ultimately a question of optimization.

Implementing SRM in the real world would necessarily entail selecting values for a number of control parameters, so that system operators could 'turn the knobs' to preferred settings. These parameters include how much reflectant to use, where to disperse it (latitude, longitude, altitude), how often to disperse it, how long to use it and so on. These are hardly trivial questions, as the specific details of any actual deployment would have significant consequences in terms of regional effects. The regional distribution of harms, benefits and risks resulting from SRM, in other words, would not be fixed, but rather would vary depending on the particular choices made by decision-makers. In technical terms, 'Introducing multiple spatial and temporal degrees of freedom has the potential to improve how well SRM can compensate for $CO_2$-induced climate change, and thus reduce concerns over the resulting regional inequalities' (MacMartin et al. 2013: 365). Yet while this claim may be physically realistic, any serious discussion of how solar geoengineering might be fine-tuned to achieve an optimal geographic distribution of harms and benefits (however defined) is clearly premature.

In the larger context of choices between different climate response instruments, it is true that the use of SRM today might come at the opportunity cost of future mitigation benefits that would otherwise accrue to the entire global population. Hence, even a justly designed SRM deployment scheme may harm the poor in the long term if resources are diverted from mitigation in the present. Yet this possibility makes the issue of harm to the most vulnerable a complicated trade across time, not a simple trade between rich and poor. To assert that solar geoengineering would harm developing countries most of all, as the Hurts the Global Poor argument would have it, both obscures this inherently complex temporal trade-off and misunderstands the existing evidence base by attributing an essential regressive quality to SRM technology where none appears to exist.

## 'SOLAR GEOENGINEERING WOULD SHIRK RESPONSIBILITY'

The other, more nuanced, global distributive justice argument against SRM claims that conducting research on SRM, and possibly deploying the technology, represents a means for the rich world to avoid meeting its historical climate justice commitments to the poor. In other words, principles of justice require that the global North, which is primarily responsible for climate change, take primary responsibility for mitigating the problem, which as noted above disproportionately affects the global South. The fullest, and most morally correct, way to accomplish this is for the global North to take on the (costly) burden of emissions reduction. SRM is an imperfect substitute for emissions mitigation but appears to be less expensive, by orders of magnitude. The temptation for industrialized countries to 'take the easy way out' by pursuing SRM rather than a substantive programme of decarbonization is obvious. The justice implications of opting for the 'quick fix' of SRM over more demanding but ethically satisfactory mitigation efforts, however, make solar geoengineering morally dubious. As Stephen Gardiner argues (albeit from a virtue ethics perspective), 'One way in which our lives might be tarnished would be if the commitment to geoengineering becomes a vehicle through which we (e.g. our nation and/or our generation) try to disguise our exploitation of other nations, generations, and species' (Gardiner 2011: 392).[2] Clive Hamilton puts it in more direct distributive justice terms: 'Installing a solar filter would cement the failure of the North in its obligations to the global South' (Hamilton 2013: 163).

The argument that SRM would represent the unjust avoidance of a moral obligation to cut emissions, which we might call Shirks Responsibility, has two significant flaws. The first relates to the so-called 'moral hazard'—or 'risk compensation' effect (Reynolds 2015)—of solar geoengineering, that is the possibility that the availability of SRM might lead individuals to reduce their efforts at emissions abatement, since SRM appears to be much less costly and easier to implement than mitigation while providing benefits that are approximate to emissions reductions. The moral hazard argument differs from the simpler opportunity cost argument presented above in that the latter pertains to the practical consequences of options foregone, whereas the former pertains to the likelihood of foregoing those options. From a theoretical perspective, there is reason to believe that an economically rational agent would indeed shift some resources away from mitigation and towards solar geoengineering if the latter were an available policy option.[3]

Interestingly, there is little empirical evidence that people would behave this way in practice. Christine Merk, Gert Pönitzsch and Katrin Rehdanz, in the first rigorous empirical analysis of the question, declare, 'We find no evidence for risk compensation at an individual level as a reaction to information on SAI [stratospheric aerosol injection]' (Merk et al. 2015: 6). Existing studies have been conducted at the level of individuals, yet critics generally make no distinction between moral hazard for individuals and for states, and to our knowledge have not presented any evidence that governments would be more susceptible than people.

However, given the limited empirical work conducted to date, generally supportive results from theoretical modelling exercises and common-sense expectations that rational actors would compensate for risk in the short term by switching effort from mitigation to solar geoengineering, we accept that 'moral hazard' in some form would be likely to occur. If so, what would be the impacts for distributive justice? In the short term, the poor would be better off in that there would be less-severe climate impacts due to the action of solar geoengineering. In the long term, the entire global population, rich and poor alike, would be worse off as a consequence of the added risk caused by lessened efforts on mitigation. The crux of the matter is the rights of the poor in the coming decades compared to the poor in the distant future.

One way out may be to assume that global economic growth will continue into the future, and therefore tomorrow's poor are likely to be better off than today's poor. With the future poor both less certain to lack resources, and more likely to be better situated than their contemporaries, it could be argued that the obligation to today's poor, and hence to use SRM, is stronger. This resolution, however, is speculative. In the end, whether or not SRM would be morally appropriate in this complex ethical landscape is a question that can be answered only by broad-based research on solar geoengineering. Indeed, to close off research into SRM is to shirk the Northern responsibility to address the full range of climate risks destined to affect the global South most of all. A more nuanced understanding of the temporal dimensions of climate risk thus has the effect of inverting the Shirks Responsibility argument and places the burden of proof on those who would seek to prevent investigation into solar geoengineering.

The second flaw in this argument, which is suggested by the language used in our critique up to now, is that its frame of reference is based on particular climate policy tools, rather than on reducing climate risk more generally.[4] By focusing on risk management tools rather than on risk management itself, critics of SRM have allowed preferences for certain policy instruments to dictate their views at the cost of addressing the complete spectrum of risks posed by climate change. Assuming that both mitigation and SRM, responsibly pursued, satisfy basic moral requirements (which we believe they do, though we acknowledge that this is contested), the refusal to countenance SRM based solely on hypothesized technical, organizational, political or other qualities necessarily comes at the expense of endeavouring to protect people in poor countries from extreme temperatures, violent storms, rising seas and other climate harms likely to manifest in the coming decades. By contrast, when managing climate risk is the framework for evaluation, ethical considerations demand that SRM be taken seriously (in addition to mitigation and adaptation). Historical obligations to the global South include mitigating harms not just in the long term, but in the near future as well; this duty cannot be fulfilled by emissions reductions alone.

## CONCLUSION

Thus, a better appreciation of climate science, including the findings from initial research on SRM, as well as the adoption of a comprehensive climate risk management framework, come together to undercut both the Shirks Responsibility and Hurts the Global Poor arguments against solar geoengineering. To repeat, we contend that a prima facie moral obligation exists to research SRM in the interest of developing countries, because SRM appears to be the most effective and practicable option available to alleviate a range of near-term climate damages that are certain to hurt the global South most of all. It is incumbent on those who oppose research on solar geoengineering to either (1) propose an alternative to SRM that would be as capable of reducing climate risks over the next several decades as solar geoengineering appears to be, or, failing that, (2) demonstrate that SRM would violate principles of global distributive justice. Since we know of no other plausible response that would be as effective in scope and scale at reducing short-term climate risks as SRM appears to be, and we regard as false the technological essentialism that underlies arguments about the supposed inevitability of unfair distributive consequences, we believe that justice requires further research on solar geoengineering.

The moral hazard argument, which underlies what we have termed the Shirks Responsibility argument against SRM, is central to a wide range of critiques of solar geoengineering (Hale 2012). Generally speaking, these critiques both originate and target audiences in the global North (Belter and Siedel 2013). Hamilton, for instance, writes that 'research is virtually certain to reduce incentives to pursue emission reductions. … Already a powerful predilection for finding excuses not to cut greenhouse gas emissions is obvious to all, so that any apparently plausible method of getting a party off the hook is likely to be seized upon' (Hamilton 2014: 167–68). The ETC Group, a civil society group critical of many emerging technologies, similarly warns against geoengineering as a 'perfect excuse', suggesting 'Geoengineering offers governments an option other than reducing emissions and protecting biodiversity. Geoengineering research is often seen as a way to "buy time," but it also gives governments justification to delay compensation for damage caused by climate change and to avoid taking action on emissions reduction' (ETC 2010: 33). Naomi Klein offers another example, declaring, 'the fact that geoengineering is being treated so seriously should underline the urgent need for a real plan A—one based on emission reduction, however economically radical it must be' (Klein 2014: 283). She continues: 'How about some other solutions ... like taking far larger shares of the profits from the rogue corporations most responsible for waging war on the climate and using those resources to clean up their mess? Or reversing energy privatizations to regain control over our grids?' (ibid., 284).

At the risk of oversimplification, this line of argument essentially involves rich-country commentators criticizing solar geoengineering in an effort to shore up mitigation as their priority domestic climate policy, while ignoring the potentially huge distributional advantages SRM might confer on the world's poorest in the global South. Their deeper motives vary, from a sense of moral indignation over shirking (Hamilton) to neo-Luddism (ETC Group) to anti-corporate ideology (Klein) and beyond. Whatever the reasons, the resulting admonition not to research SRM for fear of its policy implications for industrialized countries, at the expense of possibly enormous welfare gains in developing countries, is ethically disturbing in a global moral context.

We agree with these critics that, since long-term climate risks can only be reduced through mitigation, the present generation has a duty to future generations to implement major reductions in carbon emissions, whatever the efficacy of solar geoengineering turns out to be. But we part ways with them in their neglect of the short term, during which millions of the world's most vulnerable people will suffer harms from climate change that simply cannot be mitigated by emissions cuts. Given the very strong evidence that SRM would significantly reduce global temperatures and thereby limit climate impacts, particularly in the developing world, we view research on SRM as a moral imperative.

Fundamental principles of justice require that, all things being equal, the disadvantaged should not suffer from the results of actions benefitting the better off. Opponents of research into the possible benefits (*and harms*) of solar geoengineering threaten to violate this requirement in at least two ways. First, failing to conduct research puts the global South at risk of paying the highest near-term price for rich-world industrialization and the historical emissions associated with it. And second, stopping research may advance some rich-world political agendas in which geoengineering is at most a tangential issue, but it would come at the cost of assured suffering by poor countries confronting immediate threats that are largely absent from such agendas. Supporting research on solar geoengineering offers the best way to avoid these unjust outcomes.

## NOTES

1. For robust evidence of the efficacy of SRM in reducing global mean temperature, see Kravitz et al. (2014).
2. It is important to note that Gardiner is primarily concerned with the implications of geoengineering for individual character rather than its specific distributional consequences. While we disagree with Gardiner's proposition that researching and/or implementing geoengineering might ultimately be a reflection of "moral corruption," we do not consider his argument further here.
3. See, for example, Heutel et al. (2015).
4. For an articulation of the rationale for approaching climate change as an issue of risk management, see Schneider (2001).

## BIBLIOGRAPHY

Belter, Christopher W., and Dian J. Seidel. 2013. 'A Bibliometric Analysis of Climate Engineering Research,' *WIREs Climate Change* 4: 417–27.

Bunzl, M. 2011. 'Geoengineering Harms and Compensation.' *Stanford Journal of Law, Science & Policy* 4: 70–76.

Cohen, Joshua and Charles Sabel. (2006) 'Extra Rempublicam Nulla Justitia?' *Philosophy & Public Affairs* 34: 147–75.

Davies, Gareth. 2010. 'Framing the Social, Political, and Environmental Risks and Benefits of Geoengineering: Balancing the Hard-to-Imagine Against the Hard-to-Measure,' *Tulsa Law Review* 46: 261–82.

ETC Group. 2010. *Geopiracy: The Case Against Geoengineering*. ETC Group Communique #103. http://www.etcgroup.org/content/geopiracy-case-against-geoengineering.

Gardiner, Stephen G. 2011. *A Perfect Moral Storm: The Ethical Tragedy of Climate Change* Oxford, UK: Oxford University Press.

Hale, Ben. 2012. 'The World That Would Have Been: Moral Hazard Arguments Against Geoengineering.' In *Engineering the Climate: The Ethics of Solar Radiation Management*, edited by Christopher J. Preston, 113–31. Lanham, MD: Lexington Books.

Hamilton, Clive. 2013. *Earthmasters: The Dawn of the Age of Climate Engineering.* New Haven, CT: Yale University Press.

Heutel, Garth, Juan Moreno-Cruz, and Soheil Shayegh. 2015. 'Solar Geoengineering and the Price of Carbon.' *NBER Working Paper Series*, Working Paper 21355. Cambridge, MA: NBER.

Keith, David W. 2009. 'Why Capture $CO_2$ From The Atmosphere?' *Science* 325: 1654–55.

Klein, Naomi. 2014. *This Changes Everything: Capitalism vs. the Climate*. New York: Simon & Schuster.

Kravitz, Ben, Douglas G. MacMartin, Alan Robock, Philip J. Rasch, Katharine L. Ricke, Jason N.S. Cole, Charles L. Curry, Peter J. Irvine, Duoying Ji, David W. Keith, Jon Egill Kristjansson, John C. Moore, Helene Muri, Balwinder Singh, Simone Tilmes, Shingo Watanabe, Shuting Yang, and Jin-Ho Yoon. 2014. 'A Multi-Model Assessment of Regional Climate Disparities Caused by Solar Geoengineering,' *Environmental Research Letters* 9 doi:10.1088/1748-9326/9/7/074013.

MacMartin, Douglas G., David W. Keith, Ben Kravitz, and Ken Caldeira. 2013. 'Management of Trade-Offs in Geoengineering Through Optimal Choice of Non-Uniform Radiative Forcing,' *Nature Climate Change* 3: 365–68.

McClellan, Justin, David W. Keith, and Jay Apt. 2012. 'Cost Analysis of Stratospheric Albedo Modification Delivery Systems.' *Environmental Research Letters* 7. doi:10.1088/1748-9326/7/3/034019.

Merk, Christine, Gert Pönitzsch, and Katrin Rehdanz. 2015. 'Knowledge about Aerosol Injection Does Not Reduce Individual Mitigation Efforts.' Kiel Institute for the World Economy. Working Paper No. 2006. https://www.ifw-members.ifw-kiel.de/publications/knowledge-about-aerosol-injection-does-not-reduce-individual-mitigation-efforts/KWP%202006%20Merk%20Ponitzsch%20Rehdanz.pdf.

Moreno-Cruz, Juan B., Katharine L. Ricke, and David W. Keith. 2011. 'A Simple Model to Account for Regional Inequalities in the Effectiveness of Solar Radiation Management.' *Climatic Change* 110: 649–68.

Park, Jisung. 2016. 'Will We Adapt? Temperature Shocks, Labor Productivity and Adaptation to Climate Change in the United States (1986–2012).' *Harvard Project on Climate Agreements*, Discussion Paper 16–81. Cambridge, MA: Harvard Kennedy School.

Preston, Christopher. 2012. 'Solar Radiation Management and Vulnerable Populations: The Moral Deficit and its Prospects.' In *Engineering the Climate: The Ethics of Solar Radiation Management*, edited by Christopher Preston, 77–93. Lanham, MD: Lexington Books.

Rawls, John. 1999. *A Theory of Justice*. Cambridge, MA: Harvard University Press.

Reynolds, Jesse. 2015. 'A Critical Examination of the Climate Engineering Moral Hazard and Risk Compensation Concern.' *The Anthropocene Review* 2: 174–91.

Ricke, Katharine L., Juan B. Moreno-Cruz, and Ken Caldeira. 2013. 'Strategic Incentives for Climate Geoengineering Coalitions to Exclude Broad Participation.' *Environmental Research Letters* 8. doi:10.1088/1748-9326/8/1/014021.

Robock, Alan, Luke Oman, and Georgiy L. Stenchikov. 2008. 'Regional Climate Responses to Geoengineering With Tropical and Arctic $SO_2$ Injections,' *Journal of Geophysical Research Atmospheres* 113: D16101. DOI: 10.1029/2008JD010050.

Schneider, Stephen H. 2001. 'What Is 'Dangerous' Climate Change?' *Nature* 411: 17–19.

Svoboda, Toby, Klaus Keller, Marlos Goes, and Nancy Tuana. 2011. 'Sulfate Aerosol Geoengineering: The Question of Justice,' *Public Affairs Quarterly* 25: 157–80.

## Chapter 7

# Why Aggressive Mitigation Must Be Part of Any Pathway to Climate Justice

## Christian Baatz and Konrad Ott

This contribution's aim is twofold: on the one hand, we argue that wealthy high-emitting countries are obligated to radically lower their greenhouse gas (GHG) emissions, and if undertaken properly, this will very likely not over-burden their respective citizens (section "Mitigation duties and associated burdens"); on the other hand, we defend the primacy of mitigation duties arguing that possible obligations to adopt further supplementary strategies do not diminish these duties (section "Mitigation Duties and climate engineering options"). Please note that we do not claim that mitigation alone will be able to limit temperature increase to 'well below 2 degrees' as the Paris Agreement states, and we remain agnostic on which carbon dioxide removal (CDR) technologies should back up mitigation efforts (but think that some of them are necessary). We also do not comment on what might in future justify a high-risk climate engineering (CE) technology deployment. Finally, note that we use 'mitigation' as a shortcut for the reduction of anthropogenic GHG emissions, considering all forms of sink enhancement as CDR.

## MITIGATION DUTIES AND ASSOCIATED BURDENS

It is widely agreed that global GHG emissions ought to be limited. From the moral point of view, every person is entitled to some part of the remaining emissions budget, and this can be referred to as a person's fair share (FS) of emissions entitlements (Caney 2012; Shue 2014: 311). In an ideal situation, no one exceeds her FS, and the total past, present and future emissions budget does not cause harmful climate change. By contrast, if a sufficient number of agents do exceed their FS, they collectively cause harm (Baatz 2014).

Our so-called FS argument stipulates that A's GHG emissions are morally wrong if:

(1) A exceeds her FS of emissions entitlements, and
(2) by emitting, A contributes to a harmful activity.

We have explained the argument elsewhere, but we assume that criterion (2) holds for all present emissions (in detail Baatz 2016; Baatz and Voget-Kleschin 2016).

In this contribution, we are primarily concerned with the duties of executive and legislative bodies that represent the citizens of a given country (though we believe that the argument equally applies to individuals). According to our argument, these agents ought to limit emissions to their FS, meaning that they ought to adopt measures that appropriately limit the emissions of those they represent.

Climate change is a collective action problem, though. Institutional solutions are both more effective and more efficient compared to a situation in which each agent is expected to reduce its contribution unilaterally (Neuteleers 2010; Ostrom 2015). It is thus equally important that agents try to bring about effective and just institutions (Bell 2011; Cripps 2013). Although this argument is usually made with respect to individuals, it can also be applied to collective agents. That is, national governments ought to work towards the establishment of international/global institutions that are capable of limiting emissions and justly distributing associated burdens. First steps in this direction have just been undertaken in Paris. Thus, when adequate institutions are lacking, governments (and parliaments) are obligated both to lobby for them and to reduce the contribution of their countries to harmful climate change by not emitting more than their FS.[1]

To what extent agents ought to reduce their emissions depends on how FSs are determined. We certainly cannot settle this issue here but will try to provide at least some clarifications that will allow for a meaningful conclusion.

Determining FSs requires, first, determining the overall emissions budget and, second, distributing the emissions budget among agents. Given the necessity to limit cumulative GHG emissions in order to avoid 'dangerous' climate change, future emissions budgets will be very small compared to present ones. Whether or not these budgets will be distributed in an egalitarian or anti-egalitarian fashion, current high emitters exceed their FS by far (Baatz 2014; Baatz and Ott 2016). We consider the claim that non-poor high emitters have far-reaching mitigation duties as an important upshot of two decades of debates in climate ethics and justice (Gardiner et al. 2010). On the other hand, there is the worry that radically lowering future emissions will heavily burden many people. We think that mitigation duties can be overridden when an agent's own well-being is seriously affected; Cripps refers this as the limits of demandingness (2013). That is, one may plausibly claim that an agent has mitigation duties only as long as this, in conjunction with other duties, does not push her below a sufficiency threshold. If so, a lot depends on how the threshold is defined, and each definition will be contested. Rather than endorsing a specific proposal, we will argue that wealthy high emitters will remain far above any plausible sufficiency threshold, whether determined in terms of needs, rights or capabilities.

Our claim is that fast and far-reaching mitigation (FFM) does not necessarily generate unjust burdens for wealthy nations and that there also is considerable mitigation potential in emerging economies. We use FFM as a catch phrase for deep emission cuts over the next 50 years; for example, if the European Union reduces its emissions by around 80%.

We focus on how burdensome FFM will be for citizens of developed countries, taking Germany as our case study.[2] A widely cited study of the 'Fraunhofer-Institut für Solare Energiesysteme' analysed the levellized cost of electricity of renewable energy technologies in Germany in 2013 (Kost et al. 2013). The levellized cost of electricity indicates the average yearly costs for construction and operation of a power plant in relation to the electricity generated per year. It is a good indicator of the total costs of different electricity-generating technologies. According to the study, the levellized cost for onshore wind power is roughly the same as those for hard coal and combined combustion gas turbine power plants (around 7 cent/kWh), while brown coal is slightly cheaper and photovoltaic power plants slightly costlier (for detailed numbers, see Kost et al. 2013). By comparison, the British government just signed a deal with the industry and Chinese investors to build a new nuclear power plant guaranteeing the operators a feed in tariff of 19 cent/kWh for the next 35 years. This is considerably more than the average levellized cost for all renewable energies including biomasss and offshore wind power in Germany in 2013. Moreover, renewable energies will soon become fully competitive in all likelihood. While costs of renewable energy will go down further, costs of conventional energy will go up. For example, the Fraunhofer ISE study calculates that even small rooftop photovoltaic systems will be able to compete with fossil fuel power plants and that photovoltaic 'utility-scale power plants in Southern Germany will drop considerably below the average cost for all fossil fuel power plants by 2030' (ibid., 3).

In a similar vein, the German Advisory Council on the Environment (SRU) says that a renewable electricity supply system will become cheaper than a system based on conventional energy between 2030 and 2040 (2011). And even if costs for RE do not fall as expected, the point in time where RE systems gets cheaper is reached 'somewhat later' (2011, 332). In a pessimistic scenario which assumes that all energy needs to be generated within Germany, the levellized cost of a 100% renewable electricity supply by 2050 is around 9–12 cent/kWh plus 1 cent/kWh for the expansion of the grid (ibid.). Even if taken to be very optimistic, these numbers indicate that decarbonizing the German electricity sector would only moderately increase electricity bills, if at all.

Whether increased electricity costs are significant burdens depends on how the overall economic situation of households changes over time. If the overall economic situation results in a net increase in average incomes, increased costs may affect only a fraction of higher incomes. Even if increased costs would reduce average purchasing power slightly, this should be assessed in relation to (a) price changes of other commodities and services and (b) saving rates. If saving rates are high, as in Germany, the decarbonization might only result in consumption being postponed. The only problematic case in terms of overburdening would be if overall cost structures are profoundly affected in ways that purchasing power declines dramatically. So far, there is no evidence that this will happen in Germany.

Broadening the scope beyond electricity generation, a recent study undertaken by the Wuppertal Institute—a leading think tank working on the issue for decades—assessed different decarbonization scenarios for Germany (Hillebrandt, Samadi, and Fischedick 2015). It concludes that GHG emissions reduction of 90% or more compared to 1990 are possible and that the required reduction strategies are available. The scenarios do not assume (i) a sudden change in social and economic parameters, (ii) drastic changes in lifestyles, (iii) groundbreaking technological development, (iv) a deindustrialization or (v) a major economic crisis. And the scenarios do not consider nuclear energy use beyond 2022. Another recent study concludes that reducing all energy-related $CO_2$ emissions by 85% by 2050 will increase costs by 25% compared to a continued use of the current energy system, which would amount to 0.8% of today's GDP (Henning and Palzer 2015). This is based on the assumption that fossil fuel prices and costs for carbon emissions do not go up. If a 3% p.a. cost increase of fossil fuels is assumed, decarbonizing the energy system will cost no more than continued use of the current system (ibid.).

Broadening the focus, increasing competitiveness of renewable energy is not something that could be only a German phenomenon (in detail cf. Trancik 2014; IPCC 2014a, 46–47). Renewable energy could easily replace conventional energy systems in other wealthy countries as well, particularly given that the conditions for renewable energy supply are often more favourable than in Germany. For example, in the United States many regions have much more sunshine and there is more space for wind farms and solar power plants. Given its size, fluctuations in renewable energy supply can be compensated more easily.[3] Furthermore, renewable energies are associated with considerable co-benefits (reduction of air pollution, local employment opportunities, improved energy access and security) that can be subtracted from the costs associated with their deployment (IPCC 2014a, 47).

Deep emission cuts are likewise feasible in the building/household sector (IPCC 2014a, 58) and the land-use sector allows for considerable reductions, in particular when meat consumption is reduced (Knopf et al. 2012, 148) (See Kortetmäki and Oksanen, this volume). In the industry and transport sector, deep emissions cuts will be more challenging and thus costly (IPCC 2014b, Chapters 8–9, Long, this volume), though a recent study just published in *Science* argues that transport-related emissions can be reduced by 50% by 2050 with measures available today (Creutzig et al. 2015).

The transformation required to achieve deep cuts in total emissions is indeed enormous. However, the obstacles seem policy driven than rather technological (Wagner et al. 2015, 28).[4] First, large upfront investments are needed that require new patterns of investment (IPCC 2014a, 96; WBGU 2011,146; Fabian 2015, 28). Shifting investments, second, is in need of proper regulation (Trancik 2014, 300). In addition to technology policies such as R&D subsidies or renewable energy quotas, emissions pricing is needed. Introducing a price on carbon is associated with considerable benefits, even if implemented unilaterally. Edenhofer et al. summarize multiple possible benefits for different countries and groups of countries associated with a moderate carbon price (2015).

A further important aspect concerns fossil energy subsidies that currently amount to half a trillion USD per year globally (Wagner et al. 2015, 27). Reducing the subsidies can achieve significant emission reductions at negative social cost in the light of climate, health and new energy economy benefits (IPCC 2014a, 88). The funds can instead be used to benefit poor people in much more direct ways and to support R&D of low-carbon technologies.

Our overall point is that if there were sufficient political willingness to introduce proper regulation, FFM would not create unreasonable burdens in wealthy countries. The capital available in these countries is capable of realizing the necessary transformation (Fabian 2015). Mitigation costs are to a great extent costs of delayed growth of GDP. We do not see how delayed GDP growth brings citizens of wealthy countries near any plausible sufficiency threshold. This argument may be strengthened by bearing in mind that GDP growth is a poor proxy for welfare once a certain level of material well-being and monetary income is reached (Max-Neef 1995). Also note that taxing emissions rather than employment, and so on, could mean that there is no net social cost, even before counting climate benefits (MacKay et al. 2015). FFM can (and should) be accompanied by a tax reform compensating additional burdens to poor households (Edenhofer et al. 2015, 138).

In conclusion, and to the extent that the above considerations turn out to be correct, wealthy countries have duties to reduce their emissions by (very roughly) 60–90%, depending on particular circumstances, within the next 50 years in order to meet their FS of emissions entitlements.[5] The less wealthy and the lower per-capita emissions are in a country, the less stringent mitigation duties are (e.g. Mexico is not required to make cuts as deep as Canada but still has considerable duties). We therefore support that the distinction between Annex I and Non-Annex I countries has been given up in Paris and that most countries now have some obligations.

Due to lack in space, we conclude this section with only a few brief remarks on less-wealthy countries, starting with China. It is one of the few global powers in both economic and military terms. Its saving rates are high. China can easily invest in low-carbon technologies and has already done so. Given the accumulation of wealth and the availability of reductions at negative or low costs, China is able to undertake significant mitigation measures (see also Harris and Mele 2014). Mitigation commitments would also be beneficial for modernizing the Chinese economy and for the life prospects of Chinese citizens. Thus, China should not be exempted from mitigation duties but is not obliged to undertake FFM for the time being, given Chinese citizens' small per-capita emissions in the past and the still large number of very poor people. Similar considerations hold for South Africa as well as Brazil, and to a lesser extent for India.

The situation is different for poor countries. To the extent that they have low per-capita emissions, they very likely have not exceeded their fair share and, hence, do not have mitigation duties. In addition, replacing structures based on fossil fuels is difficult once they have been installed. To the extent such installation still can be avoided, establishing low-carbon economies is cheaper ('leapfrogging') (IPCC 2014a, 90). Achieving general access to energy requires huge investments anyway. The IPCC thus concludes that 'the costs for achieving nearly universal [energy] access are between USD 72–95 billion per year until 2030. The contribution of renewable energy-to-energy access can be substantial. Achieving universal energy access reduces air pollutants emissions ... and yields large health benefits but only negligibly higher GHG emissions from power generation' (2014a, 38).

Given the overall financial assets, generating roughly 100 billion USD per year will certainly not overburden the international community, even if this needs to be supplemented by additional resources to finance adaptation. Revenues to assist least-developed countries might be generated by taxes on consumption or wealth; for example, Bell proposes a 1.5% annual wealth tax on the richest 1% of the global population (2011). Here, we do not take a stance on whether these financings should be realized as investments, credits, transfers or a mix of these. In principle, transfers/investments of low-carbon technologies to the global South can be financed in ways that are not unfair according to any plausible theory of global distributive justice.

Calculations of future energy costs are based on a host of assumptions, and many uncertainties remain (Schmid, Pahle, and Knopf 2013). We do not think that the uncertainties compromise the big picture that FFM will only create moderate burdens for wealthy countries, all things considered. Those disagreeing can argue that FFM might be overburdening.[6] We do not think that the fact that FFM *might* turn out to be overburdening is a good reason not to enter an FFM pathway in the first place (in detail Pissarskoi 2014). At the beginning, rigorous mitigation is associated with no regret options. It is usually assumed that the more a society moves towards complete decarbonization, the more difficult, and hence costly, the measures will get. Should a society realize that FFM turns out to be much more burdensome than assumed above, it could slow the decarbonization process again and thereby lower associated burdens. If this is correct, not starting with FFM *now* because it could turn out that mitigation measures will overburden wealthy societies *in future* is unconvincing. Instead, governments and the citizens they represent are obligated to undertake FFM *until* this becomes too burdensome. Note that our criteria explicitly allow for such moves: agents ought to mitigate as long as they do not fall below a sufficiency threshold. If FFM becomes too burdensome, they are entitled to slow mitigation efforts to a level that does not push them below the threshold.

## MITIGATION DUTIES AND CLIMATE ENGINEERING OPTIONS

So far, we have argued that collective agents representing the citizens of a country ought to ensure that their 'total fair share', so to say, is not exceeded and they ought to lobby for the establishment of proper institutions. The key moral reason for these duties is the entitlement of others not to be harmed by excessive emissions. However, there also is a considerable time lag between potentially harmful emission-generating activities and actually harmful events. Thus, there is more time to prevent the harm from occurring compared to many everyday harmful activities. This is the reason why, in addition to mitigation, there are more strategies to prevent harmful climatic impacts. These include adaptation, SRM and CDR.[7]

The important question here is whether the potential to adopt these further strategies sets aside or diminishes the primary obligations for mitigation. We do not think so, as we will briefly try to argue now.

We start with the claim that all three strategies, adaptation, CDR and SRM, are imperfect substitutes for mitigation. We define substitutability as 'Y is a substitute for X if Y achieves the same aim as X'. Broadly understood, the aim of mitigation is to avoid climatic changes that have negative effects. Strategy

Y is a perfect substitute for mitigation if it avoids all negative climatic effects resulting from GHG emissions, without thereby creating other harms or risks. Thus defined, none of the above strategies is a perfect substitute. We do think, however, that this claim is both modest and widely shared. Successfully adapting to changing climatic conditions is a very complex process, and it seems far fetched to assume that adaptation is able to prevent all harm. SRM does not address all negative effects of rising GHG concentrations, creates large, partially unknown risks and, hence, is frequently called 'imperfect' (e.g. Keith 2013). Given that CDR lowers net emissions, some (small-scale) low-risk measures/technologies might be considered as an almost perfect substitute. But given its limited potential and further drawbacks such as costs, land and water requirements, effects on ecosystems and so on (Smith et al. 2016), at least large-scale CDR measures seems rather imperfect as well.

It might be the case, however, that the three strategies constitute a perfect substitute once combined. Again, we do not think so. If GHG emissions do not go down, a further increase in atmospheric concentrations cannot be halted by CDR measures alone, which would imply considerable SRM plus adaptation. A CDR–SRM–adaptation mix might therefore be able to significantly reduce harm compared to a business-as-usual scenario (see Horton and Keith, this volume), but it would create additional risks associated with large-scale CDR and SRM measures and seems unable to prevent all negative consequences (see Barrett et al. 2014; Keller et al. 2014; Morrow and Svoboda 2016).

Rather than defending this claim, we shift the burden of argument to those who think that a particular technology mix is a perfect substitute for mitigation.[8] We do not think that the controversial part of the argument is our 'imperfectness-claim' but what we believe follows from it.

The imperfect nature of adaptation, CDR and SRM does not imply that these strategies should not be adopted. For instance, it is widely acknowledged that the imperfect nature of adaptation would be a bad reason to not endorse it as a mitigation supplement.[9] We instead argue that, due to the imperfectness, their availability does not diminish duties with respect to mitigation.

Consider the following thought experiment: A part of Peter's daily routine, simply called X, causes harm to Jane at some later point in time. Peter learns about the harmful effect of X and adopts countermeasure Y before Jane is harmed. Y reduces Jane's harm but also harms Mike. Now, can Peter continue with X given the availability of Y? If we assume that it is possible for Peter to avoid X, he ought to do so. Jane and Mike are entitled not to be harmed by Peter, and since Y is unable to honour their entitlements (they are still harmed), the duty to not do X remains in place.

Bringing in climate change again, one may challenge our argument on the ground that mitigation, too, will be unable to avoid all harm. Climate change is already happening, leading to an increase in the frequency and intensity of harmful extreme weather events, reduced available of fresh water, spread of vector-borne diseases and so on. However, the fact that mitigation will be unable to avoid all harm is because too little mitigation has been undertaken in the past. In principle, mitigation would have been able to avoid all harm. This is different for the other strategies as briefly suggested above.

A further challenge to our argument is that a country cannot reduce harms to zero (like Peter) but can only reduce its contribution to the problem. Thus, the argument goes, a given country can make up for exceeding its FS by reducing overall harm via adaptation, CDR and SRM. This might be justified if the country's measures reduce overall harm by a fraction that corresponds to the country's contribution to harm (here, we ignore the problem how this could be calculated). To the extent a country's CDR measures are more or less risk free and reduce net emissions to its FS, we think that the counterargument can be convincing. We do not think so regarding large-scale CDR and SRM technologies. We believe that others are also entitled not to live with the threat of being seriously harmed (Bell 2011). By exceeding its FS the country illegitimately contributes to this threat, and the technologies employed to make up for the excess do not avoid imposing risks.[10]

The upshot of our argument so far is that even if an agent undertakes adaptation, CDR and SRM, she acts immorally if exceeding her FS of emissions entitlements. If adopting these strategies does not reduce mitigation-related obligations, nor does researching them, then the claim that researching CE is no reason to reduce mitigation efforts (e.g. Barrett et al. 2014) should be specified as *researching CE does not reduce obligations regarding mitigation, which include the obligation to not exceed one's FS and to lobby for institutional solutions.*

Our argument also implies that mitigation is the first-best strategy to respond to climate change: Mitigation duties are primary and duties to adopt further strategies are derivative. They originate from the fact that too little mitigation has been undertaken in the past that cannot be fully compensated by doing more mitigation in present and future. In short, then, mitigation duties are *supplemented* by further duties that aim at minimizing harm that will occur even if full compliance with present and future mitigation duties is assumed.

If, in the end, excessive emissions do cause harm, the representatives of a citizenry have further compensatory duties. This can be justified by reference to the Polluter Pays Principle (PPP) (Caney 2010; Baatz 2013). Drawing on the PPP also implies that compensatory duties are limited: rather than compensating all harm, 'polluters' must compensate according to their emissions levels (ibid.). Given the time lag between emissions and harmful events, some measure of compensation can often be realized in advance via financing adaptation. Ideally, this form of ex ante compensation avoids actual harms and hence rectificatory payments. In sum, then, a country ought to reduce emission to their fair share and lobby for institutional solutions. Institutions must limit total emissions, distribute remaining emissions fairly and, if it is already too late to prevent all harm, must contain a compensatory scheme (e.g. via financing adaptation).[11]

Thus, country A's overall response to climate change is morally legitimate only if:

1. A does not exceed its fair share of emissions entitlements (or has adopted mitigation measures sufficient to reach its fair share within a reasonable transition period)
2. A promotes and contributes to maintaining effective global institutions that allocate mitigation duties justly, and
3. A promotes and contributes to maintaining a global compensatory scheme.

In case of criteria (2) and (3), the successful establishment of institutions is very likely outside the power of A. The correct yardstick is whether A tries to a sufficient degree rather than the outcome of A's trying. This is different for criterion (1). Still, given current emissions levels, criterion (1) allows for a transition period (though this might be criticized as being too generous towards high emitters). Thus, it is also relevant what domestic mitigation efforts are considered to be sufficient in a given period of time.

Hence, all three criteria contain a qualifier that refers to the idea of efforts considered to be sufficient. We believe that this vagueness is not fatal to our proposal. First, the criteria can be specified to some extent in future. We hinted at how relevant conclusions can nevertheless be derived from criterion (1) in the previous section. Second, though it might be difficult to say when A has done enough, it might be less difficult to determine whether A has done too little in order to legitimately research CE. For example, if A blocks or does not push international negotiations and does not reduce her emissions though exceeding its FS, she acts illegitimately whether or not launching a CE research programme.

This concludes the argument on morally legitimate responses to climate change. It is, however, unclear what this means for the moral legitimacy of a CE research programme as such. By way of concluding this section, we identify directions for future research.

We think that the criteria raise the bar for convincing justifications of CE research programmes. For instance, if such a programme is justified with reference to obligations towards those vulnerable to climate change (Svoboda 2016; Horton and Keith, this volume), the justification is not credible if one does not meet the criteria: not meeting the criteria means failure to honour one's duties towards those very persons who are supposed to benefit from the research. The present failure to fulfil one's duties undermines the justification. Also, if an agent does not fulfil the above criteria but instead researches a technology believed to quickly reduce temperatures, this further raises suspicions that the technology is actually supposed to be more like a replacement rather than a supplement. And, due to the agent's bad faith regarding climate change–related duties so far, she should perhaps be considered unsuitable to responsibly handle a risky technology such as sulphate aerosol injections.

To put it the other way around, fulfilling the criteria means that one can demonstrate being serious about one's climate-related duties, rather than just asserting it. Given how much is at stake, it might be worthwhile to consider whether assertions are insufficient in order to legitimately research very risky CE technologies. If so, researching these technologies should be made conditional on the above criteria.[12]

We acknowledge that any such conclusion would need much more argument than we can offer here. But we believe that a debate of this issue is important.

## CONCLUDING REMARKS

We have argued that countries' representatives are obligated to ensure that their citizens' total FS of emissions entitlements is not exceeded and to work towards the establishment of adequate global institutions. Based on this, we further argued that wealthy countries ought to undertake fast and far-reaching mitigation. Finally, we offered a brief argument according to which the possibility to research and deploy CE technologies and to undertake adaptation does not diminish original obligations with respect to mitigation—given present conditions of high atmospheric GHG concentrations. This result also underlines the relevance of the so-called moral hazard argument (Baatz 2016). While it has been argued that less mitigation might not pose a hazard if supplemented by CE technologies (Goeschl, Heyen, and Moreno-Cruz 2013), our analysis shows that reduced mitigation efforts will mean noncompliance with moral duties in many cases.

We are certainly not the first to insist on the fulfilment of mitigation duties. Adopting a certain political realism, one may wonder what the moral criteria developed above are worth, given that relevant agents will likely ignore it anyway. We thus conclude this contribution with a quick comment on political feasibility.

What should ideally be done always is an indispensable yardstick for assessing the less-ideal outcomes and also for choosing among different less-ideal options. In our case, the more ideal considerations help determine better and worse ways to research CE, as argued above. Even if it is very likely that some agents will not comply with their moral duties, giving up the normative yardstick itself seems like a bad idea to us. Moreover, continued mitigation failure should not turn into a self-fulfilling prophecy. Lack in political feasibility is not a static phenomenon. Focusing on the presently feasible may ignore abilities for political action: what has a very low feasibility now may become significantly more feasible in the future if steps to expand political abilities are undertaken (Gilabert 2016). It is therefore crucial to think about how the lack in feasibility can be overcome.

First, different ways have been suggested how meaningful policies can evolve over time. For example, Edenhofer et al. show how governments, even if largely concerned with maximizing their short-term benefits, might agree on international carbon pricing (2015; see also the contributions in Heyward and Roser 2016). Carbon pricing, in turn, has the potential to significantly increase global cooperation by avoiding the difficulties associated with agreeing on national emissions reductions (MacKay et al. 2015). Second, cheaper low-carbon technologies will help erode political blockages, which is another reason for spending more on low-carbon R&D. Third, mitigation efforts increase considerably in many places at the regional and national level. A significant change in values can be observed in Germany and elsewhere (WBGU 2011). Victor observes that a 'norm against polluting nature is spreading' that could heavily impact on what people want and thus what governments can implement (2014, 854). Once the Paris Agreement enters into force, binding international law establishes that the fossil fuel era shall end within this century. National ambitions for emissions reductions are scheduled to ratchet upwards every five years. Perhaps, the agreement will be most valuable for sending such a clear signal. We think that this will affect political feasibility to a considerable extent in the mid- and long run, positively influencing all three aspects just mentioned.

## ACKNOWLEDGEMENTS

We are indebted to David Morrow for commenting on an earlier version of the manuscript and to Christopher Preston for numerous helpful suggestions. This work has been funded by the German DFG Priority Program "Climate Engineering: Risks, Challenges, Opportunities?" (SPP 1689).

## NOTES

1. A justification for why agents have both types of obligations when institutions are lacking is offered in Baatz and Voget-Kleschin (2016).

2. At the end of this section we also briefly comment on China and poor countries.

3. For options regarding a complete decarbonization of the U.S. economy, see Prentiss (2015) and Jacobson et al. (2015).

4. Given that the potential losers of FFM are (still) more powerful than its potential winners, they successfully blocked many policy changes (see also Shue 2014, 140).

5. We think that this at least holds for most European countries, Japan, Australia, the United States, Canada and probably Russia, and also includes wealthy oil-exporting countries such as Saudi Arabia, among others.

6. Very recently, Keary argued that most models used to calculate mitigation costs rely on questionably optimistic assumptions regarding technological change (2016). He concludes that rather than hoping for further technological change along the current growth trajectory, societies ought to leave this trajectory now and reorganize production and consumption in a way that allows for low emissions with existing technologies (ibid.). We do not comment on whether FFM is achievable with sustained economic growth on a global level; we just argue that FFM is feasible within reasonable limits of demandingess, something Keary seems to agree with. Also note that technological pessimism regarding mitigation—where part of this change could already be witnessed—does not go well with technological optimism regarding so far mostly nonexistent CE technologies.

7. For a slightly different classification, see Boucher et al. (2014).

8. We are not aware that such an argument has already been made apart, perhaps, from Teller et al. (2002).

9. Note that matters would be different if it were still possible to fully avoid climate change via mitigation.

10. A specific argument why undertaking adaptation does not reduce mitigation duties has been offered by Vanderheiden (2011). He concludes that 'it would seem that climate justice requires fully adequate action in mitigation and in adaptation, rather than some fungible overall national burden that can be divided at will between the two' (ibid., 70). We also side step the issue whether or not paying others to emit less is permissible. We think that it depends on the circumstances.

11. We do not address the questions whether agents ought to finance adaptation unilaterally in the absence of a compensatory scheme. If our assumption that they ought not to is wrong, the criteria below need to be supplemented by such a duty.

12. A further criterion for the legitimacy of a CE research programme might consist in the non-participation of any agent that blocked mitigation efforts in the past.

# BIBLIOGRAPHY

Baatz, Christian, and Konrad Ott. 2016. 'In defense of emissions egalitarianism?' In *Climate Justice and Historical Emissions*, edited by Lukas Meyer and Pranay Sanklecha, Cambridge: Cambridge University Press. (forthcoming)

Baatz, Christian, and Lieske Voget-Kleschin. 2016. 'Individual Duties Regarding Global Environmental Problems: The Example of Climate Change.' *unpublished paper draft*.

Baatz, Christian. 2013. 'Responsibility for the past? Some thoughts on compensating those vulnerable to climate change in developing countries.' *Ethics, Policy & Environment* 16 (1): 94–110.

Baatz, Christian. 2014. 'Climate Change and Individual Duties to Reduce GHG Emissions.' *Ethics, Policy & Environment* 17 (1): 1–19.

Baatz, Christian. 2016. 'Can we have it both ways? On potential trade-offs between Mitigation and Solar Radiation Management.' *Environmental Values* 25 (1): 29–49.

Baatz, Christian. 2016. 'Reply to my Critics: Justifying the Fair Share Argument' *Ethics, Policy & Environment*. (forthcoming)

Barrett, Scott, Timothy M. Lenton, Antony Millner, Alessandro Tavoni, Stephen Carpenter, John M. Anderies, F. Stuart Chapin III, Anne-Sophie Crepin; Gretchen Daily, Paul Ehrlich, Carl Folke, Victor Galaz, Terry Hughes, Nils Kautsky, Eric F. Lambin, Rosamond Naylor, Karine Nyborg, Stephen Polasky, Marten Scheffer, James Wilen, Anastasios Xepapadeas and Aart de Zeeuw. 2014 'Climate engineering reconsidered.' *Nature Climate Change* 4 (7): 527–29.

Bell, Derek. 2011. 'Does anthropogenic climate change violate human rights?' *Critical Review of International Social and Political Philosophy* 14 (2): 99–124.

Boucher, Olivier, Piers M. Forster, Nicolas Gruber, Minh Ha-Duong, Mark G. Lawrence, Timothy M. Lenton, Achim Maas, and Naomi E. Vaughan. 2014. 'Rethinking climate engineering categorization in the context of climate change mitigation and adaptation.' *Wiley Interdisciplinary Reviews: Climate Change* 5 (1): 23–35.

Caney, Simon. 2010. 'Climate Change and the Duties of the Advantaged.' *Critical Review of International Social and Political Philosophy* 13 (1): 203–28.

Caney, Simon. 2012. 'Just Emissions.' *Philosophy & Public Affairs* 40 (4): 255–300.

Creutzig, F., P. Jochem, O. Y. Edelenbosch, L. Mattauch, D. P. van Vuuren, D. McCollum, and J. Minx. 2015. 'Transport: A roadblock to climate change mitigation?' *Science* 350 (6263): 911–12.

Cripps, Elizabeth. 2013. *Climate Change and the Moral Agent: Individual Duties in an Interdependent World.* 1st edition. Oxford: Oxford University Press.

Edenhofer, Ottmar, Michael Jakob, Felix Creutzig, Christian Flachsland, Sabine Fuss, Martin Kowarsch, Kai Lessmann, Linus Mattauch, Jan Siegmeier, and Jan C. Steckel. 2015. 'Closing the emission price gap.' *Global Environmental Change* 31: 132–43.

Fabian, Nathan. 2015. 'Economics: Support low-carbon investment.' *Nature* 519 (7541): 27–29.

Gardiner, Stephen M., Simon Caney, Henry Shue, and Dale Jamieson, eds. 2010. *Climate Ethics: Essential Readings.* New York: Oxford University Press.

Gilabert, Pablo. 2016. 'Justice and Feasibility: A Dynamic Approach.' In *Political Utopias: Contemporary Debates*, edited by K. Vallier and M. Weber: Oxford University Press.

Goeschl, Timo, Daniel Heyen, and Juan Moreno-Cruz. 2013. 'The Intergenerational Transfer of Solar Radiation Management Capabilities and Atmospheric Carbon Stocks.' *Environmental and Resource Economics* 56 (1): 85–104.

Harris, Paul G., and Elias Mele. 2014. 'Individual Duties to Reduce Greenhouse Gas Emissions in China.' *Ethics, Policy & Environment* 17 (1): 49–51.

Henning, Hans-Martin, and Andreas Palzer. 2015. 'What will the Energy Transformation Cost? Pathways for transforming the German energy system by 2050.' https://www.ise.fraunhofer.de/en/publications/veroeffentlichungen-pdf-dateien-en/studien-und-konzeptpapiere/study-what-will-the-energy-transformation-cost.pdf.

Heyward, Clare, and Dominic Roser (eds.). 2016. *Climate Justice In A Non-ideal World*. Oxford: Oxford University Press.

Hillebrandt, Katharina, Sascha Samadi, and Manfred Fischedick. 2015. 'Pathways to deep decarbonization in Germany.' http://wupperinst.org/en/projects/details/wi/p/s/pd/505/.

IPCC. 2014a. 'Technical Summary: In: Climate Change 2014: Mitigation of Climate Change. Contribution of Working Group III to the Fifth Assessment Report of the Intergovernmental Panel on Climate Change.' Accessed October 14, 2015. http://mitigation2014.org/report.

IPCC. 2014b. 'Climate Change 2014: Mitigation of Climate Change. Contribution of Working Group III to the Fifth Assessment Report of the Intergovernmental Panel on Climate Change.' http://mitigation2014.org/report/publication/.

Jacobson, Mark Z., Mark A. Delucchi, Guillaume Bazouin, Bauer, Zack A. F., Christa C. Heavey, Emma Fisher, Sean B. Morris, Piekutowski, Diniana J. Y., Taylor A. Vencill, and Tim W. Yeskoo. 2015. '100% clean and renewable wind, water, and sunlight (WWS) all-sector energy roadmaps for the 50 United States.' *Energy & Environmental Science* 8 (7): 2093–117.

Keary, Michael. 2016. 'Message in a model: Technological optimism in climate change mitigation modelling.' *Environmental Values* 25 (1): 7–28.

Keith, David W. 2013. *A Case for Climate Engineering*. Boston: Boston Review.

Keller, David P., Ellias Y. Feng, and Andreas Oschlies. 2014. 'Potential climate engineering effectiveness and side effects during a high carbon dioxide-emission scenario.' *Nature Communications* 5: 3304.

Knopf, Brigitte, Martin Kowarsch, Ottmar Edenhofer, and Gunnar. Luderer. 2012. 'Climate Change Mitigation: Options, Costs and Risks.' In *Climate change, justice and sustainability: Linking climate and development policy*, edited by Ottmar Edenhofer, 139–50. Dordrecht [u.a.]: Springer.

Kost, Christoph, Johannes N. Mayer, Jessica Thomsen, Niklas Hartmann, Charlotte Senkpiel, Simon Philipps, Sebastian Nold, Simon Lude, Noha Saad and Thomas Schlegl. 2013 'Levelized Cost of Electricity Renewable Energy Technologies.' https://www.ise.fraunhofer.de/en/publications/studies/cost-of-electricity.

MacKay, David J. C., Peter Cramton, Axel Ockenfels, and Steven Stoft. 2015. 'Price carbon—I will if you will.' *Nature* 526 (7573): 315–16.

Max-Neef, Manfred. 1995. 'Economic growth and quality of life: a threshold hypothesis.' *Ecological Economics* 15 (2): 115–18.

Morrow, David R., and Toby Svoboda. 2016. 'Geoengineering and Non-Ideal Theory.' *Public Affairs Quarterly* 30 (1): 85–104.

Neuteleers, Stijn. 2010. 'Institutions versus lifestyle: do citizens have environmental duties in their private sphere?' *Environmental Politics* 19 (4): 501–17.

Ostrom, Elinor. 2015. *Governing the commons: The evolution of institutions for collective action.* Canto classics. Cambridge, MA: Cambridge University Press.

Pissarskoi, Eugen. 2014. *Soziale Wohlfahrt und Klimawandel: Umgang mit normativen Annahmen und Ungewissheiten bei der klimaökonomischen Politikberatung.* Hochschulschriften zur Nachhaltigkeit. München: oekom verlag.

Prentiss, Mara G. 2015. *Energy revolution: The physics and the promise of efficient technology:* Harvard University Press.

Schmid, Eva, Michael Pahle, and Brigitte Knopf. 2013. 'Renewable electricity generation in Germany: A meta-analysis of mitigation scenarios.' *Energy Policy* 61: 1151–63.

Shue, Henry. 2014. *Climate justice: Vulnerability and protection.* 1st edition. Oxford: Oxford University Press.

Smith, Pete, Steven J. Davis, Felix Creutzig, Sabine Fuss, Jan Minx, Benoit Gabrielle, Etsushi Kato et al. 2016. 'Biophysical and economic limits to negative $CO_2$ emissions.' *Nature Climate Change* 6 (1): 42–50.

SRU (German Advisory Council on the Environment). 2011. 'Pathways towards a 100 % renewable electricity system.' http://www.umweltrat.de/SharedDocs/Downloads/EN/02_Special_Reports/2011_10_Special_Report_Pathways_renewables.html.

Svoboda, Toby. 2016. 'Aerosol geoengineering deployment and fairness.' *Environmental Values* 25 (1): 51–68.

Teller, Edward, Roderick Hyde, and Lowell Wood. 2002. 'Active Climate Stabilization: Practical Physics-Based Approaches to Prevention of Climate Change.' http://www.geoengineeringwatch.org/library/research%201970-2009/16%20Geoengineering%20Active%20Climate%20Stabilization%20-%20Teller%202002.pdf.

Trancik, Jessika E. 2014. 'Renewable energy: Back the renewables boom.' *Nature* 507 (7492): 300–302.

Vanderheiden, Steve. 2011. 'Globalizing Responsibility for Climate Change.' *Ethics & International Affairs* 25 (1): 65–84.

Victor, David G. 2014. 'Copenhagen II or something new.' *Nature Climate Change* 4 (10): 853–55. doi: 10.1038/nclimate2396.

Wagner, Gernot, Tomas Kåberger, Susanna Olai, Michael Oppenheimer, Katherine Rittenhouse, and Thomas Sterner. 2015. 'Energy policy: Push renewables to spur carbon pricing.' *Nature* 525 (7567): 27–29.

WBGU (German Advisory Council on Global Change). 2011. 'World in Transition—A Social Contract for Sustainability.' http://www.wbgu.de/en/flagship-reports/fr-2011-a-social-contract/.

*Chapter 8*

# Bringing Geoengineering into the Mix of Climate Change Tools

## Jane Long

Climate change represents the greatest challenge facing the human species. The probability of humans being able to weather this change would improve if the widest possible set of strategic choices and tools are available. Climate engineering (CE), intentional modification of the climate, may be one of those tools. But having this type of tool available—or eliminating it from consideration—requires conducting research and bringing some international control to possible deployment. This chapter discusses the energy and climate context that indicates a possible role for CE, how CE might be used as part of a strategic portfolio to control climate impacts, cultural issues associated with starting research on this topic and some thoughts about moving towards international control.

### THE CLIMATE AND ENERGY CONTEXT

Although people have caused climate change, they did not design this change. Lots of everyday motivations, actions and choices add up to a slowly emerging catastrophe. Changes to the energy system could dramatically reduce emissions that might return the world, if not to safety, then hopefully to a manageable state. But important components of the solution are expensive (e.g. battery storage), unpopular (e.g. nuclear power) or not yet available (e.g. carbon-free fuel). The transition also requires dramatic policy changes to overcome the everyday motivations, actions and choices that got us here.

There are fundamentally four sets of technical actions applied to the energy system that can eliminate emissions (Long and Greenblatt 2012). These are the physical actions the world must pin their hopes on if we are to eliminate emissions from the energy system. And until the world does eliminate emissions, the risks associated with climate change will continue to grow. Unfortunately, each of these measures will be difficult and possibly slow, and some may not produce the required results.

First, measures can be taken to decrease energy intensity; in other words, increase energy efficiency to allow the same work to be done with less energy. Houses can be built to use less energy; vehicles and appliances can be made more efficient. Theoretically, such actions reduce the demand for energy, but historically, this has not happened. More-efficient machines, buildings, appliances, cars, etc., have meant that people tend to use more energy to do more, not less energy to do the same. If it costs less to maintain a house or drive a car, people build larger houses or drive more. Energy economists credit this result to the fact that efficiency essentially makes energy services less expensive and therefore increases demand (Smil 2003). Perhaps, higher energy costs would offset this effect. But if all the technically available efficiency measures were deployed without this 'Jevons paradox', it could reduce the size of the problem dramatically. The technology to do this is available, but the actions require a large shift in policy, significant investments and, perhaps most importantly, changes to behavioural norms. Although efficiency measures alone cannot solve this problem of drastically reducing emissions, they could make the problem much easier to solve.

Secondly, electrification, mostly of transportation, could be useful. Currently, nearly all our transportation is run on fossil fuel and nearly all the oil we produce is used in transportation. Mobile fuel use might be reduced if cars run on electricity instead of fuel. Electric cars produce no greenhouse gases as they are driven and electricity is easier to decarbonize than mobile use of fuel. So if the electricity supply system is decarbonized (see below), then electric cars are part of the solution. Batteries could allow cars to run on electricity, but require overcoming range problems and high costs. Electrification won't solve all transportation problems. Heavy-duty transport is difficult to electrify and aeroplanes will not likely work on batteries any time soon. Efficiency and electrification can change the size and nature of the problem, but these are hard to do practically.

Two other measures reduce the carbon intensity of the *sources* of energy, namely in electricity and fuel. Plans for decarbonizing electricity have mostly been limited to increasing the amount of renewable energy, but this energy is intermittent. Solar and wind power are not available when the sun doesn't shine and the wind doesn't blow. Back-up energy generation has largely been done with natural gas turbines that do create emissions. Other solutions such as expanding the interconnectedness of the grid are possible, but expensive and novel. Batteries could solve some of this problem but will also be very expensive and unable to solve problems such as seasonal variation in wind and solar power or maintain system stability. The engineering feasibility of a 100% renewable electricity system has not been established (Loftus et al. 2015). Nuclear power and the use of fossil fuel generation with carbon capture and underground storage of the emitted $CO_2$ could provide large-scale carbon-free electricity, but are not squarely on the table yet, and also might be quite expensive.

Perhaps the hardest of the measures and in some way the most important is to decarbonize fuel. Some uses of fuel, such as in heavy-duty transport, will be hard to avoid. The only substitute for fossil fuel currently under concerted development is biofuel. But current biofuels create nearly as many emissions as fossil fuels, and it make take decades to make them better. Biofuel production can also create an issue in justice as it can (and has) created competition with food in a world with a rapidly expanding population. European low-carbon fuel standards have caused a shortage of cooking oil in south Asia. Ethanol requirements in the United States have increased the price of corn for food. There could be enormous land-use issues associated with the massive use of biofuels. The expansive use of biofuels might be neither effective nor socially acceptable.

Other fuel pathways include using hydrogen to run vehicles. In this case the hydrogen has to be made without emitting carbon dioxide. Hydrogen is mostly made by reforming methane, and the $CO_2$ produced in this process would have to be sequestered for this pathway to help the climate; such sequestration projects have proven difficult to start. Hydrogen also has other technical and infrastructure issues. Especially given very inexpensive fossil fuel, substituting lower carbon fuels is going to be difficult to achieve.

The energy system is also vast with very large capital investments in technology that emits greenhouse gasses (GHGs) and slow to change. Worse, if we succeed in changing to a near-zero emission energy system very quickly, a large proportion of the population would likely not get the energy they need to emerge from abject poverty. This well-known issue of justice has been the source of conflict between the developing world and the developed world in global climate negotiations.

Mitigation must be the world's first priority, but it will not be easy or quick. The latest IPCC assessment results reflect this situation. Figure 8.1 shows IPCC projections from emissions scenarios used to predict possible temperature outcomes. For even the most aggressive mitigation scenarios, all models predict that negative emissions will be required by mid-century if the globe is to stay below the target of 2 degrees of warming.

Each line in Figure 8.1 represents a different global climate model result. Each cluster of lines represents a mitigation scenario with the mean of the model results shown by a bold line. The most optimistic scenario is at the bottom which is the scenario most likely to keep average temperature increase less than 2 degrees but would likely require intervention (shown as negative emissions) by mid-century to stay within this range (Fuss et al. 2014). What

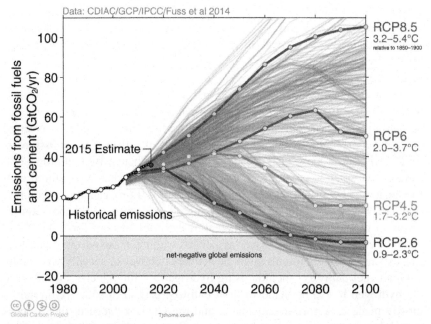

Figure 8.1 The IPCC Fifth Assessment scenarios for the quantity of $CO_2$ emissions per year, called "representative concentration pathways" (RCPs), showing the various range in resulting average temperature increases. *Source*: Fuss, S. et al. 2014. "Betting on Negative Emissions." *Nature Climate Change* 4: 850–853 doi:10.1038)

this means is that all models required *negative* emissions—that is, removal of $CO_2$ from the atmosphere—in order to keep temperature change less than 2 degrees.

This means that even if emissions are brought under control, and especially if they are not, there is a lot of global warming that is now unavoidable and we are not yet sure how well we can adapt. This is the context for thinking about intentional management of the climate. Although mitigation is the primary strategy, the energy system is very hard to change and we are already committed to very high concentrations of GHGs. So, the assumption that climate change will proceed (no matter what commitments have been made in Paris) is a very reasonable assumption. Only the rate and magnitude of mitigation can be controlled. Climate change itself can no longer be "eliminated"; it can only be managed.

## STRATEGY

CE is a fundamentally strategic choice. Figure 8.2 shows a diagram based on one sketched by Prof. John Shepherd, who chaired the Royal Society's

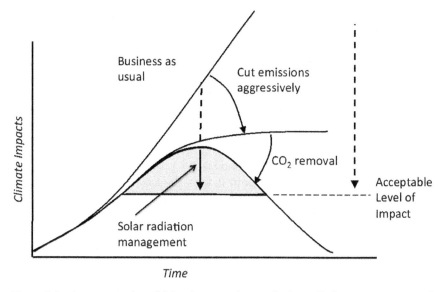

**Figure 8.2    A conceptual model for the strategic use of solar radiation management and carbon dioxide removal to address climate change impacts.** [Proposed by John Shepherd and redrawn by Douglas McMartin and Jane Long (Long and Shepherd 2014)]

study of CE, showing the possible utility of CE. Prof. Shepherd imagined that solar radiation management, the idea of injecting reflecting particles into the stratosphere, might be used to cool Earth for a finite time if necessary while mitigation is completed, followed by carbon dioxide withdrawal from the atmosphere to return conditions similar to that of the early twentieth century for example.

This figure illustrates one concept for a strategy to combat climate change. The diagram shows why solar radiation management is not a replacement for mitigation. A horizontal line shows an acceptable level of impact. If mitigation does not proceed, climate impacts will continue to grow as shown in the upper business-as-usual line, and the amount of intervention required to remain at an acceptable level of impact will grow at the same rate. The requirements for cooling the Earth will grow (this is the distance between the business-as-usual and acceptable-level-of-impact lines) and the SRM choice will become increasingly dangerous. CO2 has a very long retention time in the atmosphere (over 1000 years), thus risks are cumulative, that is, they grow until emissions stop. When emissions stop, then the risks will not stop, they will just stop growing. At the point that mitigation eliminates emissions, the risks will stay constant.

The strategy this diagram proposes includes aggressive mitigation, with solar radiation management added to avoid peak temperatures until subsequent carbon dioxide removal returns the atmosphere to something closer to a pre-industrial level of CO2 at which point, solar radiation management can end. Exactly how this would be done remains to be researched, but conceptually, it represents a way to use solar radiation management to avoid the worst impacts while mitigation and carbon dioxide removal return the planet to a safer zone.

Unfortunately, the climate problem is politically fraught and the concepts are complex, and this means strategic approaches to managing this problem are elusive. The strategic use of CE as part of a global policy and technical vision for managing climate change does not yet exist. This fact makes permission for research of CE difficult. In turn, the lack of research means that the strategic inclusion of CE in policy is not possible. Identification of specific scientific culture and policy reasons for this vicious cycle provides the context for potentially overcoming the situation and commencing research to examine the effectiveness and advisability of CE concepts.

We can and should view the CE research agenda as a way to learn how to be strategic in managing our planet because the survival of ecosystems and populations will likely depend on the ability to proactively manage our global problems whether or not CE is part of that process. This future cannot be managed based on what has happened in the past; it is terra incognito. To prepare, we need every possible technical tool. So, what will it take to build that capacity?

## CULTURAL ISSUES IN STARTING RESEARCH

Currently, not very much work has been funded to study the possible strategic use of CE as part of an approach to managing climate. For example, in the United States, NSF funds scientists to model rather limited and nonstrategic evaluations (e.g. the GeoMIP set of studies) which are largely designed to identify problems with CE. Although research that highlights problems has important validity, research designed to show how CE might be useful is also valid (Long and Scott 2013).[1] As IPCC reports are based on public literature, they have not been able to review any strategic use of CE, such as might be imagined in 'John Shepherd's napkin'. If there were more strategic modelling studies illustrating explicit strategic uses such as, but not limited to, John Shepherd's napkin strategy, these publications would then be assessed through IPCC and would enter the stream of information reaching policymakers and negotiations.

The number of climate scientists involved in addressing climate change worldwide is very large, but the number of those interested in CE is relatively small. Meanwhile, climate science has struggled to maintain funding, and many climate scientists ascribe to a view of environmental problems that focuses on the idea that human intervention in nature is the cause of problems and that a 'return to Nature' is the solution. The idea of intentional modification is an anathema to many climate scientists, and scientists who feel that way dominate the peer review of CE proposals. So for both financial and ideological reasons, climate scientists themselves do not welcome research on this topic, and this makes it hard for scientists trying to study strategic uses of CE to get their work published. The consequence is that papers on CE are hard to publish.

A chicken-and-egg phenomenon results. Without the science, the policymakers don't have a good idea about this topic, but without them asking for work, the scientists are not producing it. Consequently, policymakers do not see compelling strategic information on CE. What they do see is that the topic is at best a complication and at worst a distraction in the horribly difficult negotiations to limit emissions. This is not irrational on their part. But CE may be necessary, and it would be better to know more about it than less should that time come. We should—must—pursue mitigation as vigorously as possible. But we also should simultaneously research CE as another potential tool in the box addressing climate change.

A useful entrée to learning about how to accept the idea of CE may derive from the concept of the Anthropocene and an examination of what being in the Anthropocene means about environmentalism. Earth scientists define the Anthropocene as that geologic age when the dynamics of Earth have become dominated by human actions. If humans have dominant impacts on Earth and fundamentally can make *choices,* then what should guide these choices?

More directly than any other climate strategy, CE forces the same questions. What should the goal of intervention be? What does successful intervention look like? How do you describe success in ideological terms that ordinary humans can understand? If prudence dictates the need to know more about geoengineering and society begins to discuss and research ideas for geoengineering, this exploration could in fact force discussion of these questions and this in turn might help humanity manage many anthropogenic problems.

If there is to be a new environmental ideology of the Anthropocene, what would be at its core? The very concept of the Anthropocene begs identification of success in this age. What does thriving in the Anthropocene look like? What critical ideological shifts could provide a basis for thriving in the Anthropocene? Perhaps at the core of mid-century environmentalism was the attractiveness—or aesthetic—of 'returning to nature', which is fundamentally about removing human influence. In a way, 'going back to Nature' is a kind of abdication of management responsibility. 'Nature' will take care of herself in her mysterious and highly complex ways if humans just get out of the way. But by definition, the Anthropocene represents an age of human influence. In the case of climate, choosing to manage this problem means our influence will no longer be unintentional. To act with intention implies choosing where you want to go.

The answers to these questions about goals will surely involve things such as everyone should have enough to eat, sufficient water and shelter, clean air to breathe and so on. Some parts—an amount to be determined—of Earth should be dedicated to animals or perhaps re-wilded. The identification of these goals and even the categories of goals could be and has been the topic of scientific and public engagement and deliberation. But people will also likely want or need a simpler clarifying way to think about what humanity is trying to achieve on our home planet, and to some extent, this may simply involve beauty. Many of us—but not all—find Nature beautiful. A fundamental challenge for environmentalists in the Anthropocene will be to find beauty in a managed and cultivated world. The aesthetics of a well-oiled, sweetly humming machine, the beauty of engineering or gardening, must surely be part of a new ideology for the Anthropocene. Perhaps, CE can catalyse a discussion about how a thriving and cultivated planet could be beautiful.

This is not going to be an easy discussion. A mining engineer will hang a picture of a massive open-pit mine in his office because he finds beauty in the extensive carving up of the Earth that, to him, is a glorious human-made sculpture. Currently, many would see an ugly hole in the ground. Can these people learn to see beauty, maybe not as a sculpture, but as an enterprise that produces metals needed for a healthful life? Perhaps, finding beauty would be more likely if it is accompanied by moral conviction that the activity is fundamentally good because it takes care of people's needs. In this regard, the open-pit mine provides another insight about what it will take to achieve such an understanding of goodness in utility. The mining engineer knows that the product of the mine makes people's lives better. But most people in the developed world are no longer aware of the fundamental systems that support their lives. To most, water comes from the tap, electricity from the plug and food from the store. The aquifers, electric generation stations and farms are all quite distant from modern humans. For example, 100 years ago more than 80% of the population were farmers and these people were connected tightly to the systems that produce food. Today, only a few per cent of our population is involved in farming. It is not surprising that modern citizens find it difficult to connect the metal in our cars, computers and refrigerators to the open-pit mine. Finding beauty in aspects of the world that humans have engineered will likely require a lot more common knowledge about how the anthropogenic world works in order to believe the good that is done by an engineering intervention.

## A WORLD COUNCIL ON CLIMATE ENGINEERING

Even as climate change problems accumulate, high barriers for the deployment of global climate intervention will likely persist. First the technology will always involve hard-to-predict and perhaps devastating risks, and second, no global institutions exist that could manage that risk. If geoengineering is to become a strategic tool for managing our climate, then some kind of international cooperation and likely control will be necessary. Positing that, a first step would be some kind of world council on climate engineering (WCCE). It is important to ask, then, what is required of such a council and how might this come about?

Ideally a WCCE would first and foremost keep the context of any use of CE within the more general strategic approach to climate change. It would be a disservice to humanity to consider CE as a separate and independent activity apart from mitigation and adaptation. The council should commission the evaluation of potential technologies, deliberate potential goals for their use and management, importantly rule out the use of inadvisable technologies, set up transparent procedures and reporting to make the state of knowledge clear and useful, conduct deliberations about the use of such technologies including public engagement and issue analyses that compare the risks of not deploying a promising technology against the risks of deployment. No such body exists and building this capacity seems like a very large lift. Consequently, an early version of a council might have a more limited charge of engaging about research in CE as a way to build towards a body that would be effective when and if deployment decisions are ever contemplated.

The recently concluded COP 21 Conference in Paris provides some glimmer of hope that a WCCE could be formed. With this COP, in what may prove to be a watershed for the Anthropocene, all the countries of the world agreed on a climate goal. They did not agree about how to get there, but they agreed on where they should go. They also ascribed jointly to the development of a moral framework embedded in the idea that countries have to transparently report their progress and will be 'shamed' if they don't meet their pledges. Given how complex and impactful these choices were, this achievement does seem to represent real movement, even if the commitments are currently insufficient. Perhaps the UNFCCC will evolve and form some special bodies to deal with issues of strategy such as CE. The agreements made in Paris provide new hope that such a thing could happen.

Another likely path to global management of climate intervention would be an expansion of activities needed to adapt and manage local climate emergencies. As climate changes, impacted countries and regions will likely be driven to take local actions to relieve or prevent impacts (Long 2013). These actions will likely include weather modification that could become more vigorous, long lasting and larger in scale. The actions may occur primarily in the developing world where impacts are particularly dire and where there is a likelihood of private companies selling technological solutions to desperate governments. Indonesians, for example, may have attempted to rain out oncoming storms over the ocean to avoid flooding enhanced by climate change.[2] Current research explores ideas of directing monsoons through manipulation of sea surface temperature and aerosol emissions to cool heat waves. Cloud brightening might prove effective in such a scheme. Some have developed concepts to cool regional heat waves using atmospheric aerosols (Bernstein, Neeling, and Chen 2012). What could happen is that the local or regional intervention technologies grow in scale and impact. As heat waves become more extensive, frequent and more severe, the attempted interventions become larger in scale, more pre-emptory and stronger. What starts as local adaptation could gradually morph into global intervention.

Alternatively, proposed large-scale global interventions are likely to become more sophisticated. Modellers even now are exploring methods that would involve multiple 'knobs' such as combining sea surface temperature reduction with solar radiation management or variable space and time solar radiation management. Or scientists might try to manipulate teleconnections to control specific impacts.[3] For example, if cooler ocean waters in one location are correlated to higher rainfall in another, climate engineers may want to try to create upwelling of cooler water in the first region to enhance rain in the second. These methods will essentially use local perturbations to control global climate.

Although intentional intervention as weather modification has up to now been seen as quite different from 'single knob' injection of aerosols that would cool the whole planet, these boundaries could blur. The desire to either control local impacts or use local climate 'levers' will push the technologies towards the 'middle' from either end. The 'middle' might be defined like this: local or regional interventions are deployed, but they have global impacts. In the case of global CE, the global impacts were a goal of the intervention. But sufficiently large regional weather pattern manipulation can have global impacts as well.

In either case, the more regional the intervention is, the more likely small regions or countries are to do it because procedural justice might not require a large international institution—at least initially—as a prerequisite for taking this kind of action. This likely occurrence could potentially provide an opportunity.

To the extent such regional interventions go beyond national boundaries, one or more countries would have a moral obligation to jointly deliberate about the goals for the intervention and obtain unbiased evaluations of technologies that could address or achieve these goals. The goals could be to stop floods, end droughts, maintain the monsoon, keep permanent ice in the Arctic, limit sea-level rise and so on. Clearly, some of these goals cannot yet be addressed and some could. There would have to be some kind of solicitation of technologies and an assessment of their potential efficacy, advisability, do-ability including costs and so on. Continued cooperation would require continued trust, so norms and processes for functional scientific transparency including communication about what intervention or even research about intervention is being done and why and what is known and unknown, what can be done to improve understanding and what is expected from the research results. Importantly, the process for changing priorities and direction would also require deliberation.

All of these requirements are more easily understood and implemented on smaller scales. However, there are a number of ways regional responses might morph into a global cooperation. Deployment of regional interventions might result in regional conflicts, but these also might result in successful regional cooperation to address a 'common enemy' (Ricke et al. 2013). There could be a gradual expansion of regional compacts that reaches a critical state of interconnection and a 'phase-change' to a global or quasi-global organization—like crystallization. Or conflicts between regions, untreated tragedies or a global sense of emergency with immigration conflicts, or mass starvation or deaths in storms might cause the UN National Security Council to act. Alternatively, a coalition of the capable—a bi- or tri-lateral agreement, say between the United States and China or the United States, China and European Union with open invites to others to join under the negotiated agreement—might form.

No matter how this comes about, we should be mindful of the opportunity to use smaller scale regional interactions over localized climate interventions as a model to develop just and effective norms and processes for managing climate change. Without such mindfulness, this prognosis could lead to increased conflict or subjugation of one region's choices on either nearby countries or perhaps the globe.

## CONCLUSION

Geoengineering may be needed in the future. We need research to know if it has enough promise and if the side effects can be minimized. That research may commence soon given the evolving understanding of climate and the energy transition. A strategic approach to the use of this technology is critical and research should inform that approach. As research starts, people should capture the opportunity to learn about managing the environment of the planet in a just and effective manner and how to understand and, in fact, take pleasure in doing a good job in that process. As the problem of climate change grows, the need for international interaction and coordination will also grow and early and smaller scale interventions can provide another opportunity to build the institutions required.

## NOTES

1. Long and Scott (2013) made the point that any research proposing to find the benefits of a particular climate engineering strategy should be coupled to research to find out what might be wrong with the idea. This has been labelled a red team/blue team approach.

2. See, for example, http://www.guardian.co.uk/environment/2013/feb/19/cloud-seeding-flooding-indonesia.

3. Teleconnections are observed correlations between conditions in one place and weather patterns somewhere else. Major weather anomalies associated with El Nino events are an example of a teleconnection.

## BIBLIOGRAPHY

Bernstein, D. N., J. D. Neelin, Q. B. Li, & D. Chen. 2012. 'Could Aerosol Emissions be Used for Regional Heat Wave Mitigation?' *Atmospheric Chemistry and Physics Discussions* 12: 23793–828.

Fuss S., J. G. Canadell, G. P. Peters, M.Tavoni, R. M. Andrew, P. Ciais, R. B. Jackson, C. D. Jones, F. Kraxner, N. Nakicenovic, Corinne Le Quéré, M. R. Raupach, A. Sharifi, P. Smith & Y. Yamagata. 2014. 'Betting on Negative Emissions.' *Nature Climate Change* 4: 850–53 doi:10.1038/nclimate2392.

Loftus P. J., A. M. Cohen, J. C. S. Long and J. D. Jenkins 2015. "A Critical Review of Global Decarbonization Scenarios: What Do They Tell As About Feasibility?" *WIREs Climate Change* 6: 93–112. doi: 10.1002/wcc.324.

Long, Jane C. S. 2013. 'A Prognosis—or Perhaps a Plan—About Geoengineering.' *Carbon and Climate Law Review* 7 (3): 177–86.

Long, Jane C. S. and J. Greenblatt. 2012. 'The 80% Solution: Radical Carbon Emission Cuts for California' *Issues in Science and Technology* 28 (3) (Spring). http://www.issues.org/28.3/long.html.

Long, Jane C. S., and Dane Scott. 2013. 'Vested Interests and Geoengineering Research.' *Issues in Science and Technology* 29 (3) (Spring). http://issues.org/29-3/long-4/.

Long, Jane C. S., and J. G. Shepherd. 2014. 'The Strategic Value of Geoengineering Research.' In *Global Environmental Change: Handbook of Global Environmental Pollution* , vol. I, edited by Bill Freedman, 757–70. Springer: Dordrecht, NL. doi: 10.1007/978-94-007-5784-4_24.

Ricke, K. L., J. B. Moreno-Cruz, and K. Caldeira. 2013. 'Strategic Incentives for Climate Geoengineering Coalitions to Exclude Broad Participation.' *Environmental Research Letters* 8 (1): 014021. doi: 10.1088/1748-9326/8/1/014021.

Smil, Vaclav. 2003. *Energy at the Crossroads: Global Perspectives and Uncertainties.* Cambridge, MA: MIT Press.

*Chapter 9*

# Food Systems and Climate Engineering

## *A Plate Full of Risks or Promises?*

Teea Kortetmäki and Markku Oksanen

In 2030, Joe's lunch plate may have interesting novelties like the Climate-Fighter® curry meal. Its rice comes from special genetically modified (GM) high-albedo crops that also emit less methane than traditional crops. Vegetables are grown in a farm that is certified for actively promoting soil carbon sequestration. Energy-efficient mycoprotein has replaced the meat. While eating this climate-friendly meal, Joe hears from the news that the global agreement has been made on starting aerosol-based climate engineering all over the world, but food justice movements protest against it and require governments to subsidize ClimateFighter® varieties and traditional mitigation policies on agriculture instead.

Whether this fictive story realizes itself or not, important and difficult questions arise from interactions between climate engineering, climate mitigation, and food production and consumption. On the one hand, global warming makes the objectives of food justice—securing the right to food and ensuring that food system activities, such as production and retail, are fair in their distribution of benefits and burdens—even more difficult to reach. On the other hand, there are ways in which 'next generation food systems' could contribute to mitigating emissions and engineering the climate.

This chapter analyses the ethical challenges, risks and opportunities that result from the complex relations between food systems and climate engineering. As a normative point of departure, we take it there is an obligation to secure sufficient (and sustainable) food production that meets the human nutritional needs and is culturally acceptable. The chapter has a conjectural tone since engineering the climate (with agricultural means or otherwise) still lies some way off in the future. However, the critical task of environmental philosophy is also to consider possibilities in advance, even if they may never be realized.

Our comparative approach aims to answer the following questions: Are there ways that food production could contribute to, or be tied into, climate engineering? Conversely, how does climate engineering affect food systems? Moreover, we study whether climate engineering might create adverse effects or serious risks that hamper promoting food justice and, hence, justice in climate matters as well—or whether climate engineering could help promote food justice.[1] For the purposes of this chapter, we distinguish between agricultural and non-agricultural geoengineering. The former refers to climate engineering that is based on the use of plants, animals and microbes in food production; the latter denotes other techniques with no food-related intentions. 'Climate engineering' without qualifications refers to the whole field of climate modification, unless the context clearly indicates otherwise.

## THE BACKGROUND: FOOD SYSTEMS AND CLIMATE POLICIES

Feeding people will be a challenging task in the future. According to the IPCC *Synthesis Report*, 'Global temperature increases of ~4°C or more above late 20th century levels, combined with increasing food demand, would pose large risks to food security globally (high confidence)' (IPCC 2014a, 13). Climate change will affect the production and transportation of food, increasing the risks of malnutrition and famines, as well as the inequalities with regard to food production, rural livelihoods and access to food. Meanwhile, food systems are a significant source of greenhouse gases (GHGs): food accounts for 25–30% of total GHG emissions when the related energy-use and land-use changes are taken into account (Garnett 2011; IPCC 2014b). The most debated singular source is the livestock sector. It contributes 18% to overall anthropogenic GHG emissions and is responsible for more than 50% of the emissions related to land use, forestry and agriculture (Steinfeld et al. 2006). The emissions from rice farming are also remarkable, and rice is responsible for almost 20% of anthropogenic methane emissions (Chen and Prinn 2006). Emissions are also produced in the transportation, processing, packaging, retailing and consumption of food, not to mention food waste itself.

There is significant potential for emission reductions in the global food system (IPCC 2014b), and it is very unlikely that overall GHG emissions could be sufficiently reduced without addressing food sector. In other words, changes in the food system probably have to be an essential part of any emissions mitigation strategy. What this implies is by no means self-evident.

Many common-sense ideas about food-related emissions are misplaced: neither organic nor local food is unequivocally a superior choice, packaging matters relatively little after all and transportation from store to home counts usually more than all earlier transportation phases (Foster et al. 2006). Emission reductions in the food system then require particular policies. This raises questions we are going to address: could farming be harnessed to advance emission mitigation or climate engineering?

In our discussion, the concepts of food systems and food justice play key roles. A food system is a network that defines and structures the production and consumption of food. Food systems consist of food system activities (from seed to fork), actors (from industry to political institutions) and drivers such as sociopolitical factors and global environmental change that together shape these activities (Ericksen 2008). There are global, regional and local food systems: borders cannot be strictly drawn and systems overlap. International trade agreements, for example, affect food systems on all levels. Therefore, the concept of the food system is used in a plural form.

The notion of food justice is used here broadly. First, food justice is a normative criterion for evaluating food systems ethically and politically. Its crux is the requirement to satisfy the food-related needs of human beings[2] now and in the future. Second, in a sociological analysis, Gottlieb and Joshi (2013, 4) characterize food justice as something that aims at 'ensuring that the benefits and risks of where, what, and how food is grown and produced, transported and distributed, and accessed and eaten are shared fairly'. Accordingly, among the persistent issues of the food justice debate are working conditions, gender inequalities and agricultural trade policies. Therefore, food justice is a framework that aims to expose the existing power relations and assess their legitimacy in food system activities (Alkon and Agyeman 2011). Moreover, food justice has also been associated with non-distributional issues of justice such as representation and recognition (see Hourdequin, this volume). The ethics and politics of food are not insulated from wider social issues.

As we see it, climate change and food issues are inseparable: when the anthropogenic climate change contradicts the requirements of food justice, it harms people as well. Similarly, climate engineering has implications for food justice, and several considerations must be born in mind in recognizing the linkages between the two types of harms: changing the climate constitutes an unjust action that reduces the possibilities to maintain food system activities in a way that promotes food security and fair conditions for farmers and labour. It will turn out that some themes discussed within the 'agricultural geoengineering vs. food justice' framing are also important for the 'mitigation vs. food justice' framing, such as bioenergy versus food production and issues related to GM crops.

## FROM FARM TO AIR: INCORPORATING
## GEOENGINEERING INTO AGRICULTURE

Food systems have a dual role with regard to climate change: although they are major GHG emitters, agriculture also provides a significant carbon sink, in both the short and long term. This is evident in the seasonal variation of $CO_2$ concentration in the atmosphere famously detected in the Mauna Loa observatory (the Keeling Curve graph), which shows that during the summer of the Northern Hemisphere, terrestrial plants promote considerable carbon uptake through photosynthesis. Some of this carbon uptake is stored in the soil over long periods. Through these mechanisms, carbon is constantly being captured and removed from the atmosphere. The duration of these sinks depends on the future use of the plants and land. Vegetation can also reflect radiation away from the Earth,[3] and this albedo effect can possibly be utilized to decrease regional temperatures (Singarayer et al. 2012).

The deliberate utilization of these techniques to affect the atmosphere's carbon concentration is called bio-geoengineering and, when linked with food production, could be called agricultural geoengineering, though not all bio-geoengineering is agricultural in the sense of being intended to produce food (e.g. tree planting and farming nonfood plants like cotton and tobacco). In what follows, we evaluate two forms of agricultural geoengineering, one related to SRM and another to CDR. The question on which we focus is whether their utilization (either as alternatives or as complements to non-agricultural climate engineering) would promote food and climate justice.

### Bio-geoengineering Through the Albedo Effect

The reflectivity (albedo) of plant material varies greatly between different plant species and even between different strains of the same species. There is a growing interest in utilizing this phenomenon, and some researchers find crop albedo geoengineering a promising technique for decreasing regional or local temperatures. Singarayer et al. (2012) estimate that by choosing strains (and in some areas by changing cultivated species) with higher reflectivity, it would be possible to achieve ca. 1–1.6°C regional cooling in Europe in summer, while in South Asia the cooling effect is smaller and occurs during winter. Further, there might be positive impacts on food productivity in particular cropland regions due to decreased heat stress, though these effects are estimated to remain regional.

From the viewpoint of just climate policies, albedo geoengineering would have several benefits as a climate engineering technique. It has low risks (unlike many other SRM methods) and low implementation costs, as the required infrastructure is ready in the farms. It is estimated, with some caveats we will discuss later, to have no significant negative effect on productivity and food security, and there might be beneficial precipitation increases in certain areas such as Europe (although this varies by region) (Ridgwell et al. 2009; Singarayer et al. 2012). Regional cooling might alleviate other problems such as heat wave–related diseases or mortality, hence promoting justice in climate matters in a more general sense. However, there are three other concerns for food justice: (1) issues of creation and distribution of varieties (including availability, intellectual property rights and genetic modification); (2) threats to agricultural diversity and biodiversity; and (3) undiscovered threats to food security.

## Challenges with Plant Modification Approaches

Before the deployment of albedo-based geoengineering can be carried out, crop varieties would have to be developed that have the desired qualities, are safe for human consumption and are available for large-scale use. These novel varieties could result from either traditional plant breeding, whereby their use might not face significant legal or political obstacles, or genetic engineering. In this latter case there are various regulatory protocols to be met and further ethical issues that could arise. The acceptability of genetically modified varieties in food production is a widely discussed and contested topic (especially in Europe). Even though an increasing amount of agriculture relies on GM varieties, the opposition to them is staunch. The creation of plant varieties for agricultural geoengineering through GM also raises ethical issues characteristic of the 'traditional' GM food discussions, such as health risks related to GM products, the right of the consumer to know and the public interest to protect the food system from GM products.

Let us assume here that GM varieties gain legal and social acceptance and that they are safe. Even then, further obstacles to their use might emerge from geopolitics, as states might be reluctant to engage with the technology transfer and want to retain their hold on strategic varieties. Moreover, there are powerful private interests involved in the form of intellectual property rights. Although the rights holders may not always benefit from preventing anyone from using GM varieties, conflicts of interests are commonplace. Consider the eagerly anticipated Golden Rice. It relied on many inventions that were protected by intellectual property rights, but the rights holders showed goodwill and allowed for their subsistence use (Potrykus 2001). Golden Rice developers have also established the idea of 'Humanitarian Use License' that provides 'free access for those who need it'.[4] However, due to reasons that vary from regulative issues to objections by environmental movements, Golden Rice has not reached fields despite its availability since 2000. Acceptance from farmers is vital. What this example points out is that even though suitable varieties could become available, their use might face serious social, legal and political hindrances.[5]

Agricultural geoengineering based on plant modification, whether genetic or not, also constitutes a biodiversity-related risk of 'bio-perversity'. Adopted from forestry research, bio-perversity refers to situations where climate-motivated reforestation policies have decreased diversity, because policy evaluations have considered the ecological consequences of reforestation policies too narrowly (Lindenmayer et al. 2012). We find this risk conceivable in agriculture if efficient new SRM varieties are promoted extensively. This can be in conflict with farmers' sovereignty, if the alternatives are circumscribed and the farmers are compelled to choose a certain crop variety against their own desires. As we argued earlier, SRM varieties should be broadly available, yet their use should not be too extensive (this, however, reduces their effectiveness at a global level), and the opportunities for the choice in farming should be protected.

Another diversity-related worry concerns the effects of SRM-type agricultural geoengineering on landscapes. A rural landscape, shaped by agricultural activities, is highly valued in many parts of the world and considered as an important part of traditional biodiversity (even though there are huge areas of monocultures that have mainly economic, rather than cultural, value). Deploying agricultural SRM might affect these landscapes. Although it is too early to say whether people would find this positive or negative, this dimension should not be neglected.

Problems of another kind would arise if new SRM strains were efficient in terms of their albedo effect but had some other unpredicted and undesired properties. Although Singarayer et al. (2012) do not consider albedo engineering to significantly risk food security, they acknowledge that there are uncertainties concerning the actual operational yields and disease or drought resistance of albedo crops. Were such trade-offs realized, it would invoke problems similar to the 'biofuels versus food production dilemma', although with less mutually exclusive alternatives. Is it justifiable to use arable land for climate crops that produce less food but more climate benefits? If it is, to what extent? This problem is a very conjectural one, however, unless future research suggests that there are trade-offs between albedo and other agriculturally important properties of the plants.

## Soil Carbon Sequestration and Agricultural Production

Much attention has recently been paid to soil carbon sequestration. Sequestration methods within food production include field management (such as reduced tillage, erosion control and cover crops) and biochar (biomass-based charcoal used as soil amendment). BECCS or bioenergy with carbon capture and storage is a sequestration method in which energy crops are combined with carbon capture and storage, producing negative emissions

(IPCC 2014b). BECCS is admittedly non-agricultural bio-geoengineering (as it does not involve food-related intentions), but we discuss it here because of its indirect yet important relation with food production through the utilization of arable land.

The first 30 cm of soil contains three times as much carbon as all of the global ground vegetation (Powlson et al. 2011). Some estimate that carbon sequestration could therefore have huge potential, removing up to 50 ppm carbon equivalent from the atmosphere in the next century (Lal 2013). Yet, others are more cautious about the significance of this method and warn that the most optimistic calculations have been too simplified (Powlson et al. 2011). Despite disagreement on the effectiveness, soil sequestration is considered to be a 'no-regrets' policy. Risks are low, and 'any measure that increases [soil carbon] content is likely to have beneficial impacts on soil properties and functioning' (Powlson et al. 2011, 53). Biochar is broadly agreed to improve soil fertility in addition to its carbon-sequestering effects (Conte 2014). Improved soil functioning in turn often affects food production positively and hence improves long-term food security.

Some might argue that soil carbon sequestration is not a climate engineering method at all. On the other hand, a technique that adds biomass to the soils and makes possible the revegetation of degraded land while at the same time sequestering carbon seems like a highly desirable practice, whether or not you choose to call it climate engineering. Other revegetation activities such as large-scale afforestation and reforestation usually are considered a CDR technique (Preston 2012, 2), which speaks in favour of also counting more permanent soil carbon enhancements as a CDR technique. A more detailed article on the distinctions between mitigation, adaptation and climate engineering activities (Boucher et al. 2014, 32) proposes categorizing these kinds of techniques as territorial or trans-territorial removal of atmospheric $CO_2$ and other long-lived GHGs to distinguish them from emission reduction practices. That being said, how does this method look like from the climate and food justice viewpoint?

By definition, 'no-regrets' policies are expected to be relatively safe and have predictable consequences. Furthermore, especially plant-based agricultural geoengineering practices are easy to cancel due to their annual renewal. With view to harms, sequestration within food production seems to be a solution that at least does not raise any major doubts of injustice and, moreover, potentially meets the need for negative emissions. One objection that needs consideration, however, concerns the efficacy and costs of these actions. What is the accepted additional price for the sequestered carbon, if the permanency of sequestration is uncertain (and depends not only on natural factors but on future policies and the actions of future farmers)? Another question is, who should pay the costs of these actions in the developing countries: those most responsible for climate change (the global North) or those benefitting from the actions (the global South)?

In contrast, BECCS appears unviable in relation to food justice. It inherits the ethical dilemmas of the 'energy vs. food' debate. In the context of scarce fertile arable land, reserving it for energy crops to a significant extent is likely to risk food security and, accordingly, impede food justice. There is a possible exception to this: sourcing biomass from agricultural waste and side streams instead of dedicated energy crops might make BECCS a justifiable addition to the policy toolbox.

From the food justice viewpoint, it is arguable that compared with SRM-related agricultural geoengineering, CDR through soil management is indeed more favourable and promotes food justice better. Lal (2013) has argued that soil carbon sequestration also addresses food security in developing countries by increasing their agricultural productivity (in a sustainable way). If this argument is sound, there are chances that at least in some cases, carbon soil sequestration is a win-win solution with important co-benefits: enabling climate engineering in a way that at the same time promotes food justice.

## NON-AGRICULTURAL CLIMATE ENGINEERING AND FOOD SYSTEMS: HARMS OR SYNERGIES?

Non-agricultural climate engineering can have consequences for all aspects of food systems. Neither agriculture itself nor food processing, transportation, marketing and consumption are safe from the different hydrometeorological changes and side effects associated with climate engineering. Arising from this, we next address whether non-agricultural climate engineering is acceptable from the viewpoint of food justice. When it is compared with emission mitigation through more sustainable food systems, which alternative is likely to promote food justice most?

### Risks and Uncertainties

Both the estimated effects of and uncertainties related to non-agricultural climate engineering are relevant when these policies are to be evaluated by the food justice approach. In addition, it is important to consider how the expected benefits and harms are distributed among different communities. Climate engineering is here compared with more traditional mitigation policies in food systems. Which issues of justice arise when these two alternatives are compared, and do they make any difference for food justice?

The estimates for mitigation potential (excluding agricultural geoengineering) in food systems vary enormously. Agricultural production has the potential for 7.2–11 $GtCO_2eq$/year reductions by 2030 (through cropland management and restoration of organic soils), and the demand side potential estimates vary between 0.76 and 8.6 $GtCO_2eq$/year (IPCC 2014b) (through reducing food waste and changing diets). Given that the global emissions were 49 $GtCO_2eq$ in 2010 (IPCC 2014b), 'greening the food systems' significantly contributes to GHG mitigation policies.

Some mitigation options in food systems are problematic in that they can impede food justice. These include policies that threaten food production or increase overall food prices globally or locally, such as the promotion of biofuel crops and regulations that might violate the food sovereignty of local communities by, for example, restricting their freedom to define their own food ways. It could also be argued that the individual right to control one's own food and nutrition practices would be to some extent violated if the policies set *de facto* constraints on the opportunities to consume climate-burdening food items. However, the food justice discourse itself strongly endorses environmental sustainability and acknowledges (at least to some extent) that food sovereignty should be exercised within ecologically sound limits (see Gottlieb and Joshi 2013, 226; Holt-Giménez 2011), so we suggest at least the majority of GHG mitigation in food systems is compatible with food justice. These mitigation options include but are not limited to more sustainable cropland management practices, the restoration of organic soils and reducing food waste.

Non-agricultural climate engineering strategies differ greatly in terms of their effectiveness, predictability and reversibility. CDR methods are considered generally safer, more predictable and more safely reversible, but also significantly less efficient, in comparison with SRM. Keller et al. (2014) contend that CDR methods are unable to prevent warming from continuing well above 2°C and are predicted to have a modest impact at best. Both CDR and emission mitigation in food systems are then partial solutions.

To our knowledge, non-agricultural CDR techniques such as artificial trees usually have no significant direct effect on food systems overall. They would reduce $CO_2$ (hence having a slightly negative effect on yields) but also reduce temperature stress (hence having a positive effect on yields) (cf. Pongratz et al. 2012). The indirect effects of CDR in alleviating or slowing down climate change can contribute to promoting food justice by two mechanisms: (1) allowing more time for adaptation and (2) reducing yield losses in the long run (by diminishing the impacts of climate change). The total contribution of these techniques is then likely to be slightly positive in terms of food justice.

While SRM has greater potential to prevent warming, it also carries significantly higher risks. A few model-based predictions have been made on the effects of SRM strategies on agriculture. Decreases in precipitation, possibly up to 9% in a global scale and even more in particular tropical regions (Keller et al. 2014, 8), might threaten food production. This would violate food justice by degrading food security and by increasing inequalities between communities, depending on their adaptive capacity. On the other hand, Keith (2013, 9–10) asserts that moderate SRM with sulphates would actually reduce crop losses in the hottest areas (in comparison with the same GHG levels but no SRM). Pongratz et al. (2012) propose that SRM has generally positive yet limited effect on yields, but some regions may face undesired impacts and yield losses that threaten their local food security. Moreover, the authors remark that 'SRM poses substantial anticipated and unanticipated risks by interfering with complex systems that are not fully understood' (Pongratz et al. 2012, 104). This makes them conclude that the potential of SRM to reduce the overall risks of climate change on food security is not established and that emission mitigation is still the safest climate policy option with regard to global food security.

Another question is whether uncertainties related to SRM can be decreased. Robock et al. (2010) argue that even testing aerosol-based SRM would require full-scale implementation that could seriously disrupt food production and affect the food supplies of more than 2 billion people due to changes in precipitation. Risks related to precipitation changes caused by SRM are serious. It is possible that some future plant varieties can handle drought and variations in the timing of precipitation; drought-resistant plants are already being studied (Ling and Jarvis 2015). Some proponents of SRM have also asserted that these risks are partly exaggerated and misunderstood, at least if SRM is deployed to a moderate extent only (Keith 2013).

An argument for effective, full-extent SRM is that it would make mitigation in food systems unnecessary, hence being the best option for securing food sovereignty and consumer autonomy. This proposal, however, is problematic because climate engineering cannot tackle other environmental problems of food production (such as habitat loss, soil degradation and water eutrophication), and the need to restrict or change environmentally harmful food activities is likely to remain. Therefore, we contend that full-scale SRM at least (such as extensive stratospheric sulphate aerosol injection) is likely to have too substantial risks and relatively narrow benefits from the food justice viewpoint and in comparison with other available strategies. Yet, it is possible that future research shows these risks to be controllable and rather insignificant, which would in turn require changes in these ethical considerations on SRM and food justice.

Non-agricultural engineering of the climate could, in the worst case, function as a trigger for an unpredictable global-scale humanitarian crisis. Such a crisis could come about if the deployment of full-scale climate engineering turned out to disrupt the food production of 2 billion people, realizing a risk discussed by Robock et al. (2010). Such a disruption would increase food prices and cause food insecurity, which would likely inflict (food) refugee floods and political unrest around the world due to scarce food supplies and increased food prices. This 'trigger risk' provides strong grounds for following the precautionary principle with regard to deploying the riskiest SRM methods in a large scale. Consequently, especially techniques that are hard to reverse are barely acceptable from the viewpoint of food justice, if there are alternative mitigation or engineering strategies that are together sufficiently effective.

## CONCLUSION

Although the importance of food might not always be recognized in climate policies, there are no reasons for overlooking it. Agricultural climate engineering provides a good example of how emission mitigation and climate engineering can be combined (see Fragnière and Gardiner, this volume), though it is unclear whether global cropland area is sufficient to provide effective global mitigation. On the other hand, certain climate engineering techniques can have significant impacts on global food security and food justice. As we see it, this creates a moral obligation to consider the effects of climate engineering on food systems with open eyes.

Agricultural activities can contribute to climate engineering mainly by SRM geoengineering and enhanced soil carbon sequestration methods. Non-agricultural CDR and SRM techniques vary significantly in their effects on food systems. Evaluating these alternatives with regard to food justice requires considering both how these techniques promote or impede food justice and their effectiveness in decreasing the harmful effects of climate change to food systems. These alternatives and their estimated benefits and costs, as regards food justice, are summarized in Table 9.1.

We concur with the argument that while some climate engineering strategies can be considered as complements to mitigation policies, $CO_2$ mitigation is still the most effective way to tackle climate change (cf. Keller et al. 2014, 9). This concerns the great potential of mitigation in food systems as well. One reason that makes mitigation in food systems a superior alternative to (particularly non-agricultural) climate engineering is that due to other environmental impacts of food systems, climate engineering cannot replace the need to address the environmental effects of food systems whereas food system mitigation could partly address these as well, providing a valuable co-benefit.

More research on climate geoengineering is, however, needed. It is possible that in future some geoengineering techniques will prove to be useful for promoting food justice, if they safely decrease yield losses particularly in the poor or vulnerable communities as Keith (2013, 9–11, 58–60) has suggested with regard to (non-agricultural) SRM. It is necessary to find the ways to resolve or manage the risks related to non-agricultural SRM techniques

**Table 9.1　A Comparison of Climate Engineering Methods in Regard to Food Justice**

| Method | Benefits to Food Justice | Harms/risks to Food Justice | Efficiency in Reducing Climate Harms |
|---|---|---|---|
| SRM in agriculture | + Safe, cheap, reversible<br>+ Local cooling effect decreases heat wave–related harms<br>+ May increase productivity | − Property rights or GM-related threats to justice<br>− Risk of "bio-perversity"<br>− Relatively unknown risks | Unknown |
| CDR in agriculture | + Safe, cheap, reversible<br>+ Promotes food security by increasing production | − Price of sequestered carbon requires consideration | Modest |
| SRM, non-agricultural | + Very effective and quick<br>+ Mitigation in food systems would become unnecessary<br>+ Cheap | − May risk food security widely<br>− Unequally distributed harms<br>− Substantial anticipated and unanticipated risks<br>− Termination has high risks | Very high |
| CDR, non-agricultural | + Rather safe<br>+ Few risks to food security | − Possibly high costs<br>− Termination has high risks | Modest |
| Mitigation in food systems | + Safe and rather effective<br>+ Most policy options are compatible with food justice<br>+ Other environmental problems in food systems are addressed | − Poorly designed policies might impede food justice<br>− Costs may be high (at least in the short run) | Relatively high |

(cf. Pongratz et al. 2012; Robock et al. 2010). It is also important to keep in mind that full-scale and moderate implementation of such techniques are different in their effects and related risks.

Considering how significantly climate change threatens food justice and food security, there are reasons for being cautiously positive towards those climate engineering strategies that are safe in terms of food justice and food security. Within our current knowledge, soil carbon sequestration, small-scale CDR techniques (with the exception of BECCS) and perhaps albedo geoengineering, with some reservations, already fulfill this condition. Soil-based CDR can be considered as the most justifiable option in these respects, because it will improve food production and food security regardless and the effects in terms of carbon sequestration will be either positive or neutral.

## NOTES

1. There are food-related human engineering issues such as modifying the human size through the diet or funnies like engineering human digestive systems to make them less gaseous; these are aside the main theme.

2. The place of animals in food systems is thought provoking; some species are important as sources of food, but pure companion animals are merely consumers. This issue is not discussed here.

3. This is not true of all vegetation: temperate forests (in, for instance, the United States, Canada and Russia) absorb heat significantly, which is a concern about large-scale afforestation (see Swann, Fung and Chiang 2011).

4. http://goldenrice.org/Content1-Who/who4_IP.php—accessed 12 October 2015.

5. Similar problems have disturbed the use of patented drugs in the global South.

## BIBLIOGRAPHY

Alkon, Alison H., and Julian Agyeman, eds. 2011. *Cultivating Food Justice: Race, Class, and Sustainability.* Cambridge: The MIT Press.

Boucher, Olivier, Piers M. Forster, Nicolas Gruber, Minh Ha-Duong, Mark G. Lawrence, Timothy M. Lenton, Achim Maas, and Naomi E. Vaughan. 2014. 'Rethinking Climate Engineering Categorization in the Context of Climate Change Mitigation and Adaptation.' *WIREs Climate Change* 5 (1): 23–35. doi:10.1002/wcc.261.

Chen, Yu-Han, and Ronald G. Prinn. 2006. 'Estimation of Atmospheric Methane Emissions Between 1996 and 2001 Using a Three-Dimensional Global Chemical Transport Model.' *Journal of Geophysico-chemical Research* 111: D10307. doi: 10.1029/2005JD006058.

Conte, Pellegrino. 2014. 'Biochar, Soil Fertility, and Environment.' *Biology and Fertility of Soils* 50 (8): 1175.

Ericksen, Polly J. 2008. 'Conceptualizing Food Systems for Global Environmental Change Research.' *Global Environmental Change* 18: 234–45. doi: 10.1016/j.gloenvcha.2007.09.002.

Foster, Chris, Ken Green, Mercedes Bleda, Paul Dewick, Barry Evans, Andrew Flynn, and Jo Mylan. 2006. *Environmental Impacts of Food Production and Consumption: A Report to the Department for Environment, Food and Rural Affairs.* Manchester Business School. Defra, London. http://randd.defra.gov.uk/Document.aspx?Document=EV02007_4601_FRP.pdf.

Garnett, Tara. 2011. 'Where Are the Best Opportunities for Reducing Greenhouse Gas Emissions in the Food System (Including the Food Chain)?' *Food Policy* 36: 523–32. doi: 10.1016/j.foodpol.2010.10.010.

Gottlieb, Robert, and Anupama Joshi. 2013. *Food Justice.* Cambridge: The MIT Press.

Holt-Giménez, Eric. 2011. 'Food Security, Food Justice, or Food Sovereignty?' In *Cultivating Food Justice: Race, Class, and Sustainability,* edited by Alison H. Alkon, and Julian Agyeman, 309–30. Massachusetts: MIT Press.

IPCC. 2014a. Climate Change 2014: Synthesis Report. *Contribution of Working Groups I, II and III to the Fifth Assessment Report of the Intergovernmental Panel on Climate Change* [Core Writing Team, R. K. Pachauri and L. A. Meyer (eds.)]. Geneva: IPCC.

IPCC. 2014b. Summary for Policymakers, In: Climate Change 2014, Mitigation of Climate Change. *Contribution of Working Group III to the Fifth Assessment Report of the Intergovernmental Panel on Climate Change* [Edenhofer, O., R. Pichs-Madruga, Y. Sokona, E. Farahani, S. Kadner, K. Seyboth, A. Adler, I. Baum, S. Brunner, P. Eickemeier, B. Kriemann, J. Savolainen, S. Schlömer, C. von Stechow, T. Zwickel and J. C. Minx (eds.)]. Cambridge University Press, Cambridge, United Kingdom and New York, NY, USA: Cambridge University Press.

Keith, David. 2013. *A Case for Climate Engineering*. Cambridge: The MIT Press.

Keller, David P., Ellias Y. Feng, and Andreas Oschlies. 2014. 'Potential Climate Engineering Effectiveness and Side Effects During a High $CO_2$-Emission Scenario.' *Nature Communications* 5: 3304. doi:10.1038/ncomms4304.

Lal, R. 2013. 'Abating Climate Change and Feeding the World Through Soil Carbon Sequestration.' In *Soil as World Heritage*, edited by David Dent, 443–57. London: Springer.

Ling, Qihua, and Paul Jarvis. 2015. 'Regulation of Chloroplast Protein Import by the Ubiquitin E3 Ligase SP1 Is Important for Stress Tolerance in Plants.' *Current Biology* 25 (19): 2527–34. doi:10.1016/j.cub.2015.08.015.

Lindenmayer, David B., Kristin B. Hulvey, Rirchard J. Hobbs, Mark Colvyan, et al. 2012. 'Avoiding Bio-Perversity from Carbon Sequestration Solutions.' *Conservation Letters* 5: 28–36. doi:10.1111/j.1755-263X.2011.00213.x.

Pongratz, J., D. B. Lobell, L. Cao, and K. Caldeira. 2012. 'Crop Yields in a Geoengineered Climate.' *Nature Climate Change* 2: 101–5. doi:10.1038/nclimate1373.

Potrykus, Ingo. 2001. 'Golden Rice and Beyond.' *Plant Physiology* 125 (March): 1157–61.

Powlson, David S., A. P. Whitmore, and K. W. T. Goulding. 2011. 'Soil Carbon Sequestration to Mitigate Climate Change: A Critical Re-Examination to Identify the True and the False.' *European Journal of Soil Science* 62 (1): 42–55. doi:10.1111/j.1365-2389.2010.01342.x.

Preston, Christopher J., ed. 2012. *Engineering the Climate: The Ethics of Solar Radiation Management*. Lanham, MD: Lexington Press.

Ridgwell, Andy, Joy S. Singarayer, Alistair M. Hetherington, and Paul J. Valdes. 2009. 'Tackling Regional Climate Change by Leaf Albedo Bio-geoengineering.' *Current Biology* 19 (2): 146–50. doi:10.1016/j.cub.2008.12.025.

Robock, Alan, Bunzl, Martin, Kravitz, Ben, and Stenchikov, Georgiy L. 2010. 'A Test for Geoengineering?' [Perspectives text] *Science* 327: 530–31. doi: 10.1126/science.1186237.

Singarayer, J. S., and T. Davies-Barnard. 2012. 'Regional *Climate Change Mitigation with Crops: Context and Assessment.' Philosophical Transactions of the Royal Society A: Mathematical, Physico-chemical and Engineering Sciences* 370: 4301–16. doi:10.1098/rsta.2012.0010.

Steinfeld, Henning, Gerber, Pierre, Wassenaar, Tom, Castel, Vincent, Rosales, Mauricio, and De Haan, Cees. 2006. *Livestock's Long Shadow*. Rome: FAO.

Swann, A. L., Fung, I., and Chiang, J. C. 2011. 'Mid-Latitude Afforestation Shifts General Circulation and Tropical Precipitation.' *Proceedings of the National Academy of Sciences of the United States of America* 109 (3): 712–16. doi: 10.1073/pnas.1116706108.

*Part III*

# GEOENGINEERING JUSTICE IN FRAMES, SCENARIOS AND MODELS

*Chapter 10*

# Framing Out Justice

## *The Post-politics of Climate Engineering Discourses*

### Duncan McLaren

This chapter compares climate engineering with established responses to climate change in terms of the predominant ways in which climate engineering is presented or framed in media discourses. It argues that these frames divert attention away from questions of justice that are central to other climate responses.

The chapter begins with a brief review of existing climate change discourses. Building on ideas derived from Dryzek (2013), it highlights competing climate change discourses of technological *Prometheanism*, *eco-modernization* and *green radicalism*. It then reviews the findings of previously published studies of climate engineering discourses to identify common frames: three of which are explicit—'technological optimism', 'political realism' and 'avoiding catastrophe'—and one implicit—the 'clean sheet' with respect to justice. These frames are compared and contrasted with those found in climate change discourses, highlighting ways in which climate engineering is adopting and reinforcing certain expressions of the eco-modernization and Promethean climate discourses.

The chapter also contrasts the ways in which solar radiation management (SRM) and carbon dioxide removal (CDR) approaches match these discourses, locating the former primarily within *Prometheanism* and the latter within *eco-modernization*. This further highlights the disconnect between the largely 'post-political' discourses of climate engineering and *green radical* climate discourses, which place questions of politics and justice more centrally, and largely reject climate engineering (at least as it is commonly defined and understood).

The chapter concludes with a philosophical analysis of the implications of the 'clean sheet' framing which is common to climate engineering, but not broader climate discourses. Some mechanisms by which this framing is sustained and reproduced are suggested, including post-political ideologies, silence about power and persistent comparison of climate engineering with unabated climate change (rather than with the outcomes of other climate responses). The section argues that a richer and deeper treatment of justice than currently found in climate engineering discourses would likely reject consideration of climate engineering as an alternative to mitigation and adaptation, rather than a supplement (see Fragnière and Gardiner, this volume). It also suggests that better consideration of justice could helpfully illuminate key questions regarding the research, funding and governance of potentially appropriate techniques for climate engineering as part of a portfolio of climate responses.

As space is limited, this chapter necessarily simplifies geographic, cultural and disciplinary complexity. It focuses on public discourses—ways in which people discuss and make sense of a topic—in an effort to identify the most salient and prevalent approaches to the description and analysis of climate engineering across media and academic debate. Discourses are a largely coherent way of talking about an issue, a collection of narratives and storylines, viewed through specific frames—which may be issue specific or of broader application. Discourses around particular issues typically act to establish competing approaches and prescriptions for action. The chapter draws on a range of published content analysis, mainly focused on media coverage as the space in which academic, public and policymaker understandings are shaped and intersect. It highlights specific 'frames' deployed within discourses as 'a means of interpreting an object or issue' (Benford and Snow 2000, Gerhards 1995) or of establishing 'a particular construction of a problem and its solution' (Entman 1993). *Issue frames*, used by actors to promote a particular interpretation of an object or a problem, are distinguished from *master frames*, which tend to apply a broader ideological or discursive stance across a range of issues and which therefore may appear in multiple discourses (Dombos et al. 2012). Narratives and storylines are understood as processes that—deliberately or unintentionally—communicate the values inherent in particular framings and help to construct and reconstruct those framings. Discourses and frames are highly relevant to outcomes for policy and justice. They not only represent and mobilize particular attitudes to justice with respect to the topic at hand; they also typically embody existing power imbalances among those able to influence the discourse. Issues and framings that go unrecognized or are excluded can be as important as those that explicitly appear.

## DISCOURSES OF CLIMATE CHANGE

Public debate frames climate change as potentially catastrophic, its solutions as primarily technological in nature and the challenge as raising

Table 10.1 Comparison of Key Discourses in Climate Change

|  | *Prometheanism* | *Eco-modernization* | *Green Radicalism* |
|---|---|---|---|
| **Overview** | Free-market neo-liberalism. Actively advocating disruptive technological innovation | Social democracy, with managed capitalism and markets. Positive but selective and managerial view of technology | Green and socialist politics, collectivist economics. Critical and precautionary towards technology |
| **Discursive contests** | Sceptical - - - - - versus - - - - Scientific | Reformist - - - - - - versus - - - - - - Radical |  |
| **Concepts of justice** | Background: libertarian ideals of justice as desert | Part of debate: utilitarian and liberal models of justice, with limited redistribution | Foreground of debate: egalitarian ideals of justice |
| **Application to climate change (Example)** | May doubt the issue. Assumes that free markets and technology can solve any problem (Breakthrough Institute) | Accepts climate change as potential threat to capitalism, seeks reformist solutions through carbon markets and green investment (New Climate Economy) | Sees problem as symptom of (neo-liberal) capitalism. Seeks political, social and behavioural solutions (ETC group) |

*Note*: These environmental discourses were first described by Dryzek (2013) as *Prometheanism* (and *economic rationalism*); *Ecological Modernisation* (and *green Keynesianism*) and *Green radicalism* (*green consciousness* and *green politics*) respectively.

important questions of justice yet somehow transcending or superseding politics (Anselm and Hultman 2014, Methmann et al. 2013). The dominant mainstream discourse (see also Table 10.1)—widely deployed in international climate negotiations—can be described as one of ecological moderniza-tion (Dryzek 2013), hereafter 'eco-modernization'. In its typical corporatist social democratic forms, eco-modernization offers a systemic response to catastrophic environmental threats while maintaining the essence of industrial capitalism. To address climate change it relies heavily on low-carbon tech-nologies such as renewables, nuclear power and carbon capture and storage (CCS), alongside state intervention in both technological development and consumer behaviour.

Eco-modernization discourses deploy utilitarian and liberal concepts of justice. For instance, concerned that mitigation might harm existing econo-mies or prevent future growth in poorer countries, they seek internationally coordinated climate action, under the rubric of 'common but differentiated responsibility'. But disagreements over the extent of historical responsibility and differentiated duties for mitigation and financing of adaptation continue to hamper climate negotiations (Pickering et al. 2012). At national levels the distributional implications of climate policy measures, especially on adaptation, have often been critical to their design and success (Bickerstaff et al. 2013).

Despite the accepted significance of justice, eco-modernization however de-emphasizes political debate around climate change in at least two ways. Internationally, it seeks multilateral consensus around significant climate action as a universal threat, harnessing capitalism and globalization to deliver technological solutions—largely subjugating political differences to a dominant ideology of market capitalism. Nationally, it tends to individualize and depoliticize the problem, offering carbon markets and green consumption as solutions—which turns climate policy into a matter of consumer choice guided by economic markets. In this respect it has been criticized for its limited engagement with social justice and the distribution of wealth (Baker 2007).

Eco-modernization can therefore be seen as 'post-political' (Zizek 1999, Ranciere 2004) in multiple senses. As both the description and the critique of the late-twentieth-century ideological convergence around neo-liberal capitalism, 'post-politics' identifies and critiques the ways in which conventional democratic spaces of electoral and activist politics have been sidelined and disempowered. It highlights a series of shifts including a cultural individualization in which a focus on identity displaces concerns about class and a public debate in which risks feature more prominently than distribution. Climate change is understood as one of those risks, whose universal apocalyptic potential is paradoxically appropriated to defend corporate capitalism (Swyngedouw 2010).[1]

The central eco-modernization discourse is challenged from two directions, however: by a global Northern-centred discourse of denial and scepticism and a more Southern-centred one of green radicalism and anti-globalism.

In the global North, and particularly the United States, climate sceptics mobilize a 'Promethean' discourse to resist public action on climate change as an undesirable constraint on individual freedoms and free markets (Hoffman 2011a,b). While eco-modernization emphasizes the scientific basis of the challenge of climate change, Center for Promethean argue that *if* climate change is a problem, technological solutions will be found to address it. In such discourses, technological ingenuity gives humanity dominion over nature, with both the right and the capacity to control it (Dryzek 2013). Contemporary expressions of Prometheanism include the ideas of a 'good Anthropocene' advocated by the Breakthrough Institute (Asafu-Adjaye et al. 2015).[2] Like previous Promethean discourses these are aggressively post-political, placing both problem definition and solutions in an optimistic scientific and technocratic frame (Hamilton 2015). This leaves little space for questions of justice

(Collard et al. 2015) and assumes rather a libertarian ideal, in which inequality is accepted or celebrated as meritocratic.

Elsewhere, more radical discourses—such as 'eco-socialism' (Anselm and Hultman 2014) and 'green consciousness' or 'green politics' (Dryzek 2013)—are arguably the main challenge to eco-modernization. In green radical discourses, catastrophic climate change can only be averted—or survived—by transforming economic and political systems. Capitalism and corporate globalization are the problem, and solutions are seen in collective, politically driven lifestyle and behaviour change. Egalitarian concepts of justice are central to such discourses. Effective adaptation and mitigation is understood as necessarily being of a form that embodies justice, not just economically or technically efficient. Such perspectives are widespread, but generally subordinate to eco-modern approaches, except perhaps in some Southern countries, notably in Latin America.[3]

## WHAT DISCOURSES DOMINATE CLIMATE ENGINEERING?

This section turns to the question of whether the same public discourses can be identified regarding climate engineering. It relies on secondary analysis of a corpus of discourse analyses, which considers the emergence and development of coverage of climate engineering in a range of media (Anselm and Hansson 2014a and b, Buck 2013, Loukkanen et al. 2012, Nerlich and Jaspal 2012, Porter and Hulme 2013, Sikka 2012, Scholte et al. 2013).[4] These analyses highlight some common and evolving discourses and narratives that echo some of those in extant climate policy debates. Systematic comparison of these analyses suggests a handful of highly persistent master frames which span otherwise distinctive climate discourses.[5]

Three *explicit* master framings can be identified from the climate engineering discourses: technological optimism, political realism and catastrophe-avoidance. Below (and in Table 10.2), each is outlined and its expression in climate engineering compared with that in broader climate discourses. The analysis also reveals one *implicit* master frame: the clean sheet. Subsequently, each of the frames is examined in more detail to identify contrasting aspects.

*Technological optimism* refers to the presentation of climate engineering as controllable, feasible and practical. The planet is often portrayed as a reparable machine or body, and the technologies as analogues of natural processes such as volcanic eruptions. This master frame includes both Promethean innovation and eco-modern technical managerialism.

*Political realism* claims that conventional approaches to mitigation and adaptation are incapable of responding swiftly enough—if at all—to the challenges of climate change. This 'post-political' master frame also appears

in different flavours, including eco-modern forms of 'pragmatism' that position climate engineering as a necessary Plan B, capable of apolitical delivery,
and Promethean celebrations of entrepreneurial market-based technological
'solutions' that make restrictions on free markets unnecessary.

*Avoiding catastrophe* frames climate engineering as an—often *the only*—
alternative to the catastrophic impacts of unabated climate change. This master frame appears in all forms of climate and climate engineering discourse,
whether Promethean or eco-modern. In many earlier sources, it appears as
an 'emergency' framing, supported by claims regarding the risks of climate
'tipping points'. In contrast, the risks inherent in climate engineering are typically portrayed as knowable and calculable, '*relative to the risks of unmitigated anthropogenic climate change*' (Porter and Hulme 2013: 347).

The prevalence of catastrophic portrayals of unabated climate change does
not mean that climate engineering is necessarily portrayed as safe as well as
practical. In fact, ambivalence about the technology (Scholte et al. 2013) and
the idea that climate engineering is a distinctively 'post-modern' technology
(Anselm and Hansson 2014a)—research into which is advocated despite
serious risks—are notable in the analyses. Nonetheless, although debate and
contestation are noted in these analyses, the typical conclusion is that there
is a dominant discourse incorporating some or all of the main elements set
out above.

Table 10.2 elaborates on how each of these frames appears in climate and
climate engineering discourses.

The analyses considered here largely focus on explicit aspects of the
debate. But what is unsaid or implicit can be just as important. In contrast
with mainstream climate discourses, in climate engineering, justice is notice-
able by its absence. Searching the climate engineering analyses for reference
to justice, and related concepts such as fairness, equity, distribution, winners
and losers, and gains and losses, reveals virtually no mentions, never mind
discussion of its salience, even where reference is made to norms or ethics.
Porter and Hulme (2013) identify 'morality' and 'justice' as among the three
least prevalent of the frames they identified in written UK media coverage. In
most other analyses, justice is occasionally hinted at, especially in procedural
forms related to governance, but never takes centre stage. Buck (2013) also
explicitly considers justice concerns, but finds reference to them in just 12%
of print media articles and about twice that proportion of Internet articles.
She confirms (2013: 176) that 'the justice issue is seldom considered; even
when it was present, it was rarely the dominant frame. ... The antagonist in
the dominant frames is $CO_2$, which mundanely threatens everyone, making
questions of justice invisible.'[6]

This mechanism is perhaps the key way in which the emerging climate
engineering discourse has implicitly framed justice out of the public debate.

**Table 10.2 The Dominant Framings of Climate Engineering and Their Relationship to Expressions of the Main Climate Discourses**

| Master Frames | Discourses | | |
| --- | --- | --- | --- |
| | *Promethean* | *Eco-modern* | *Green Radical* |
| | *In both climate- and climate engineering discourses* | | *Climate discourses only* |
| **Technological optimism** | Dominant: Hubristic advocacy of high-tech, large-scale "solutions" such as nuclear fusion and SRM. Society is expected to inevitably adjust to technology. | Strong: Industrial technologies like CCS, electric vehicles and CDR are practical and essential. Risks of technology exist but can be negotiated and accommodated. | Weak: Social change is more important. "Appropriate" technology (renewables, passive buildings etc.) is endorsed, but "high-risk" technologies should be rejected. |
| **Political realism** | Strong: Post-political, technological solutionism. Politics is not only dysfunctional but undesirable—free markets are preferable. | Moderate: Politics must become managerial with consensual approaches between stakeholders and internationally within capitalist system. | Moderate: State politics is dysfunctional, but system change is possible and desirable. Individual and community action is required. |
| **Catastrophism** | Strong: Mobilized to support technological solutions and to sideline politics. In denialist variants the "catastrophe" to be avoided is state "takeover". | Moderate: Severity of impacts justifies serious interventions (and maintenance of core of industrial capitalism). | Strong: Severity of impacts justifies radical system change ("emancipatory" catastrophism) |
| **Clean sheet** | Absolute: No looking back. Future justice concepts go no further than desert and weak forms of procedural justice. | Strong: "End of history". Some regard for distributive justice looking ahead, and some concern for most vulnerable. Limited recognition. | Moderate: Even radical egalitarian rights-based approaches and "contraction and convergence" tend to downplay history. Broad recognition. |

*Note:* The origins of the master frames in the climate engineering literature are detailed in Table 10.4 in the notes to this chapter.

Climate engineering advocates typically insist that mitigation and adaptation can no longer avoid dangerous climate change ('political realism') and thus that any harms arising from climate engineering should be contrasted with unabated climate change. Catastrophe therefore faces us all, and in this context, we are likely to consider distributional and other political questions to be of only secondary importance (cf. Swyngedouw 2010).

It is as though climate engineering proposals were emerging on a *'clean sheet'* where impacts of and responsibilities for climate change were not already unevenly distributed and contested. This implicit *clean sheet* is arguably the most distinctive part of the framing of climate engineering in contrast with climate change discourses generally. Its presence helps marginalize green radical framings of opposition and rejection, which appear only as a relatively weak alternative discourse with few active proponents (Anselm and Hansson 2014b, see also Markusson 2013). Although some scholars have attempted to integrate localized and small-scale approaches to climate engineering with socially just strategies for climate protection (Buck 2012, Olson 2012, Martindale 2015), such narratives are almost invisible in the public debate among green radical discourses that reject climate engineering (e.g. ETC 2010, Klein 2014).

There are also important differences in the ways climate change and climate engineering discourses apply the three *explicit* master frames. Detailed analysis suggests that the presentation of climate engineering—and especially SRM—within these frames often takes an exaggerated form that fits most closely with technological Prometheanism (as shown in Table 10.2).

In climate engineering discourses, *political realism* drives suggestions that climate engineering might be deployed unilaterally or by a small 'climate engineering club'. The difficulties of political action and the high leverage of the technologies are emphasized to justify avoiding collective negotiations, rather than to trigger a search for compromise. Some expressions of *technological optimism* in climate engineering discourses are also arguably more extreme. While leading CDR technologies [such as Bioenergy with CCS (BECCS) or Direct Air Capture of carbon dioxide] and their dependence on carbon markets closely reflect the managerial styles and industrial technologies of eco-modernization, SRM implies extreme Promethean hubris regarding human capacity to understand and control complex Earth systems.

Finally, in their treatment of *catastrophe*, climate engineering discourses—especially those advocating SRM—often emphasize urgency. They deploy an 'apocalyptic' form of catastrophism (Asayama 2015), designed to legitimate a 'techno-fix' to protect industrial modernity, as opposed to the 'emancipatory' and openly political form used by green radicals to argue for socially disruptive ways of responding to climate change. An apocalyptic threat potentially justifies 'securitization' of an issue and deployment of 'exceptional', even military measures' (Corry 2014). While Prometheans denigrate much state intervention, they are, however, remarkably supportive of state action and expenditure on national defence and security. Consideration of climate engineering might therefore further enable climate change to be incorporated into a Promethean discourse that has previously sympathized with a sceptical perspective motivated by 'small-state' political ideology.[7]

In summary, the discourses of climate engineering are often reminiscent of mainstream climate discourses, especially in their central eco-modern form, but with all three *explicit* framings—political realism, technological optimism and avoiding catastrophe—exaggerated to a significant degree, in particular when discussing SRM. The chapter now turns to focus explicitly on the contrasts between SRM and CDR in these discourses.

## CONTRASTS BETWEEN SRM AND CDR

This section elaborates on the differences between framings of CDR and SRM identified above and identifies some implications Table 10.3 summarizes this analysis.

Analyses of general media discourses typically find little distinction between SRM and CDR (e.g. Porter and Hulme 2013), although specific techniques—notably stratospheric aerosol injection (SAI) as a form of SRM and ocean iron fertilization (OIF) as a form of CDR—are often discussed. SAI has been widely positioned as *the* exemplary climate engineering technology since the Royal Society report (Shepherd et al. 2009), while OIF has seen some active experimentation and controversy over governance. Both fit the broader narratives of high-tech natural analogues, with high leverage

Table 10.3 Application of Key Climate Discourses in Climate Engineering

| | Prometheanism | Eco-modernization | Green Radicalism |
|---|---|---|---|
| **Attitude to climate engineering** | Supportive of research and development | Supportive of research and selective development | Largely opposed to research and development |
| ***Application to SRM*** | Supportive, even in some cases as an alternative to mitigation | Seen as last resort, requires research and careful risk assessment | Opposed: even to extent of preferring adaptation in some cases |
| ***Application to CDR*** | May be supportive if low-cost. Likely to oppose subsidies | 'Negative emissions' are important in managerial approach. Fits with carbon price/markets | Opposed to large-scale technologies such as OIF or industrial-scale BECCS and afforestation |

and scope for unilateral action, and considerable uncertainty about the risks involved. These two technologies therefore arguably suit media agendas, in which some controversy is desirable.

There are other generic similarities between SRM and CDR: both carry risks of moral hazard, for example. Nonetheless, much scholarly and policy work—as well as noting the diversity of techniques in both categories—has begun to construct narratives that distinguish rather than conflate SRM and CDR (McNutt et al. 2015a,b, Shepherd et al. 2009). SRM is often described as rapid, low cost, high risk and (perhaps) less natural. CDR is slow, high cost, low risk and (to some degree) more natural. These distinctions have significant implications for the ways in which dominant discourses affect the approaches. In these rather caricatured forms, CDR would appear to better match eco-modernization discourses, and in fact, the New Climate Economy initiative (NCE 2014)—an excellent example of the contemporary eco-modernization discourse—already encompasses support for improved management of land-based carbon sinks.

On the other hand, SRM—and especially SAI—fits more neatly in technological Prometheanism. If we recognize the Promethean discourse as rooted in part in climate scepticism, it is easy to see why. SRM has already been advocated as the best 'insurance policy' if climate is an issue by sceptical Prometheans such as Dubner and Levitt (2010) and Lomborg (2009). In this form SRM could performatively define an acceptable 'climate problem' in which the capability to control climate outcomes can be sought even without acknowledging a link with $CO_2$ emissions, and the 'solution' does not involve large-scale intervention in free markets or restrictions on the use of fossil fuels. CDR, on the other hand, remains inextricably linked with $CO_2$ emissions, even if its costs can be somehow managed by incorporating it into markets, for example in carbon utilization.

Yet as a rapid and high-leverage technique, SAI is not just a potentially marketable insurance policy but also appears to fit catastrophic and emergency framings—allowing humanity to respond when (and only when) it is clear that climate change is a clear and present danger. Advocacy for SRM research by high-profile climate scientists such as Paul Crutzen, David Keith and Ken Caldeira (Caldeira and Keith 2010; Crutzen 2006; Keith 2014) is arguably a product of their belief that such severe impacts are already otherwise unpreventable (in contrast to Baatz and Ott, this volume).

In eco-modernization discourses, a similar catastrophist framing—in the form of analysis showing the impracticality of achieving the 2°C target without negative emissions—is being deployed to support arguments for urgent investment in and development of CDR techniques. But at the same time, the incorporation of CDR in climate models (typically in the form of BECCS) helps sustain the claim of eco-modernization that climate change can be tackled through low-carbon technology and carbon markets, without overturning capitalism.

CDR might also feature in green radical discourses, but only in certain forms. Ocean iron fertilization is seen as Promethean in its hubris, while at a large scale, BECCS and even biochar are rejected because they are seen as industrializing forests (ETC Group 2010). However, some techniques, especially forms of soil carbon restoration or localized enhanced weathering, might be perceived as acceptable 'no-regrets' options within green radical discourses (Martindale 2015).

The next and final section turns to the central question of the chapter: what are the implications of these Promethean and eco-modern discourses and their post-political, market-based, technological and solutionist framings for justice?

## IMPLICATIONS FOR JUSTICE

We saw above that the implicit 'clean sheet' frame is prevalent in climate engineering discourses, but not in climate change discourses in general. This section outlines three broad implications and highlights some critical mechanisms by which they are reproduced in the discourses. It argues that creating a clean sheet erases historical obligations; detracts attention from power and vested interests, and the ways in which future generations' options might be constrained; and insofar as justice appears at all, implicitly inscribes particular cultural and ideological concepts of justice in the discourse.

Historical obligations related to climate change are not uncontroversial but might arise in diverse ways and forms. Fundamentally, many proposals for responses to climate change seek to respond to historic injustice. Arguments for 'contraction and convergence' (Mayer 2000), 'greenhouse development rights' (Baer et al. 2010) or repayment of a 'climate debt' (Athanasiou and Baer 2011, Blomfield 2015) rest on the historically disproportionate use of fossil fuels and carbon sinks by some nations and groups. Disproportionate resource use has fuelled a process of uneven development in which wealthier countries now enjoy much greater capacities and financial resources to undertake mitigation and adaptation, and in which poorer countries' greater vulnerability to climate impacts is exacerbated by the legacy of colonialism and underdevelopment (Adger et al. 2006). Moreover, the structural processes that have enabled uneven development continue to exist (Blomfield 2015).

In current climate politics, these concerns have fuelled debate over the extent and financing of relative obligations to reduce emissions, maintain carbon sinks, support adaptation and enable migration and relocation, among others. Southern nations perceive a twofold injustice—first that the impacts of climate change harm them disproportionately, and second, that in pursuit of global mitigation, their capacity to develop based on the use of fossil fuels will be unfairly curtailed (see, e.g. Luwesi, Doke, and Morrow this volume). As a result, those disadvantaged by carbon-fuelled underdevelopment have sought forms of compensation or rectification from the winners—rooted in corrective or restorative, as well as distributive, concepts of justice. All these understand the growing impacts of climate change as—to a major degree— the product of historic and ongoing unfairness in the distribution of fossil fuel use and carbon emissions.

In contrast, by emphasizing the ineffectiveness of political solutions, climate engineering discourses deemphasize historical responsibility. Comparisons with scenarios of unabated emissions growth, rather than more realistic trajectories of partial mitigation, portray any negative distributional effects of climate engineering as insignificant in the face of the catastrophic outcomes of unabated climate change. Moreover, because these scenarios are presented (within the 'averting catastrophe' and 'political realism' master frames) as an inevitable context for the consideration of climate engineering, rather than a morally loaded choice, this also implies that the distributional consequences of unabated climate change are somehow of less moral consequence.[8] The construction of climate engineering models and the narratives derived from their findings thus deflect attention from the historic causes of climate injustice. The more it is presented as impractical and politically unrealistic to avoid a high greenhouse gas world, and the more focus is drawn to technological means of avoiding the extremes of climate impacts, the less attention is paid to any moral obligations arising from historic emissions. Compensatory obligations on historic emitters do not appear in the public discourse.[9] Even a weak obligation on developed nations to fund mitigation and adaptation in poorer ones—based in the ability to pay (Caney 2010), rather than any confession of culpability or complicity—is, in SRM advocacy, potentially traduced into a push for a 'lower cost', economically more-efficient alternative whose higher risks rebound on the victims of climate change. In other words, SRM is presented as more acceptable precisely because it imposes fewer financial costs on the very countries responsible for the majority of past emissions.

Not only is state responsibility largely invisible, but so is corporate responsibility and power. In contrast to mitigation discourses, in some of which proposals seek to focus obligations on the largest corporate polluters and extractors of fossil fuels (Klein 2014, Tickell 2008), in climate engineering discourses the power of the (corporate and national) fossil fuel lobbies—built on a history of colonialism and resource extraction—is typically concealed. The post-political nature and technological optimism of climate engineering narratives also pushes questions of power and interests further into the background.

These framings are reproduced in discourses presented predominantly by scientists and experts. In her study of geoengineering in print news media from 1990 to 2010, Buck (2013) reports that 70% of assertions on the topic of geoengineering were made by scientists (of varying types), and only nine scientists were responsible for 36% of the assertions.[10] Eli Kintisch (2010) describes this small and highly influential group of mainly U.S. scientists as 'the geo-clique'. While the 'geo-clique' is likely as much a creation of media imperatives (and laziness) as it is any form of conspiracy, we must be alert to the risk that such a group might share ideological beliefs as well as scientific discussion. Insofar as in discourse making, statements from such a group are intermingled with those from libertarian, anti-regulation, climate sceptic lobby groups (Sikka 2012), we cannot ignore the possibility of a campaign to co-opt geoengineering as a tool to promote continued profits from fossil fuels, rather than as a potentially useful adjunct to accelerated mitigation.

In presenting climate engineering as a post-political technocratic solution, the discourses also understate the extent to which the current climate policy is an exercise of power with respect to future generations. Future people are particularly vulnerable to domination by the present generation (Smith 2012), and the deployment of climate engineering would strongly structure the choices available to them. Arguably, such domination of future generations is a case of failure of recognition: we treat future people as less than fully our moral equals. This is a particular problem if the development of climate engineering techniques also results in reduced action to mitigate carbon emissions, transferring risks onto those same future people. Yet the more climate engineering is understood and embedded as a means to maintain industrial modernism, the greater this risk becomes. This is a feature of both SRM and CDR. CDR enables further delay in mitigation in the belief that the same future $CO_2$ concentrations can be achieved by later action to draw down carbon from the air. Its inclusion in climate models allows eco-modernists to resist pressure from green radicals for accelerated emissions reductions. SRM similarly empowers those who would argue against mitigation as too expensive or ideologically undesirable.

In particular, any idea that fair and effective climate responses might instead require structural social change is pushed to the margins. Responses to climate change rooted in locally just and resilient communities (Hopkins 2008, Klein 2014) are typically ignored or dismissed as 'fuzzy thinking' (Keith 2014). At the same time, particular embedded and implicit ideological and cultural framings of justice are reproduced without explanation or question. In the Promethean discourse we see a narrow libertarian concept of 'justice' as freedom to pursue economic and commercial interests without fear of redistribution or expropriation. It is 'justice' as (rhetorical) equality of opportunity without regard for initial capabilities or endowments. In more eco-modern discourses the implicit concepts of justice are utilitarian, liberal and sometimes distributional. Justice here is individualistic, but inequality and even exploitation—for example of indigenous communities resisting the conversion of forests into carbon storage plantations—are tolerated, or ignored insofar as they help increase aggregate well-being.

The climate engineering discourses, whether Promethean or eco-modern, exclude green radical concepts such as climate justice (Athanasiou and Baer 2011)—understood as equal rights to climate resources which therefore demand far deeper emission cuts than appear *politically realistic*, and recognition (Schlosberg 2009, Hourdequin, this volume)—with its requirement that we acknowledge differential vulnerability and different values systems in our approaches to procedural justice. More mainstream capabilities- and rights-based approaches are nodded to in some narratives, which feature calls for better public participation and consultation. But in practice the discourses are shaped by findings from research and scenarios constructed by climate modellers and academic experts with virtually no consultation of publics.[11] This privileges academic and modelling expertise (a form of epistemic injustice) and reconstructs justice, insofar as it appears at all, as something done to the public by elite institutions, rather than something with democratic, participatory and other procedural elements (McLaren et al. 2013).

In considering the framing-out of historical responsibility and climate justice, we have seen how the dominant climate engineering discourses are reproduced by comparisons with unabated climate change, by silence over power (which leaves the powerful also determining narratives and framings) and by the broader embrace of post-politics which excludes alternative framings and debate over them by appeals to singular 'objective' truths revealed by science and addressed by technology.

This is not to argue that climate engineering could not be deployed in ways that respect and even enhance justice (see Horton and Keith, this volume), rather that in the dominant framings such forms of deployment are unlikely. SRM's speed might allow near-term distributed climate impacts to be ameliorated (in contrast with CDR, which would have limited effect on climate outcomes for many decades), and some have argued that it could be targeted in ways that minimize negative distributional side effects (Moreno-Cruz et al. 2012) and ramped down to reduce termination risks. But such deployment implies global governance and effective complementary mitigation, neither of which features strongly in the framings identified here. Similarly, while CDR could conceivably be funded by historic high-emitting countries and/ or companies—thus taking account of historical responsibility—the mainstream framings suggest that large-scale BECCS, with rich nations importing biomass to fuel power stations and using the $CO_2$ for enhanced oil extraction, would be a more likely model. This could exacerbate past injustices and worsen food insecurity (cf. Kortetmäki and Oksanen, this volume) by transferring agricultural and forest lands from local and indigenous subsistence uses to serve the interests of rich-country populations for cheap energy (McLaren 2012).

In both carbon dioxide removal and solar radiation management variants then, technological and commercial feasibility structures current climate engineering debate, rather than justice considerations. *Technological optimism* about climate engineering serves to sideline questions about the distribution of the resources needed and about how to govern it fairly (rather than simply how to enable it). In contrast, political and social discussion of the design of mitigation and adaptation practices often brings justice into the centre of the debate. It is critical that future analysis of climate engineering examines the details of specific techniques, specific funding and specific governance mechanisms if justice is to be properly considered.

## CONCLUSIONS: BRINGING JUSTICE TO THE CENTRE OF CLIMATE ENGINEERING

Overall, media frames typically imply that geoengineering would be practical and controllable, contrast it as a climate response with continued insufficient mitigation and describe the decision as one to be made in the face of potentially catastrophic climate change. They frame out active consideration of justice, presenting rather a post-political 'clean sheet' for climate policy.

These framings rebut any prospect of radical emissions cuts, denying 'climate justice', and exclude consideration of processes of underdevelopment, past responsibility for dangerous emissions and the role of vested interests in climate policy. They place decision-makers on the horns of a dilemma (where neither choice is fair or ethical), sideline procedural justice in favour of 'emergency powers' and downplay distributional implications, implying such a large-scale problem that 'we are all in it together'.

These discourses strengthen particular extant climate policy discourses, with CDR approaches to climate engineering matching well with narratives of eco-modernization and SRM fuelling a revived technological Prometheanism which can even be embraced by climate sceptics. In comparison, climate engineering does not obviously support green radical discourses that are open to integrating narratives of climate protection with those of social justice, and more typically such discourses reject climate engineering. Indeed, insofar as climate engineering discourses spread, they bolster a trend of active depoliticization of the climate debate.

Looking both backwards and forwards in time, this chapter has drawn attention to both intra- and intergenerational consequences and obligations arising with respect to climate policy. It has argued that these must inform decisions about climate engineering. In particular, it has argued that climate engineering's implications must be compared with those arising from effective mitigation and adaptation, not just with those arising from unabated climate change. Yet the discourses and framings set around climate engineering discourage such comparisons. Thicker and deeper treatments of justice are needed in climate engineering discourses. Such approaches would likely reject consideration of climate engineering as an alternative to mitigation and adaptation, rather than a supplement. Better consideration of justice could also helpfully illuminate key questions regarding the research, funding and governance of potentially appropriate techniques for climate engineering as part of a portfolio of climate responses.

Moreover, the power of narrative is itself also an issue of justice. Those who construct the narrative and set the frames determine the scope and terms of any debate. Different perspectives and epistemologies are not admitted, or at least not on equal terms. Yet for climate engineering we have seen that particular groups, disciplines and nations predominate in the discourses. This helps reproduce the discourses, alongside post-political ideology and the tendency to compare the effects of climate engineering only with unabated climate change. Wider public debate and deliberation would clearly be valuable in ensuring greater consideration of questions of justice.

In turn, this might offer the possibility of ending the domination of climate debate by discourses that sustain existing injustices—particularly those arising from the failure to recognize historic roots to injustice and the way elite lifestyles and cultures act to constrain capabilities in the global South. Otherwise it seems we face the prospect of climate engineering as an expression of neo-colonialism, extending domination by the global North, in contrast with the potential for fuller realization of human capabilities under a portfolio of climate responses shaped by a goal of climate justice.

## ACKNOWLEDGEMENTS

I wish to thank Gordon Walker, Nils Markusson, Christopher Preston, Olaf Corry, Adam Corner and Martin Hultman for their insightful and constructive comments on various earlier drafts of this piece. Errors, as ever, remain my responsibility.

## NOTES

1. Anselm and Hultman (2014) describe how neo-liberal managerial approaches to climate policy in Sweden (bolstered by the failed Copenhagen talks) resisted an opening-up of the debate in response to eco-socialist ideas of justice and redistribution

which had begun to penetrate the eco-modern centre-left discourses (bringing proposals such as work-sharing as well as green job creation) in the period 2006–2009.

2. The title of the Breakthrough Institute's 'Ecomodernist Manifesto' (Asafu-Adjaye et al 2015) is (probably deliberately) misleading, in that [as highlighted by critiques such as Hamilton (2015), Latour (2015) and Collard et al. (2015)] its market individualism, strongly antipolitical ideology and extreme technological hubris are more clearly aligned with Promethean discourses as described here and by Dryzek (2013). Its aim is presumably to convince the eco-modern mainstream to accept these more ideologically extreme positions.

3. In Sweden, Anselm and Hultman (2014) show that green radical narratives of equality also influenced the more mainstream eco-modern 'green Keynesian' discourses of the opposition centre-left parties.

4. These analyses are summarized in Table 10.4.

5. The application of the term 'master frame' is not intended to suggest that the climate engineering and broader climate discourses are completely separate; rather that within these discourses, the Promethean, eco-modern and green radical discourses can be distinguished, yet all display elements of the same master frames. It also seems likely that these master frames may also be reproduced in discourses around other issues such as food supply and the role of genetically modified crops.

6. The lack of justice in the public discourse does not mean it is also overlooked by academics. Scholars such as Gardiner (2010), Preston (2012), Smith (2012) and Burns (2013) have drawn attention to various aspects of justice among wider ethical concerns.

7. This discussion implies that climate engineering technologies are easily accommodated in industrial modernism. Although Anselm and Hansson (2014a) argue that climate engineering has a uniquely 'post-modern' character as a risky response to a modern hazard (a narrative of a 'double fear'), we might question the distinctiveness of climate engineering in this respect: arguably technologies such as nuclear power and genetic modification have also been promoted by Prometheans and eco-modernizers despite acknowledged risks. Moreover, as Anselm and Hansson themselves identify, a storyline of 'mimicking nature' has come to supplant that of the 'double fear' in an active attempt by advocates to 'integrate geoengineering into the logic of industrial modernity' (Anselm and Hansson 2014b: 117).

8. Methmann and Oels (2015) suggest a similar case in adaptation policy. In the presentation of climate change as an immutable fact, they argue, resilience discourses focused on climate-induced migration become post-political, depriving subjects of their rights, side-stepping questions of compensatory funding for adaptation and facilitating a shift of responsibility from the global North to the South.

9. This is broadly the case for academic consideration also, with the contributions to this volume from Habib and Jankunis, and Baard and Wikman-Svahn offering largely unprecedented efforts to consider SRM as a potential form of, or contribution to, historical recompense.

10. Buck notes that the 'loudest silence, so to speak, was from women' (p. 174). Space does not permit me to argue this further, but it would also seem reasonable to suggest a gendered preference for technological and politically negotiated responses to men and women respectively.

Table 10.4 Review of Consistent Themes in Climate Engineering Discourse Analyses

| Source | Technological Optimism | Political Realism | Avoiding Catastrophe | Coverage |
|---|---|---|---|---|
| **Loukkanen et al. (2012)** | *Mechanisms, Health & Controllability* metaphors often carry such implications | *Controllability* metaphors such as "Plan B" are responses to limited political action | *War and Fight* metaphors, highlighting seriousness and potential need for sacrifice | Six sets of metaphors in 88 *NYT* and *Guardian* articles (2006–2011) |
| **Nerlich and Jaspal (2012)** | *Techno fix*: metaphors of planet as body or machine in need of fixing | Do not directly identify political realism, but highlight later emergence of "Plan B" narratives | The *argument from catastrophe* itself frames techno-fix metaphors | Metaphors in 91 popular science and other trade press articles (up to 2010) |
| **Sikka (2012)** | *Technological determinism*—a utopian belief in entrepreneurial innovation to provide solutions | *Market economy*—opposition to climate engineering is portrayed as opposition to economic progress and free markets | *Philosophical exceptionalism*—climate engineering as the "only option" for avoiding "catastrophic" climate change | Four discursive frames used by mainly conservative advocates of geoengineering |
| **Buck (2013)** | *Managerial* frame draws on "ecological modernization" and relative cheapness of climate engineering | Highlights absence of discussion of prospects for political or behavioural transformation | *Catastrophic* frame combines discursive elements of "crisis" and "inevitability" | one hundred and eighty one English-language print and online media articles (1990–2010) |
| **Porter and Hulme (2013)** | *Innovation* most prevalent frame: reflecting pro-technology stance of promoters such as Royal Society | In *governance* frame, frequent references to inevitability of climate engineering from "failed negotiations". | *Risk* framing highlights high stakes in unabated climate change | Seven issue frames in 70 articles in UK media (up to 2011) |
| **Scholte et al. (2013)** | *Techno-fix* (in 46% of articles). Technology the "key solution". nature "controllable". | *Pragmatism* (in 41% of articles). Climate engineering "is practical", but "current approaches" to climate are "failing" | *Avoiding catastrophe* (in 53% of articles). Climate engineering as perhaps essential or our "only hope" to tackle climate problems | Seven common frames in 181 English-language newspaper articles (2006–2011) |
| **Anselm and Hansson (2014a and b)** | Implicit *technological salvation* supported by *natural analogies* which emphasize the practicality of the technologies | *The failure of politics* and cynical industrial fatalism suggest no political option. "Emergency" frames also "depoliticize" the issue | *Double fear*: where climate engineering is risky but the alternative is catastrophe. In later material the *naturalism* frame ameliorates the riskiness of climate engineering | Dominant storylines in 1500 media articles between 2006 and 2013 in English, German and Scandinavian languages |

11. The work of the IAGP programme (http://iagp.ac.uk/) is a notable exception, as deliberative public engagement (albeit only in the UK) influenced the research programme and helped inform the development of scenarios for comparative modelling evaluations of climate engineering technologies.

## BIBLIOGRAPHY

Adger, W.N., J. Paavola, S. Huq, M. J. Mace (eds). 2006. *Fairness in Adaptation to Climate Change*. Cambridge MA: MIT Press.

Anselm J. and A. Hansson. 2014a. 'The Last Chance to Save the Planet? An Analysis of the Geoengineering Advocacy Discourse in the Public Debate.' *Environmental Humanities*, 5: 101–23.

Anselm J. and A. Hansson. 2014b. 'Battling Promethean dreams and Trojan horses: Revealing the critical discourses of geoengineering.' *Energy Research & Social Science* 2: 135–44.

Anselm J. and M. Hultman. 2014. *Discourses of Global Climate Change*. London: Routledge.

Asafu-Adjaye, J., L. Blomqvist, S. Brand et al. 2015. *An Eco-modernist manifesto*. Available online at http://www.ecomodernism.org/manifesto-english/.

Asayama, S. 2015. 'Catastrophism toward 'opening up' or 'closing down'? Going beyond the apocalyptic future and geoengineering.' *Current Sociology* 63(1): 89–93.

Athanasiou, T. and P. Baer (2011) *Dead Heat: Global Justice and Global Warming*. Seven Stories Press.

Baer, P. with T. Athanasiou, S. Kartha and E. Kemp-Benedict. 2010. Greenhouse development rights: a framework for climate protection that is 'more fair' than equal per capita emission rights. In *Climate Ethics: Essential readings,* edited by S. Gardiner, S. Caney, D. Jamieson and H. Shue, 215–30. Oxford: Oxford University Press.

Baker, S. 2007. Sustainable development as symbolic commitment: Declaratory politics and the seductive appeal of ecological modernisation in the European Union, *Environmental Politics*, 16(2): 297–317.

Benford, R. D. and D. A. Snow. 2000. 'Framing Processes and Social Movements: An Overview and Assessment.' *Annual Review of Sociology*, 26: 611–39.

Bickerstaff, K., G. Walker and H. Bulkeley (eds). 2013. *Energy Justice in a Changing Climate: Social equity and low-carbon energy*. London: Zed Books.

Blomfield, M. 2015. 'Climate change and the moral significance of historical injustice in natural resource governance.' In *The Ethics of Climate Governance*, edited by A. Maltais and C. McKinnon, 3–22. Rowman and Littlefield International.

Buck, H. J. 2012. Geoengineering: re-making climate for profit or humanitarian intervention? *Development and Change* 43 (1): 253–70.

Buck, H.J. 2013. 'Climate engineering: Spectacle, tragedy or solution? A content analysis of news media framing.' In: *Interpretative approaches to global climate governance: (De-)Constructing the greenhouse,* edited by C. Methmann, D. Rothe and B. Stephan, 166–80. London: Routledge.

Burns, W. C. G. 2013. 'Climate Geoengineering: Solar radiation management and its implications for intergenerational equity.' In *Climate Change Geoengineering: philosophical perspectives, legal issues and governance frameworks,* edited by W. C. G. Burns and A. L. Strauss, 200–20. Cambridge, MA: Cambridge University Press.

Caldeira, K. and D. W. Keith. 2010. 'The Need for Climate Engineering Research.' *Issues in Science and Technology* 27 (1).

Caney, S. 2010. 'Climate Change and the Duties of the Advantaged.' *Critical Review of International Social and Political Philosophy* 13: 203–28.

Collard, R-C., J. Dempsey and J. Sundberg. 2015. 'The Modern's amnesia in two registers.' *Environmental Humanities* 7: 227–32.

Corner, A. and N. Pidgeon. 2014. 'Geoengineering, climate change scepticism and the 'moral hazard' argument: an experimental study of UK public perceptions.' *Philosophical Transactions of the Royal Society A*; DOI:10.1098/rsta.2014.0063.

Corry, O. 2014. 'The Politics of Direct Intervention: Climate Engineering and Security Dynamics in Climate Politics' Paper presented at *Climate Engineering Conference*, August 2014, Berlin.

Crutzen, P. 2006. 'Albedo Enhancement by Stratospheric Sulfur Injections: A Contribution to Resolve a Policy Dilemma?' *Climatic Change* 77 (3–4): 211–20.

Dombos, T. with A. Krizsan, M. Verloo and V. Zentai. 2012. *Critical Frame Analysis: A Comparative Methodology for the 'Quality in Gender + Equality Policies' (QUING) project.* Budapest: Center for Policy Studies.

Dryzek, J. S. 2013. *The Politics of the Earth.* 3rd edition. Oxford: Oxford University Press

Dubner, S. J. and S. D. Levitt. 2010. *Superfreakonomics.* London: Penguin Books.

Entman, R. M. 1993. 'Framing: Toward Clarification of a Fractured Paradigm.' *Journal of Communication* 43 (4): 51–58.

ETC Group. 2010. *Geopiracy: The case against geoengineering.* Online at http://www.etcgroup.org/sites/www.etcgroup.org/files/publication/pdf_file/ETC_geopiracy_4web.pdf.

Gardiner, S. M. 2010. 'Is 'Arming the Future' with Geoengineering Really the Lesser Evil? Some Doubts about the Ethics of Intentionally Manipulating the Climate System.' In *Climate Ethics: Essential readings,* edited by S. Gardiner, S. Caney, D. Jamieson and H. Shue, 284–312. Oxford: Oxford University Press.

Gerhards, J. 1995. 'Framing dimensions and framing strategies: contrasting ideal and real-type frames.' *Social Science Information*, 34 (2): 225–48.

Hamilton, C. 2015. The theodicy of the 'Good Anthropocene'. *Environmental Humanities* 7: 233–8.

Hoffman, A. J. 2011a. 'Talking Past Each Other? Cultural Framing of Skeptical and Convinced Logics in the Climate Change Debate.' *Organization Environment* 24 (1): 3–33.

Hoffman, A. J. 2011b. 'The culture and discourse of climate skepticism.' *Strategic Organization* 9 (1): 77–84.

Hopkins, R. 2008. *The Transition Handbook. From Oil Dependency to Local Resilience.* Green Books.

Keith, D. 2014. *A Case for Climate Engineering.* A Boston Review Book, MIT Press.

Kintisch, E. 2010. *Hack the Planet: Science's Best Hope - or Worst Nightmare - for Averting Climate Catastrophe.* London: Wiley.

Klein, N. 2014. *This Changes Everything.* London: Allen Lane.

Latour, B. 2015. 'Fifty shades of green.' *Environmental Humanities* 7: 219–25.

Lomborg, B. 2009. 'Climate engineering: It's cheap and effective.' *The Globe and Mail.* August 14, 2009. Available online at http://www.theglobeandmail.com/globe-debate/climate-engineering-its-cheap-and-effective/article4283374/.

Loukkanen, M., S. Huttunen and M. Hildén. 2013. 'Geoengineering, newsmedia and metaphors: Framing the controversial.' *Public Understanding of Science.* DOI: 10.1177/0963662513475966.

Markusson, N. 2013. 'Tensions in framings of geoengineering: Constitutive diversity and ambivalence.' *Climate Geoengineering Governance Working Paper Series: 003.* Available online at: http://www.geoengineering-governance-research.org/cgg-working-papers.php.

Martindale, L. 2015. 'Understanding humans in the Anthropocene: finding answers in geoengineering and Transition Towns.' *Environment and Planning D: Society and Space* 33 (5): 907–24.

McLaren D., K. Krieger and K. Bickerstaff, 2013. 'Justice in energy system transitions: the case of carbon capture and storage.' In *Energy Justice in a Changing Climate: Social equity implications of the energy and low carbon relationship,* edited by K. Bickerstaff, G. Walker and H. Bulkeley, 158–81. London: Zed Books.

McLaren, D. P. 2012. 'A comparative global assessment of potential negative emissions technologies.' *Process Safety and Environmental Protection* 90 (6): 489–500.

McNutt M., W. Abdalati, K. Caldeira et al. 2015a. *Climate Intervention: Reflecting Sunlight to Cool Earth.* National Research Council of the NAS: Committee on Geoengineering Climate. Washington DC: National Academies Press.

McNutt et al 2015a and 2015b: McNutt, M. K., Abdalati, W., Caldeira, K., Doney, S. C., Falkowski, P. G., Fetter, S., Fleming, J. R., Hamburg, S. P., Morgan, M. G. Penner, J. E., Pierrehumbert, R. T., Rasch, P. J., Russell, L. M., Snow, J. T., Titley, D. W. and Wilcox, J. *Climate Intervention: Carbon Dioxide Removal and Reliable Sequestration,* National Research Council of the NAS: Committee on Geoengineering Climate. Washington DC: National Academies Press.

Methmann C., D. Rothe and B. Stephan, 2013. 'Introduction: How and why to deconstruct the greenhouse.' In *Interpretative approaches to global climate governance: (De-) Constructing the greenhouse,* edited by C. Methmann, D. Rothe and B. Stephen, 1–23. London: Routledge.

Methmann, C. and A. Oels. 2015. 'From 'fearing' to 'empowering' climate refugees: Governing climate-induced migration in the name of resilience.' *Security Dialogue* 46 (1): 51–68.

Moreno-Cruz, J. B., K. L. Ricke and D. W. Keith. 2012. 'A simple model to account for regional inequalities in the effectiveness of solar radiation management.' *Climatic Change* 110: 649–68.

NCE (New Climate Economy) 2014. *Online* at http://2014.newclimateeconomy. report/.

Nehrlich, B. and R. Jaspal. 2012. 'Metaphors we die by? Geoengineering, metaphors and the argument from catastrophe.' *Metaphor and Symbol* 27 (2): 131–47.

Olson, R. L. 2012. 'Soft Geoengineering: A gentler approach to addressing climate change.' *Environment Magazine* 54 (5): 29–39.

Pickering, J., S. Vanderheiden and S. Miller. 2012 'If Equity's In, We're Out': Scope for Fairness in the Next Global Climate Agreement. *Ethics & International Affairs*, 26(4): 423–43.

Porter, K. E. and M. Hulme. 2013. 'The emergence of the geoengineering debate in the UK print media: a frame analysis.' *The Geographical Journal*, 179 (4): 342–55.

Preston, C. J. 2012. 'Solar radiation management and vulnerable populations: the moral deficit and its prospects.' In *Engineering the Climate: The Ethics of Solar Radiation Management*, edited by C. J. Preston, 77–94. Lanham, MD: Rowman and Littlefield.

Ranciere, J. 2004. 'Introducing Disagreement.' *Angelaki: Journal of the Theoretical Humanities*, 9 (3): 3–9.

Robock, A. 2008. '20 reasons why geoengineering may be a bad idea.' *Bulletin of the Atomic Scientists* 64 (2): 14–18, 59.

Schlosberg, D. 2009. *Defining Environmental Justice: Theories, Movements, and Nature.* Oxford: Oxford University Press.

Scholte, S., E. Vasileiadou and A. C. Petersen. 2013. 'Opening up the societal debate on climate engineering—how newspaper frames are changing.' *Journal of Integrative Environmental Sciences* 10 (1): 1–16.

Shepherd et al 2009: Shepherd, J., Caldeira, K., Cox, P., Haigh, J., Keith, D., Launder, B., Mace, G., MacKerron, G., Pyle, J., Rayner, S., Redgewell, C. and Watson, A. *Geoengineering the Climate: Science, Governance and Uncertainty.* London: Royal Society.

Sikka, T. 2012. 'A critical discourse analysis of geoengineering advocacy.' *Critical Discourse Studies* 9 (2): 163–75.

Smith, P. T. 2012. 'Domination and the ethics of solar radiation management.' In *Engineering the Climate: The Ethics of Solar Radiation Management*, edited by C. J. Preston, 43–62. Lanham, MD: Rowman and Littlefield.

Swyngedouw, E. 2010. 'Apocalypse Forever? Post-political Populism and the Spectre of Climate Change.' *Theory, Culture & Society*, 27 (2–3): 213–32.

Tickell, O. 2008. *Kyoto 2: How to manage the global greenhouse.* London: Zed Books.

Zizek, S. 1999. *The Ticklish Subject: The Absent Centre of Political Ontology.* London: Verso.

*Chapter 11*

# Solar Geoengineering

## *Technology-based Climate Intervention or Compromising Social Justice in Africa?*

### Cush Ngonzo Luwesi, Dzigbodi Adzo Doke and David R. Morrow

Humans' greenhouse gas (GHG) emissions are changing the climate (IPCC 2014). GHG emissions correlate highly with the growth of per-capita gross domestic product (GDP), which represents the wealth of nations and is associated with larger carbon footprints and, often, social inequality (Hayward 2007). The world's poorest people suffer most from climate change though insignificantly contributing to the problem (UNEP 2003; Shue 2010). Africa in particular 'stands to lose the most' despite having 'contributed only a tiny fraction to overall greenhouse gases' (UNECA 2015). African leaders often blame the developed world for the large range of climate injustices experienced in the continent (Zougmore et al. 2015).

Climate injustice in Africa often results from governments' difficulties in protecting potential victims of climate change. This relates especially to the 85% of poor people living in rural areas, including men, women, their children and other vulnerable groups (Goh 2012; Rees 2014). Granting the poor their right to participation in decision-making for easy access to natural, economic and social assets is already a challenge, so how would African governments protect them against undemocratic decisions of the global carbon market? (Taylor 1997; Harris 2010; Posner and Weisbach 2010).

In their global Shared Socio-economic Pathways 4 (SSP-4) storyline, O'Neill et al. (2014) predicted a highly unequal world, dominated by a relatively small global elite, responsible for most GHG emissions. A larger, much poorer group, contributing very little to GHG emissions, would suffer the most harm of climate impacts, owing to ineffective institutional mechanisms and high poverty and inequality levels. In addition, many African countries face financial and energy constraints and lack adequate technological assets for climate adaptation and mitigation, including proposed geoengineering technologies. Hence, they already foresee an escalation of existing social injustices with the deployment of some radical forms of climate intervention (Gardiner 2011; Preston 2012; Hamilton 2013a). How will the global community ensure justice to poor farmers, women and their children, particularly those whose livelihoods are affected by drought and flooding in rural areas? That is the topic of this chapter.

## APPROACHES TO CLIMATE SCENARIO PLANNING

The uncertainties of the global coordination of climate policies are well illustrated using scenario planning. Processes for developing scenarios vary from one simulator to another, but most recent processes follow the planning methods championed by the Global Business Network (YCEI 2013). The present study first assumed that the O'Neill et al. (2014) SSP-4 storyline was the most feasible scenario process for potential climate intervention. Scenario planning was secondly linked to the stakeholder-driven food and climate scenarios for policy development in Africa proposed by Palazzo et al. (2014). To develop the base scenario for our study, in which climate change proceeds without solar geoengineering, we used these tools to predict African governments' responses to climate change. The scenario planning method was streamlined to an iterative, multistage process to derive the relevance of policy interventions to climate justice. This process encompassed four steps: (1) extending the time horizon to 2100; (2) clustering countries based on the hydrological context in which they are likely to evolve over this period (e.g. hyper-arid, arid, semi-arid, semi-wet, wet or polar conditions); (3) integrating these diverse sets of perspectives and convergent elements into a robust model featuring each future scenario in a dichotomous manifestation of events (i.e. high/low impacts from climate change versus high/low capacity for implementing climate policy); and (4) finally, the development of a two-by-two matrix comprising four groups of countries to describe as accurately as possible the likely response of each group to projected climate impacts. Countries were grouped as 'water-scarce climate proactors' (high impacts/high capacity), 'water-stressed climate prospectors' (high impacts/low capacity), 'water-rich climate defenders' (low impacts/high capacity) and 'water-rich climate reactors' (low impacts/ low capacity), according to their capacity to prevent or respond to climate injustice.

Water-scarce climate proactors are countries with *high* projected climate impacts on water and *high* capacity for implementing policies to address (potential) climate injustice. They have a very active public service that can map and manage climate impacts while attending to key stakeholders, who are directly affected by climate change. In countries categorized as water-stressed climate prospectors, most stakeholders are at risk but those who would be most vulnerable without assistance are attended to in emergencies by national and international civil society. Water-rich climate defenders, on the other hand, do not have a clear climate policy agenda but will quickly intervene to attend to the 'most critical' stakeholders. These countries also experience very *low* climate impacts but have *high* levels of policy intervention. Finally, water-rich climate reactors do not have 'priority' stakeholders, meaning those highly vulnerable to water stress, but will likely react in case of emergency to assist selected victims, if they can. Since they are experiencing very *low* climate impacts, their policy interventions may be *low*.

Countries were categorized based on a large number of secondary data obtained from the International Monetary Fund (IMF), United Nations Economic Commission for Africa (UNECA) and the World Resources Institute (WRI) among others. These data included change factors such as population, GDP, technology impacts on water, farm yield and costs, progress towards achieving natural resource management (NRM) and millennium development goals (MDGs), and other relevant factors. Each of these variables was assigned a dichotomous value ('high' or 'low') based on the specifics of the country, prior to clustering countries and predicting responses to climate injustice within each cluster.

## ANALOGIES FOR AFRICA'S RESPONSE TO SOLAR GEOENGINEERING DEPLOYMENT

To develop our second scenario, we suppose that in response to an unspecified but significant degree of climate change, one or more rich countries propose and perhaps deploy stratospheric aerosols as a form of solar geoengineering (also known as solar radiation management). We paid special attention to stratospheric aerosols' projected effects on water and related ecosystems, since these ecosystems constitute the bedrock of most rural livelihoods in sub-Saharan Africa (Nzuma et al. 2010; Anderson et al. 2013). Using the country clusters identified in the base scenario, we consider how countries in each of those clusters would be likely to react to stratospheric aerosol proposals and deployment.

To do this, the study looked at fundamental motivations that may drive each African country to respond to a call for geoengineering deployment (Moore et al. 2015), complemented by the authors' expert judgement and analogies to previous international negotiations (Olukuye and Mukanga 2007), such as the signing of the cooperative agreement framework (CFA) in the Nile Basin (Adar and Check 2011).

The present study recognized five key predictive factors for responding to a call for solar geoengineering deployment: (a) regional economic specialization; (b) priorities and expertise of decision-makers; (c) financial incentives offered by world powers; (d) the environmental impacts of the technologies on water, forest and rural livelihoods; and (e) previous attitudes towards the implementation of international treaties, protocols and agreements on climate change and environmental management. In order to project each country's response to stratospheric aerosol injection by analogy to their response to climate change (Glantz 1998), these factors were projected onto each group identified in the base scenario.

Countries in the first group, *water-scarce climate proactors*, face *high* expected climate impacts and feature a *high* capacity to implement climate policies. At the time world powers call for stratospheric aerosol injection, they will have appropriate climate adaptation/mitigation technologies and may responsibly decide, where possible, whether to support a long-term geoengineering scheme.

In countries categorized as *water-stressed climate prospectors*, with *high* expected climate impacts but *low* capacity for climate policy implementation, the climate intervention agenda is driven by nonstate actors, like nongovernmental organizations (NGOs) and the media, without a climate 'policy' per se. However, if stratospheric aerosols were deployed, domestic and international civil society would presumably be very active and may rescue the most vulnerable people.

*Water-rich climate defenders* are water-rich countries with *low* expected climate impacts and a *high* capacity for climate policy implementation, giving them the ability to devise short-term public interventions to generate income from the global carbon markets, for example, payment for environmental services (PES). If the decision to deploy stratospheric aerosols was to be taken by world superpowers, these countries would invoke potential negative effects of solar geoengineering on ecosystems and, anticipating a loss of their benefits from schemes like reducing emissions from deforestation and forest degradation (REDD+), request compensation mechanisms.

Finally, *water-rich climate reactors*, with *low* expected climate impacts and *low* capacity for policy implementation, generally lack sufficient motivation to devise high-level climate policies in the short term. By the time stratospheric aerosol injection is being proposed, they will have no adaptation strategies to curb any side effects of geoengineering. Consequently, depending on the length of time between the international proposal of geoengineering and its deployment, many vulnerable people would have to devise their own coping mechanisms to 'save themselves'.

# RESULTS AND DISCUSSION

Besides being among the poorest in the world, African countries account for the most significant casualties of climate impacts accrued from water stresses (UNEP 2003; CODESRIA and UNECA 2015). Policy interventions predicted under the current trajectory of climate impacts on water, forest and livelihoods often unintentionally add to the existing social inequities. The next four subsections discuss in more detail how different kinds of African States might respond to the proposal or deployment of solar geoengineering by rich countries, based on the groupings described in the previous section. The fifth subsection discusses how the prospects for climate justice differ between these geoengineering scenarios and the base scenario in which, despite significant climate change, geoengineering is neither proposed nor deployed.

## Self-determination: A Response from Water-scarce Climate Proactors

Most African countries are water scarce but only a few can be called 'climate proactors', that is, those with consistent climate protection mechanisms. These include countries like the Republic of South Africa, Namibia, Botswana and Lesotho (Southern Africa); Algeria; Egypt, Morocco, Tunisia, and Libya (Northern Africa); Burkina Faso, Mali, Mauritania, Niger, Senegal and Chad (Western Africa); Rwanda, Ethiopia and Djibouti (Eastern Africa); and Small Islands Independent States (i.e. Comoros, Mauritius and Cape Verde). These countries have 'self-determined' climate governance systems with proper adaptation and mitigation strategies for countering a long trend of extreme climate variability and impacts.

Most of these countries might welcome solar geoengineering under the assumption that it would improve the harsh weather conditions in the Sahara and Namib deserts, including some parts of the Sahel, the Tellel, the Horn of Africa and Southern Africa (Ricke et al. 2010; AAS and SRMGI 2013; Keith 2013). Some (e.g. Tunisia, Namibia and Egypt) have already adopted costly technological and energy-based climate mitigation innovations to ensure resource recovery, recycling and reuse for environmental protection. Others (e.g. Burkina Faso, Mali and Ethiopia) have simply adopted ecosystem-based approaches towards climate adaptation and mitigation. Some (e.g. Senegal, Algeria and Djibouti) have also developed innovative adaptive strategies for storing water underground, tapping drinking water from snow and dew, trading virtual water, using early warning systems for rapid drought alert and so on. These mechanisms are generally complemented by the enforcement of 'Polluter Pays' and 'User pays' principles, water allocation and evapo-transpiration quotas, green water credits and highly equitable pro-poor schemes like PES, as in Rwanda, Comoros, Mauritius and Cape Verde. Furthermore, these countries have increased climate preparedness at the national level and implemented clean energy and other technological mitigation measures (e.g. rainfall seeding in Morocco and the recovery, recycling and reuse of wastewater in Namibia). Such policies and mechanisms have improved climate resilience and increased social justice in those countries. However, only key stakeholders within the country (e.g. rural farmers) are recognized as direct victims of climate impacts and attended to on a regular basis, unlisted vulnerable classes usually being neglected.

With the deployment of geoengineering, countries in this cluster might request compensatory mechanisms when affected by these technologies. Due to high uncertainties arising from several factors varying from one region to another, parties to a global agreement on stratospheric aerosol injection are likely to have significantly different positions. This will make it difficult to strike a global consensus for a fair deal for compensation just like in the case of 'REDD+' (Shue 1992; Kant and Wu 2011). Richer, more stable countries will feel most comfortable negotiating. Without a consensus, they may vehemently oppose a unilateral decision by the world superpowers.

Many 'climate proactors' may doubt the value of stratospheric aerosol injection as a form of environmental protection. 'Self-determined' countries like South Africa, Namibia, Morocco and Egypt may pledge to commit the world leaders to climate mitigation agreements targeting 'no harm' of life-supporting systems. The latter entails keeping fossil fuels in the ground; protecting watersheds, forests and other ecosystems; promoting ecological farming through farmers or indigenous communities and building a global green economy that limits economic growth. Such strong positions may lead to a 'steel stand' in the negotiations surrounding stratospheric aerosol deployment.

## 'Civil Society to the Rescue': A Response from Water-stressed Climate Prospectors

Countries like Kenya, Malawi, Zambia, Zimbabwe and Madagascar are water-stressed climate prospectors and would have to depend on civil society to come to their rescue. In most instances, these governments provide inadequate climate protection because of inadequate capacity and resources, inconsistent and unclear data collection mechanisms, as well as inadequate market-based and public channels for climate information and protection. Civil society would likely oppose any form of field testing and deployment of solar geoengineering, fearing degradation of their environment, which often increases the economic and external costs of alternating water scarcity and flooding conditions (Luwesi 2010; Getachew and Melesse 2012; Maeda 2012). On the other hand, if they were convinced that solar geoengineering would help with water scarcity, they would create awareness of its benefits.

In East Africa and the Horn of Africa, Ethiopia and Djibouti have stood out among these 'climate prospectors' for building a strong 'climate-friendly public service'. However, the rest of the countries have seen increased economic inequality and deteriorated social justice across social divides. Even though they face serious climatic variability and impacts, they keep calling upon the global community to rescue their most vulnerable stakeholders. This is clearly illustrated by unresponsive governmental interventions to recurrent droughts that claimed millions of lives and triggered UN calls for global actions in 1983–1984, 1998–1999 and 2009–2010 (Shisanya 1990; Tiffen and Mortimore 2002; Luwesi et al. 2012). Faced with solar geoengineering, these countries would be unable to empower their vulnerable populations to adapt to and/or mitigate any harmful effects. Their response to proposals for or deployment of solar geoengineering will simply be a series of public outcries coupled with emergency interventions like food and water relief from national and international civil society.

## 'Cash, Carbon and Calories': A Response from Water-rich Climate Defenders

Most 'water-rich' countries in West Africa are 'climate defenders'. These include Ghana, Nigeria, Equatorial Guinea and Ivory Coast. They emphasize climate 'adaptation' rather than market-based climate 'mitigation', unless accompanied by economic incentives. They support 'Clean Development Mechanisms' (CDM), including the existing mitigation mechanisms under the REDD+ and other reforestation mechanisms, which are feasible ways of providing sinks for carbon through sustainable conservation and management of life support ecosystems. But they still perceive these mechanisms as a means of enabling 'rich polluting' countries to keep their industrialization agenda on track while keeping African industrialization ambitions on hold for the sake of global welfare (Shisanya et al. 2014).

These opportunistic water-rich climate defenders would promptly capitalize on injustices arising from solar geoengineering by seeking or trading their climate agenda in the international market via CDMs to generate 'cash, carbon, and calories'. This might result in the rise of innovative coping mechanisms among their people and enhanced self-preparedness against harmful effects of solar geoengineering. However, when an extreme event occurs, policymakers will protect only the most critically affected stakeholders.

The climate burden of other stakeholders will likely be neglected, resulting in increased inequality and poor social justice. Nonetheless, should world powers inject stratospheric aerosols unilaterally, without assurance of compensation, water-rich climate defenders (like Nigeria and Ghana), who are in search of 'cash, carbon, and calories', will put a strong case on solar geoengineering trade-offs and carbon removal credits to compensate for the loss of human lives, animals, forestlands and other flora and fauna species (Robock 2008). This might lead to strong negotiations and, later on, to resistance to further deployment of solar geoengineering, such as various states in Africa and elsewhere have already expressed in conferences of the Convention on Biological Diversity (Hamilton 2013b).

## 'Save Yourself': A Response from Water-rich Climate Reactors

Most of water-rich climate reactors enjoy quasi-normal climatic regimes and are located within the rainforest of Central Africa (including Cameroon, Central African Republic, Congo, DR Congo, Gabon and Sao Tome) or its outskirts (Tanzania and Uganda in Eastern Africa; Angola and Zambia in Southern Africa). They lack adequate climate protection and preparedness owing to fragmented public and social services (IMF 2015). This often undermines trust in public institutions and exacerbates social inequalities and injustices. Individual households thus make quick decisions to cope with climate change impacts by increasing their security measures. When facing the effects of stratospheric aerosol injection, most of these water-rich climate reactors will be in a *sauve qui peut* situation ('save yourself'). The government's response will likely be pure silence, possibly repeating the DR Congo's pathway for the implementation of the Cooperative Framework Agreement (CFA) on sharing the Nile waters.

Despite its capital role in spearheading a process that took almost a decade, the DR Congo, who was chairing the Nile Basin Initiative in 2009, silently abstained from signing the CFA, leaving all other riparian countries in a *sauve qui peut* situation (Adar and Check 2011). Water-rich climate reactors may likewise keep quiet when called to support stratospheric aerosol injection, opting for a 'business-as-usual' social model of climate governance. Their silence would likely be justified by economic and development reasons, countries like Angola, Gabon and Uganda foreseeing a potential for continuing industrialization and oil extraction after solar geoengineering deployment. Besides, they lack adequate capacity for climate negotiations as well as mechanisms to protect society from climate change. However, individual country responses will likely depend on their natural resources endowments (especially oil deposits), economic opportunities and the ability of its leaders to anticipate opportunities arising from the international arena.

## CLIMATE CHANGE, SOLAR GEOENGINEERING
## AND CLIMATE JUSTICE

Based on these predictions about how each cluster of countries will fare in the solar geoengineering scenario, as compared to the base scenario, we identify four ways in which climate justice might differ significantly between the two scenarios.

Since African countries have contributed very little to climate change, much climate change–related harm suffered in Africa involves the imposition of undeserved harm (and risk) on innocent and sometimes vulnerable parties by much wealthier, more powerful parties (Preston 2012). Solar geoengineering may reduce some of these harms (to some people) while exacerbating others (to the same people or to other people). This study is not fine-grained enough to say whether these harms will involve more or less injustice, on balance, given that this kind of injustice is likely to affect different individuals in the different scenarios.

A second kind of injustice is procedural injustice. Procedural justice requires that public policies be chosen through morally acceptable procedures. This is often taken to require procedures that give all affected parties an adequate opportunity to influence the choice of policy, though what exactly this means (or whether it is always required) remains open to debate, especially in global decision-making (Svoboda et al. 2011; Morrow, Kopp, and Oppenheimer 2013). Even without settling the details of procedural justice, the risk of procedural injustice is greater in the solar geoengineering scenario than in the no-solar geoengineering scenario because some forms of geoengineering can be deployed by a small coalition of powers, even over the objections of other states, whereas effective mitigation policies require consensus, and from an African perspective, at least, whatever procedural injustice exists in the base scenario presumably persists in the solar geoengineering scenario. Thus, it is easier to implement a more procedurally unjust decision about some kinds of geoengineering than it is to implement an equally procedurally unjust decision about mitigation. Of the various clusters, only water-scarce climate proactors are likely to have much power in negotiations over geoengineering, but even that power would be limited.

Concerns about distributive justice (i.e. about the fair distribution of resources, opportunities and other goods) point to a third type of potential injustice, especially outside the water-scarce climate proactors. As the preceding subsections show, policy and civil society responses to solar geoengineering would likely alter the distribution of such goods, though whether this would be better, worse or simply different is too hard to say.

The fourth type of justice concern is often overlooked in Anglo-American philosophy, but it is important in much African moral thought. Justice, on this view, requires us to promote social harmony (Wiredu 1992). On one reconstruction of this view, social harmony involves a sense of shared identity grounded in mutual goodwill and solidarity (Metz 2007). Insofar as a country's (lack of) response to solar geoengineering would increase inequality (e.g. by prioritizing some stakeholders over others), it would undermine social harmony and therefore cause further injustice. The discussion in previous subsections suggests that this risk is especially salient in water-stressed climate prospectors and water-rich climate defenders. Solar geoengineering could also undermine global and intergenerational solidarity (Hourdequin 2012), which would count as a form of global injustice.

## CONCLUSION

Africa is likely to experience catastrophic climate impacts if the current trajectory of climate policies is maintained. A better future is predicted for some countries after solar geoengineering deployment while others would face uncertain risks, including a reduction of rainfall with depleting rainforests. Hence, the response of African countries to injecting aerosols in the stratosphere will be diverse but cutting across major clusters. For the sake of climate justice, there is a great need for caution when considering whether or how to deploy solar geoengineering.

In effect, this study has shown that under certain climatic conditions and a specific climate intervention, African policymakers often decide to prioritize one group of stakeholders, depending on its influence in the society and interest in the climate policy outcome, with significant implications for climate justice. A focus of public climate policy on the 85% of African farmers, poorer men and women and their children, lacking resources to meet their basic needs, would generate better outcomes for climate protection in Africa in the event of solar geoengineering. Without intervention by governments or civil society, these marginalized groups are left to 'save themselves'.

By focusing on those people, African governments would better promote policies and technologies that enhance farmers' resilience and reduce climate injustice. Building such systems will require adequate infrastructure and services that are environmentally sustainable, socially equitable and economically affordable. Rather than investing in harebrained technologies with unpredictable impacts on weather systems, economic development and social well-being, African leaders need to become self-determined 'climate proactors' by developing consistent climate protection mechanisms. They should refrain from investing emotional capital in unprofitable schemes that may divert resources from the task of providing equitable and secure livelihoods for those already in need.

# BIBLIOGRAPHY

AAS and SRMGI. 2013. *Governance of Research on Solar Geoengineering: African Perspectives Consolidated Report of Three Workshops in Senegal, South Africa, and Ethiopia.* Nairobi: African Academy of Science [AAS].

Adar, K. G. and N. A Check. (eds.) 2011. *Cooperative Diplomacy, Regional Stability, National Interests—The Nile River and Riparian States.* Pretoria: Africa Institute of South Africa [AIS].

Anderson, J., M. Colby, M. McGahueye, S. Mehta. 2013. 'Leverging natural and social capital for resilient development'. *Nature, Wealth and Power* 2.0. Washington: USAID.

CODESRIA and UNECA. 2015. Reflections on Policy and Practice. *Journal of African Transformation* 1 (1): 1–156.

Gardiner, S. M. 2010. 'Is 'arming the future' with geoengineering really the lesser evil: some doubts about the ethics of intentionally manipulating the climate system'. In: S. M. Gardiner, S. Caney, D. Jamieson and H. Shue (Eds.), *Climate Ethics: essential readings,* New York: Oxford University Press, 284–312.

Getachew, H. E. and A. M. Melesse. 2012. 'The impact of land use change on the hydrology of the Angereb Watershed, Ethiopia'. *International Journal of Water Sciences*, Regular Paper.

Glantz, M. (ed.). 1998. *Societal Responses to Regional Climatic Change: Forecasting by Analogy.* Boulder, CO: Westview Press.

Goh, A. H. X. 2012. 'A literature review of the gender-differentiated impacts of climate change on women's and men's assets and well-being in developing countries.' *CAPRi Working Paper* No. 106 (September 2012). Washington, D.C.: International Food Policy Research Institute. Available at: http://dx.doi.org/10.2499/CAPRiWP106.

Hamilton, C. 2013a. 'The ethical foundations of climate engineering'. In: Burns and Strauss (eds.), *Climate change geoengineering: Philosophical perspectives, legal issues and governance frameworks.* Cambridge, MA: Cambridge University Press, 39–58.

Hamilton, C. 2013b. *Earthmasters: The dawn of the age of climate engineering.* Yale: Yale University Press.

Harris, P. G. 2010. *World Ethics and Climate Change: From International to Global Justice.* Edinburgh: Edinburgh University Press.

Hayward, T. 2007. 'Human Rights Versus Emissions Rights: Climate Justice and the Equitable Distribution of Ecological Space' *Ethics & International Affairs* 21: 431–50.

Hourdequin M. 2012. 'Geoengineering, solidarity and moral risk'. In: Preston (ed.), *Differential Treatment in International Environmental Law.* Oxford, Oxford University Press, 15–32.

IMF. 2015. 'Is the glass half empty or half full? Issues in managing water challenges and policy instruments'. *IMF Staff Discussion Note* (June 2015) SDN/15/11.

IPCC. 2014. *Climate Change 2014: Mitigation of Climate Change. Working Group III Contribution to the Fifth Assessment Report of the Intergovernmental Panel on Climate Change (IPCC).* New York, NY: Cambridge University Press.

Keith, D. 2013. *A case for climate engineering*. Boston: Boston Review Books.

Kant, P, & Wu, S. (2011). 'The REDD market should not end up a subprime house of cards: introducing a new REDD architecture for environmental integrity.' *Environmental science & technology*, 45 (19), 8176–8177.

Luwesi, C. N. 2010. *Hydro-economic Inventory in Changing Environment—An assessment of the efficiency of farming water demand under fluctuating rainfall regimes in semi-arid lands of South-East Kenya*. Saarbrüken: Lambert Academic Publishing.

Luwesi, C. N., C. A. Shisanya and J. A. Obando. 2012. *Warming and Greening - The Dilemma Facing Green Water Economy under Changing Micro-Climatic Conditions in Muooni Catchment (Machakos, Kenya)*. Saarbrüken: Lambert Academic Publishing.

Maeda, E. E. 2012. 'The future of environmental sustainability in the Taita Hills, Kenya: assessing potential impacts of agricultural expansion and climate change'. *Fennia* 190: 1, 41–59.

Metz, T. 2007. 'Toward an African moral theory.' *Journal of Political Philosophy* 15: 3, 321–41.

Moore, N., H. Benmazhar, K. Brent, H. Du, V. Lese, S. Kone, C. N. Luwesi, V. Scott, J. Smith, A. Talberg, M. Thompson and Z. Zhuo. 2015. 'Climate Engineering: Early Reflections on a Complex Conversation'. *Climate Law » Brill Online*, 5 (2–4): 295–301.

Morrow, D. R., R. E. Kopp and M. Oppenheimer. 2013. 'Political Legitimacy in Decisions about Solar Radiation Management Experiments.' In: W. C. G. Burns and A. L. Strauss (Eds.), *Climate Change Geoengineering: Philosophical Perspectives, Legal Issues, and Governance Frameworks*, Cambridge, MA: Cambridge University Press, 146–67.

Nzuma, J. M., M. Waithaka, R. M. Mulwa, M. Kyotalimye and G. Nelson. 2010. 'Strategies for Adapting to Climate Change in Rural Sub-Saharan Africa'. *IFPRI Discussion Paper* 01013.

Olukoye, G. A. and H. Mukanga. 2007. 'A review of multi-lateral agreements and their implications for environmental governance in Kenya'. *Environment and Sustainable Development* 2: 101–20.

O'Neill, B. C., E. Kriegler, K. Riahi, K. L. Ebi, S. Hallegatte, T. R. Carter, R. Mathur, D. P. van Vuuren. 2014. 'A new scenario framework for climate change research: the concept of shared socioeconomic pathways'. *Climatic Change* 122 (3): 387–400.

Palazzo, A., J. Vervoort, P. Havlik, D. Mason-D'Croz and S. Islam. 2014. 'Simulating stakeholder-driven food and climate scenarios for policy development in Africa, Asia and Latin America: A multi-regional synthesis'. *CCAFS Working Paper* No. 109: 1–94.

Posner, E. and D. Weisbach. 2010. *Climate Change Justice*. Princeton: Princeton University Press.

Preston, C. J. 2012. Solar Radiation Management and Vulnerable Populations: The Moral Deficits and its Prospects. In: C. J. Preston (Ed.), *Engineering the Climate:*

*The Ethics of Solar Radiation Management*. Lanham, MD: Lexington Books, Rowman & Littlefield.

Rees, W. (2014). *Avoiding Collapse: An agenda for sustainable degrowth and relocalizing the economy*. British Columbia: Climate Justice Project, Canadian Centre for Public Policy Alternatives (CCPPA).

Ricke K.L., M.G. Morgan and M.R. Allen. 2010. 'Regional climate response to solar radiation management'. *Nature Geosciences* 3: 537–541.

Robock A. 2008. '20 Reasons Why Geoengineering May Be a Bad Idea'. *Bulletin of the Atomic Scientists* (May/June 2008), 64 (2) 14–18, 59. DOI: 10.2968/064002006.

Shisanya, C. 1990.'The 1983-1984 Drought in Kenya.' *Journal of Eastern African Research & and Development* 20: 127–48.

Shisanya, C.A., C.N. Luwesi and J.A. Obando. 2014. 'Innovative but Not Feasible: Green Water Saving Schemes at the Crossroads in Semi-Arid Lands'. In: OSSREA (eds.), *Innovative Water Resource Use and Management for Poverty Reduction in Sub-Saharan Africa: An Anthology*, Addis Ababa, 137–72.

Shue, H. 2010. 'Global environment and international inequality'. In: S. Gardiner, S. Caney, D. Jamieson and H. Shue (Eds.), *Climate Ethics: Essential Readings*, New York, Oxford University Press, 101–11.

Svoboda, T., K. Keller, M. Goes and N. Tuana. 2011. 'Sulfate Aerosol Geoengineering: The Question of Justice.' *Public Affairs Quarterly* 25: 157–79.

UNECA. 2015. 'Is global climate governance working for Africa?' United Nations Economic Commission for Africa. Accessed February 4, 2016. http://www.uneca.org/cop21/pages/global-climate-change-governance-working-africa.

UNEP. 2003. *Africa Environment Outlook (AEO)*. Nairobi: UNEP-DEWA. Available at: http://www.unep.org/dewa/africa/publications/aeo-1/006.htm.

Taylor, P. E. 1997. 'From Environmental to Ecological Human Rights: A New Dynamic in International Law?' *Geo. Int'l Envtl. L. Rev.* 10: 309–98.

Tiffen, M. and M. Mortimore. 2002. 'Agroecosystems regaining the high ground: Reviving the Hillsides of Machakos.' *World Resources 2000-2001*: 149–58.

Wiredu, K. 1992. 'The moral foundations of an African culture.' In K. Wiredu & K. Gyekye (Eds.), *Person and Community: Ghanaian Philosophical Studies* (Washington, DC: Council for Research in Values and Philosophy).

YCEI. *2013 Scenario Planning for Solar Radiation Management. Workshop Report and Scenarios, August 2013*. Ontario: Centre for International Governance Innovation (CIGI).

Zougmore, R., A. S. Traore and Y. Mbodj. 2015. 'Paysage scientifique, politique et financier de l'agriculture intelligente face au climat en Afrique de l'ouest'. *CCAFS Working Paper* No. 118: 1–91.

*Chapter 12*

# Geoengineering and Climate Change Mitigation

*Trade-offs and Synergies as Foreseen by Integrated Assessment Models*

Johannes Emmerling and Massimo Tavoni

## MODELLING CLIMATE STABILIZATION AND GEOENGINEERING

Achieving climate stabilization is the ultimate goal of climate change policies. However, even if countries were to agree on a given long-term temperature goal—such as 2°C by the end of the century—the question remains on how a far distant objective can be translated into actionable short-term climate change strategies. The research community has responded to this policy request by developing and using models which integrate the economy, energy, land-use and climate components into a unified framework: such 'integrated assessment models' (IAMs) have been used extensively to provide ex ante assessment of national and international climate policies. For example, the latest report of the IPCC working group III (Edenhofer et al. 2014) has relied on more than 1000 scenarios generated by IAMs to evaluate the best strategies required to countervail human-made climate change. Similarly, IAMs have been used to estimate the social cost of carbon to allow for instance the U.S. agencies to incorporate the social benefits of reducing $CO_2$ emissions into cost–benefit analyses of regulatory action (Interagency Working Group on Social Cost of Carbon, U.S. Government 2013).

Geoengineering strategies—carbon dioxide removal (CDR) and solar radiation management (SRM)—have been incorporated into IAMs, though in much different degrees (Clarke and others 2014). CDR is routinely considered in IAMs, given its capacity to compensate emissions and achieve net negative emission balances needed to attain stringent climate objectives. Given its larger potential, IAMs consider mostly CDR of biological nature, such as afforestation as well as biomass energy with carbon capture and storage (BECCS) (Tavoni and Socolow 2013). Other CDR strategies, such as direct air capture, have received less attention, given the larger uncertainties about economic and technical feasibility.

The representation of SRM in IAMs is at an earlier stage and has so far been mostly implemented using a simplified framework such as the DICE model developed by William Nordhaus (Goes, Tuana, and Keller 2011), though some exceptions exist (Emmerling and Tavoni 2013). The uncertainties surrounding the costs and benefits of SRM are extremely large and thus difficult to model properly. Notably the large list of possible side effects of SRM and the uncertainties about its potential to counteract climate change in terms of regional temperatures and precipitation patterns at the current state of knowledge render the task to integrate this technology into integrated models very difficult. As a result, the modelling community has so far kept some distance from the possibility of examining the trade-offs between mitigation, adaptation and SRM: a more comprehensive assessment based on robust modelling effort is likely to materialize in the future, but only insofar as these key uncertainties will be resolved.

IAMs generate courses of action which are consistent with a given objective, such as attaining a certain level of climate protection or balancing the costs and benefits of acting on climate. As such, they allow answering questions which are relevant for climate justice. In particular, IAMs can inform about the distribution of climate change mitigation effort in both time and space, and assess policy instruments which could alleviate possible distributional tensions. For example, the issue of burden sharing of global emission goals can be assessed by models under different assumptions about equity principles. Similarly, these models can be used to provide quantitative evaluations of the stability of international climate agreements, accounting for the strategic incentives which countries face when deciding whether to join a climate treaty. This decision will depend on the benefits of joining the treaty, which will depend on how many other parties have decided to join: the solution of this game will be given by each country's best response to the others and can be modelled by IAMs by means of iterative algorithms.

In the remainder of this chapter, we focus on both the strategic and distributional issues, by exploring the results of models with respect to distributional effort and free-riding incentives when accounting for the two leading geoengineering strategies, namely CDR and SRM respectively.


## CARBON DIOXIDE REMOVAL AND THE DISTRIBUTION OF EFFORT TO ACHIEVE CLIMATE STABILIZATION

The recognition of the gravity of climate change has led the science and policy community to examine precautionary climate targets, such as that of keeping average surface temperature increase below 2°C (or even nearer 1.5°C). The fourth assessment of the IPCC contained only a handful of scenarios which were consistent with the 2°C target and which were generated by a restricted subset of models (M. Tavoni and Tol 2010). In order to address the policy question of whether 2°C can be achieved, and in which way, many new studies have focused in recent years on low-temperature targets, often including a variety of different models to ensure scientific robustness. This large set of scenarios, which constitutes a significant fraction of those reviewed in the IPCC and whose results are publicly available, have clearly identified CDR as a precondition for achieving 2°C or similar targets (Clarke et al. 2014).

With growing emissions and fossil fuel–based infrastructure on the rise, CDR provides a unique opportunity to expand the admissible carbon budget while limiting global warming to 2°C. Indeed, when it is assumed to become available in the future, IAMs rely on CDR in very large quantities, leading to up to a doubling of the available carbon budget by removing half of the emitted $CO_2$ from the atmosphere in the second half of the century (Massimo Tavoni and Socolow 2013). When CDR is not available, the economic and technical feasibility of attaining low-temperature targets is considerably reduced and the economic costs are significantly increased. Given its key role in projected climate mitigation scenarios, CDR will also have important repercussions for equity and justice between countries and generations.

As a first illustration of the distributional implications of CDR, it is instructive to look at Figure 12.1, which depicts the temporal profile of global emissions under different assumptions about CDR availability. By absorbing $CO_2$ from the atmosphere, CDR allows achieving large negative emissions later in the century. In turn, this allows for more headroom in emissions for the next 50 years. The extent of the temporal rebalancing of emissions depends crucially on the time preferences assumed in the IAMs (Rogelj et al. 2013). The role of discounting has indeed been shown to play a significant role in the cost–benefit assessment of climate change (Beckerman and Hepburn 2007; Nordhaus 2007; Stern and others 2006), but has traditionally been disregarded in cost effectiveness studies, which constitute the bulk of the literature reviewed by the IPCC. This is because cost-effective analyses are equivalent to assuming a damage parameter which tends to infinite when one surpasses the policy goal, making discounting less important. However, this ethical parameter has a significant impact on the prospects of CDR. For example, Chen and Tavoni (2013) find that setting the time preference parameter to zero as opposed to 3%, that is, giving a much higher weight to future generations, decreases the amount of CDR necessary by more than 30%. That is to say, when discounting is very low, CDR loses attractiveness given that it tends to benefit future generations at the expense of current ones.

Additional implications can be drawn, notably with respect to intergenerational justice. CDR shifts the burden of mitigating climate change from current

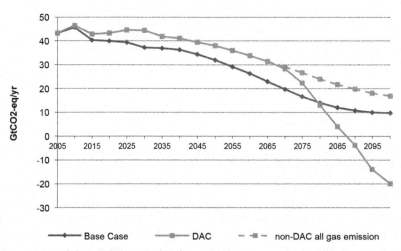

**Figure 12.1 Global emission profile for a 490 ppm-eq concentration target as produced by the WITCH IAM, with and without direct air capture (DAC).** The dashed line shows a scenario of DAC failure by year 2070. Reproduced from Chen and Tavoni (2013). *Source:* Chen, Chen, and Massimo Tavoni. 2013. "Direct Air Capture of CO2 and Climate Stabilization: A Model-Based Assessment." Climatic Change 118 (1): 59–72. doi:10.1007/s10584-013-0714-7.

to future generations. The extent of the shift depends on how a social planner discounts the future, but also on the rate of economic growth and about preferences for substituting consumption at different levels of income. Given that the marginal utility of one unit of consumption is typically declining with the level of income—as commonly assumed by IAMs—it makes sense to shift the effort forward in time if future generations will be richer. This assumption is commonly made in IAMs, which assume the rate of economic growth will outpace population growth, even when accounting for the impacts of climate change. And indeed this is what an optimization in an IAM such as the one reproduced in Figure 12.1 predicts. However, there are also counterbalancing arguments, not all of which are included in IAM simulations. For example, future generations have no say in this decision; they will inherit a much warmer planet, and by overshooting emissions in the next decades, more damage will occur before climate stabilization is attained. Moreover, future generations might have to bear the possibly high costs of CDR compared to cheaper abatement options that are available already today. Seen from this perspective, CDR appears to exacerbate intertemporal injustice.

Furthermore, one has to keep in mind that CDR is a technology which is currently not proven at the scale foreseen by models. Assumptions about technical progress drive the large deployment of CDR in the models. But technology failure cannot be excluded a priori: if we were to find that CDR cannot be deployed as we imagined and hoped it would, we would be left with more emissions and an even hotter planet, as portrayed in Figure 12.1 (dashed line). This optimism about technological progress creates a moral hazard: current generations delegate not only the burden of mitigation but also the risk of CDR failure, to the future ones. The outcome of the recent Paris accord has emphasized stringent temperature objectives such as $1.5°C$, while keeping the current level of ambition relatively modest. Achieving the long temperature objective will thus require CDR to work at enormous scale.

CDR would also have repercussions on interregional well-being. First, the higher initial $CO_2$ headroom might interplay with the way the near-term mitigation burden is shared across countries. Allocation schemes often take the current distribution of emissions across countries at face value and assume convergence to some equitable criteria (such as equal per-capita emissions) at some point in the future (See Baatz and Ott, this volume). The higher current per-capita emission rates of industrialized economies matched with more global headroom might in this case favour the better-off countries in potentially unjust ways, by endowing them with higher initial emission permit allocations. Although this can be in principle resolved by adjusting the principle of emissions rights, it would require substantial financial transfers within a potential global carbon market, which makes this option politically more difficult to achieve and therefore impractical. Very little analysis has been devoted to the assessment of CDR in the context of burden sharing, so it is difficult to tell ex ante what would be the implications. More research in this field is warranted.

Moreover, the potential of CDR is not evenly spread geographically. Especially with regard to biological CDR strategies such as afforestation and biomass energy with CCS (carbon capture and storage), the potential depends on the availability of biomass, as well as—for those options which require CCS— the availability of $CO_2$ storage reservoirs. Other CDR options, such as DAC, require substantial amounts of energy to be operated. The models indeed project that a large fraction of the biological CDR would be carried out in areas rich in biomass, creating an economic opportunity for countries closer to the tropics (Clarke et al. 2014). At the same time, a large upscale of bioenergy crops will increase pressure on land and have an impact on the prices of food staples.

The extent of this impact will depend on whether agricultural intensification will compensate for the extra demand for land due to bioenergy crops (Hertel 2011). Overall, model results indicate that technical progress will not fully compensate the additional land demand and will thus have a significant and positive effect on crop prices (Popp et al. 2014), and the economic implications will vary by region depending on whether they export food or not. Moreover, the impact on food prices might also have nonmarginal impacts on the lower income classes and on poverty (Hertel, Burke, and Lobell 2010), adding to justice concerns (see Kortetmäki and Oksanen, this volume).

In addition, expansion of arable land will put additional pressure on the eco-systems and require an increased use of fertilizers (Smith and Torn 2013).

Globally, however, CDR has the potential to lower the economic costs of achieving stringent climate targets in a significant way. The reduced mitigation costs together with potentially lower impacts due to a feasible more stringent stabilization policy will lead to a positive effect in terms of macro-economic growth. Achieving stringent climate targets such as 2°C without CDR, on the other hand, will increase economic costs several fold (Kriegler et al. 2013), or even make the climate target unattainable. Another distributional impact from CDR can be expected from initially lower energy prices when CDR is available, given the lessened mitigation effort. Given the regressivity of energy expenditures, with lower income classes spending a larger share of their income on energy than higher income ones, limiting the increase in energy prices will have positive distributional repercussions. Lower costs will increase the political feasibility of climate stabilization policies and—everything else being equal—will lead to less global warming. Given that hotter—and thus generally poorer—countries will be affected adversely by climate change (Burke, Hsiang, and Miguel 2015), this will favour developing countries. Overall, CDR brings about substantial distributional implications from different sectors, but in any case the effect must be regarded as important.

## SOLAR RADIATION MANAGEMENT AND INTERNATIONAL CLIMATE POLICY

As noted above, model-based assessments of SRM in the context of climate strategies have so far mostly relied on relatively simple IAMs. This is mainly due to the large uncertainties surrounding the costs and benefits of SRM vis-à-vis traditional strategies such as mitigation or adaptation. The economic assessment of SRM has yielded mixed and often opposing results, which is unsurprising given the difficulty of properly calibrating SRM. The economics of SRM appears to be particularly advantageous (Barrett 2008), notably also due to the low costs of implementation (Crutzen 2006). When coupled with the hypothesis—supported by climate model simulations (Caldeira, Bala, and Cao 2013; Kravitz et al. 2013; Ricke et al. 2012)—that SRM is very effective at compensating temperature increases and that it can do it fast, model-based assessments of SRM would indicate that SRM is a strong substitute to mitigation, especially if climate change is expected to be particularly harmful (Bickel and Lane 2009). However, SRM's side effects might be significant, so that it might actually be uneconomical to give up emission reductions now, only to find that SRM cannot be deployed at scale in the future (Gramstad and Tjøtta 2010; Goes, Tuana, and Keller 2011). This moral hazard argument echoes the one for CDR discussed in the previous section.

This is a problem of decision-making under uncertainty rather than risk, since it is difficult to even estimate probabilities of the costs and benefits of SRM. When accounting for uncertainty, the assessment becomes more complicated. Results from economic and modelling evaluations indicate that SRM and mitigation would still be substitutes for each other, but that the reduction in mitigation would be less marked than otherwise (Emmerling and Tavoni 2013; Heutel, Moreno-Cruz, and Shayegh 2015; Moreno-Cruz and Keith 2012).

Most of the analysis carried out so far on the economics of SRM has focused on the global implications for climate and abatement. Fewer articles have focused on the strategic implications which SRM would have on international climate policy. Yet, the biggest challenge which climate change confronts us with is that of cooperation and free-riding. The slow progress in reducing emissions is motivated by the nature of $CO_2$ emissions as an externality. Indeed, the post-2020 climate policy debate centring around the INDCs is showing us once more that the biggest obstacle is that of reaching a sustainable self-enforcing and comprehensive agreement to curb $CO_2$. By its nature, SRM has the potential to change the complicated nature of climate change negotiations, as already recognized 20 years ago (Schelling 1996). Due to the large regional heterogeneity in many dimensions, including regional economic and technological conditions, the strategic implications of SRM will depend on the regional distribution of costs and benefits. Although these are not well understood, one can expect a significant degree of regional response variation to SRM, with different countries facing different and possibly opposite incentives to invest in SRM. This creates incentives to form specific coalitions and generates an exclusivity in the governance of SRM (Ricke, Moreno-Cruz, and Caldeira 2013). Indeed, SRM can lead to an opposite result to the normal free-riding incentives of public good games such as climate change: under what has been dubbed 'free driving' (Weitzman 2012), the low costs of SRM create incentives towards unilateral geoengineering and to a problem of overprovision rather than under-provision. That is to say, the global outcome would be that of having too much SRM. The actual impact on coalition formation will depend on how the costs and benefits of SRM are distributed (Moreno-Cruz 2010). It is therefore interesting to compare the results with a case where regions act unilaterally, which can give rise to a sort of 'Tuvalu Syndrome' (Millard-Ball 2012), in which the most vulnerable countries decide to independently implement geoengineering.

Figure 12.2 reports the results of an assessment of SRM using an IAM with a game theoretic structure. The WITCH IAM (witchmodel.org) can generate optimal climate strategies under different levels of regional cooperation, ranging from situations of complete non-cooperation among countries, to the case in which all world countries work together in the best interest of the world as a whole. We present results from scenarios generated by WITCH including an SRM module. We purposely take an optimistic view of SRM, assuming a low cost of implementation and limited damages. Our interest is to assess numerically the incentives to deploy SRM, comparing a situation of full cooperation to one in which each region acts in its own interest (non-cooperative). The wedge between these two worlds reflects the 'free-driving' risk of climate engineering.

Figure 12.2 shows the optimal choice of SRM implemented by different countries and world regions comparing a cooperative and non-cooperative framework (average yearly deployment between 2050 and 2100). Given the optimistic assumptions made about SRM, the model results show that SRM would be implemented as soon as it becomes available (here assumed to be in 2050), leading to a gradual counterbalancing of the effect of global warming. However, a major difference is observed between the cooperative and non-cooperative cases, with four times more SRM deployment observed in the latter, suggesting that the 'free-driving' nature of SRM would indeed lead to an overuse.

The reason for this dismal result is that SRM, similarly to climate change, creates an additional environmental externality: SRM imposes damage and side effects also to those countries that did not implement it. This externality is taken into account in the cooperative case, which would consist of a more balanced climate strategy which would foresee a significant role of emissions reductions. On the contrary, if countries were to implement SRM unilaterally in their own interest, the resulting SRM level would by far exceed the optimal level, leading to a colder planet but more damaged planet raising numerous concerns of distributional justice.

The regional distribution of SRM effort will also be affected by the degree of cooperation among regions. In the case of full cooperation, SRM tends to be implemented in a more equal fashion among regions (see Figure 12.2, right panel). Overall, the main regions implementing SRM turn out to be the big and rich economies, mainly OECD countries, despite the fact that in relative terms the countries most affected by climate change will be the poorer developing economies. However, the size of the economies of OECD and large emerging economies creates the economic incentive to invest in SRM. Moreover, developing countries can free-ride on their effort.

The overall results of this analysis suggest that the threat of SRM is significant and could potentially lead to an outcome which is worse than the solution it is meant to cure. This underlines the importance of procedural justice and the global governance of a potential geoengineering scheme as discussed

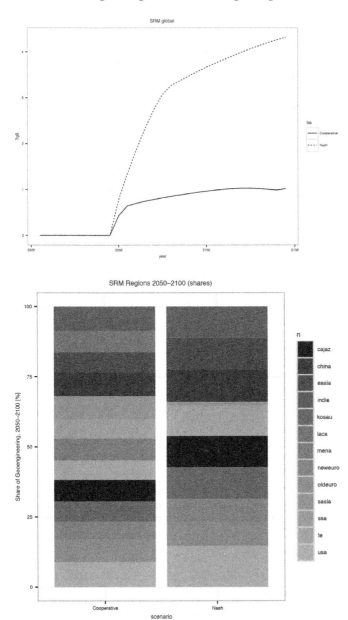

**Figure 12.2     SRM deployment in the WITCH IAM in a cooperative and noncooperative (Nash) framework.** Top: Global deployment in time. Bottom: Regional SRM post 2050. *Note*: Regional acronyms: CAJAZ: Canada, Japan and New Zealand. EASIA: South East Asia. KOS Korea South Africa and Australia. LACA: Latin and Central America. MENA: Middle East and North Africa. NEWEURO: East Europe. SASIA: South Asia (excluding India). SSA: Sub-Saharan Africa. TE: Former Soviet Union.

in Victor et al. (2009) and Virgoe (2008) and, moreover, how geoengineering should be viewed in the general climate policy mix (Bahn et al. 2015). In this respect, geoengineering should be discussed and managed by the same international institutions which deal with mitigation and adaptation, such as the UNFCC, in order to ensure a coherent picture.

## POLICY IMPLICATIONS OF MODEL-BASED ASSESSMENTS OF CLIMATE ENGINEERING

The general picture emerging from model-based assessments of CDR and SRM strategies shows some common points and some differences. Both CDR and SRM have the capacity to significantly reduce the costs of achieving low climate targets, thus representing an additional option for increasing efficiency. Both strategies raise a series of concerns, which have important consequences for equity and justice, but which are fundamentally different for CDR and SRM.

In the case of CDR, the benefits of reduced economic costs must be compared with the temporal and geographical repartition of effort. CDR would shift the mitigation burden forward in time and change its distribution among regions. CDR also brings about risks, in terms of possible technology failure, impact on food markets and so on. Although these are important concerns which need to be properly taken into account when assessing the CDR strategy, the risks can be mitigated by setting appropriate measurement and by the right policies.

On the other hand, SRM embodies a series of risks which are not easily mitigated. By altering the strategic dimension of the climate change game, SRM could lead to a cure which is worse than the disease. As we have shown in this analysis, a decentralized solution without cooperation could lead to excessive use of SRM, resulting in a worse outcome. In this sense, SRM presents a set of challenges for both equity and efficiency, which are much larger than CDR. SRM brings about potential benefits which could indeed make it a viable strategy for dealing for climate change, but more assessment is needed, especially incorporating strategic and governance elements.

## BIBLIOGRAPHY

Bahn, Olivier, Marc Chesney, Jonathan Gheyssens, Reto Knutti, and Anca Claudia Pana. 2015. 'Is There Room for Geoengineering in the Optimal Climate

Policy Mix?' *Environmental Science & Policy* 48 (April): 67–76. doi:10.1016/j. envsci.2014.12.014.

Barrett, Scott. 2008. 'The Incredible Economics of Geoengineering.' *Environmental and Resource Economics* 39 (1): 45–54. doi:10.1007/s10640-007-9174-8.

Beckerman, Wilfred, and Cameron Hepburn. 2007. 'Ethics of the Discount Rate in the Stern Review on the Economics of Climate Change.' *World Economics* 8 (1): 187–210.

Bickel, J. Eric, and Lee Lane. 2009. 'An Analysis of Climate Engineering as a Response to Climate Change.' *Smart Climate Solutions*. http://faculty.engr.utexas. edu/bickel/Papers/AP_Climate%20Engineering_Bickel_Lane_v%205%200.pdf.

Burke, Marshall, Solomon M. Hsiang, and Edward Miguel. 2015. 'Global Non-Linear Effect of Temperature on Economic Production.' *Nature* 527 (7577): 235–39. doi:10.1038/nature15725.

Caldeira, Ken, Govindasamy Bala, and Long Cao. 2013. 'The Science of Geo-engineering.' *Annual Review of Earth and Planetary Sciences* 41 (1): 231–56. doi:10.1146/annurev-earth-042711-105548.

Chen, Chen, and Massimo Tavoni. 2013. 'Direct Air Capture of $CO_2$ and Climate Stabilization: A Model Based Assessment.' *Climatic Change* 118 (1): 59–72. doi:10.1007/s10584-013-0714-7.

Clarke, L., and others. 2014. *Assessing Transformation Pathways. Climate Change 2014: Mitigation of Climate Change. Contribution of Working Group III to the Fifth Assessment Report of the Intergovernmental Panel on Climate Change.* Cambridge, UK: Cambridge University Press.

Crutzen, Paul. 2006. 'Albedo Enhancement by Stratospheric Sulfur Injections: A Contribution to Resolve a Policy Dilemma?' *Climatic Change* 77 (3–4): 211–20. doi:10.1007/s10584-006-9101-y.

Edenhofer, Ottmar, Ramón Pichs-Madruga, Youba Sokona, E. Farahani, S. Kadner, K. Seyboth, A. Adler, et al. 2014. 'Climate Change 2014: Mitigation of Climate Change.' *Working Group III Contribution to the Fifth Assessment Report of the Intergovernmental Panel on Climate Change.* UK and New York. http://report. mitigation2014.org/spm/ipcc_wg3_ar5_summary-for-policymakers_may-version. pdf.

Emmerling, Johannes, and Massimo Tavoni. 2013. 'Geoengineering and Abate-ment: A 'Flat' Relationship Under Uncertainty.' SSRN Scholarly Paper ID 2251733. Rochester, NY: Social Science Research Network. http://papers.ssrn. com/abstract=2251733.

Goes, Marlos, Nancy Tuana, and Klaus Keller. 2011. 'The Economics (or Lack Thereof) of Aerosol Geoengineering.' *Climatic Change* 109 (3–4): 719–44. doi:10.1007/s10584-010-9961-z.

Gramstad, Kjetil, and Sigve Tjøtta. 2010. 'Geoengineering - a Part of Climate Change Policies.' http://www.uib.no/filearchive/filetopic_geopaper_2901_2010_4.pdf.

Hertel, T. W. 2011. 'The Global Supply and Demand for Agricultural Land in 2050: A Perfect Storm in the Making?' *American Journal of Agricultural Economics* 93 (2): 259–75.

Hertel, T. W., M. B. Burke, and D. B. Lobell. 2010. 'The Poverty Implications of Climate-Induced Crop Yield Changes by 2030.' *Global Environmental Change* 20 (4): 577–85.

Heutel, Garth, Juan Moreno-Cruz, and Soheil Shayegh. 2015. 'Solar Geoengineering, Uncertainty, and the Price of Carbon.' Working Paper 21355. National Bureau of Economic Research. http://www.nber.org/papers/w21355.

Interagency Working Group on Social Cost of Carbon, United States Government. 2013. 'Technical Support Document: - Technical Update of the Social Cost of Carbon for Regulatory Impact Analysis - Under Executive Order 12866.' May. http://www.whitehouse.gov/sites/default/files/omb/inforeg/social_cost_of_carbon_for_ria_2013_update.pdf.

Kravitz, Ben, Ken Caldeira, Olivier Boucher, Alan Robock, Philip J. Rasch, Kari Alterskjær, Diana Bou Karam, Jason N. S. Cole, Charles L. Curry, and James M. Haywood. 2013. 'Climate Model Response from the Geoengineering Model Intercomparison Project (geomip).' *Journal of Geophysical Research: Atmospheres* 118 (15): 8320–32.

Kriegler, Elmar, Ottmar Edenhofer, Lena Reuster, Gunnar Luderer, and David Klein. 2013. 'Is Atmospheric Carbon Dioxide Removal a Game Changer for Climate Change Mitigation?' *Climatic Change* 118 (1): 45–57. doi:10.1007/s10584-012-0681-4.

Millard-Ball, Adam. 2012. 'The Tuvalu Syndrome.' *Climatic Change* 110 (3): 1047–66. doi:10.1007/s10584-011-0102-0.

Moreno-Cruz, Juan B. 2010. 'Mitigation and the Geoengineering Threat.' http://works.bepress.com/morenocruz/3.

Moreno-Cruz, Juan B., and David W. Keith. 2012. 'Climate Policy under Uncertainty: A Case for Solar Geoengineering.' *Climatic Change*. doi: 10.1007/s10584-012-0487-4.

Nordhaus, William. 2007. 'Critical Assumptions in the Stern Review on Climate Change.' *Science* 317 (5835): 201–2. doi:10.1126/science.1137316.

Popp, Alexander, Steven K. Rose, Katherine Calvin, Detlef P. Vuuren, Jan Phillip Dietrich, Marshall Wise, Elke Stehfest, et al. 2014. 'Land-Use Transition for Bioenergy and Climate Stabilization: Model Comparison of Drivers, Impacts and Interactions with Other Land Use Based Mitigation Options.' *Climatic Change* 123 (3–4): 495–509. doi: 10.1007/s10584-013-0926-x.

Ricke, Katharine L, Juan B. Moreno-Cruz, and Ken Caldeira. 2013. 'Strategic Incentives for Climate Geoengineering Coalitions to Exclude Broad Participation.' *Environmental Research Letters* 8 (1): 014021. doi: 10.1088/1748-9326/8/1/014021.

Ricke, Katharine L., Daniel J. Rowlands, William J. Ingram, David W. Keith, and M. Granger Morgan. 2012. 'Effectiveness of Stratospheric Solar-Radiation Management as a Function of Climate Sensitivity.' *Nature Climate Change* 2 (2): 92–96. doi: 10.1038/nclimate1328.

Rogelj, Joeri, David L. McCollum, Andy Reisinger, Malte Meinshausen, and Keywan Riahi. 2013. 'Probabilistic Cost Estimates for Climate Change Mitigation.' *Nature* 493 (7430): 79–83. doi:10.1038/nature11787.

Schelling, Thomas C. 1996. 'The Economic Diplomacy of Geoengineering.' *Climatic Change* 33 (July): 303–7. doi:10.1007/BF00142578.

Smith, Lydia J., and Margaret S. Torn. 2013. 'Ecological Limits to Terrestrial Biological Carbon Dioxide Removal.' *Climatic Change* 118 (1): 89–103. doi:10.1007/s10584-012-0682-3.

Stern, Nicholas, and others. 2006. *Stern Review: The Economics of Climate Change.* London: HM Treasury. http://www.hm-treasury.gov.uk/independent_reviews/stern_review_economics_climate_change/sternreview_index.cfm.

Tavoni, Massimo, and Robert Socolow. 2013. 'Modeling Meets Science and Technology: An Introduction to a Special Issue on Negative Emissions.' *Climatic Change* 118 (1): 1–14. doi:10.1007/s10584-013-0757-9.

Tavoni, M., and R. S. J. Tol. 2010. 'Counting Only the Hits? The Risk of Underestimating the Costs of Stringent Climate Policy.' *Climatic Change* 100 (3): 769–78.

Victor, David G., M. Granger Morgan, Jay Apt, John Steinbruner, and Katharine Ricke. 2009. 'The Geoengineering Option: A Last Resort against Global Warming?' *Foreign Affairs* 64–76.

Virgoe, John. 2008. 'International Governance of a Possible Geoengineering Intervention to Combat Climate Change.' *Climatic Change* 95 (1–2): 103–19. doi:10.1007/s10584-008-9523-9.

Weitzman, Martin. 2012. 'A Voting Architecture for the Governance of Free-Driver Externalities, with Application to Geoengineering.' Working Paper 18622. National Bureau of Economic Research. http://www.nber.org/papers/w18622.

*Chapter 13*

# Distributional Implications of Geoengineering

## Richard S. J. Tol

Through geoengineering, a single country can impose its preferred climate on the rest of the world. Different countries have different climate preferences and thus a different demand for geoengineering. The impacts of climate change, geoengineered or not, are very diverse. In this chapter, I do two things. First, I quantify the implications of geoengineering for all countries in the world. I then derive the optimal level of geoengineering and find progressive transfers to support that policy.

There is a substantial literature on the various technical options for geoengineering (Angel 2006, Hoffert et al. 2002, Keith 2000, Rasch et al. 2008, Vaughan and Lenton 2011, Wigley 2006) and its impacts on the climate (Bala, Duffy, and Taylor 2008, Govindasamy and Caldeira 2000, Heckendorn et al. 2009, Lenton and Vaughan 2009, Matthews and Caldeira 2007, Ricke, Morgan, and Allen 2010, Robock, Oman, and Stenchikov 2008). There are papers on the effects of geoengineering on optimal greenhouse gas emission reduction (Goes, Tuana, and Keller 2011, Irvine, Sriver, and Keller 2012, Moreno-Cruz 2015) and on the governance of geoengineering (Barrett 2008, 2009, 2014; Schelling 1996; Urpelainen 201; Victor 2008; Weitzman 2015). These papers do not, however, have a detailed representation of distribution of the impact of climate change, and may thus misjudge the various stakes. There is also a literature on the ethics and desirability of geoengineering (Crutzen 2006, Gardiner 2011, Hartzell-Nichols 2012, Heyward 2014, Horton 2014, Hulme 2015, Jamieson 1996, Liao, Sandberg, and Roache 2012, Preston 2011; Svoboda 2012, 2015, 2016, Svoboda and Irvine 2014, Tuana et al. 2012, Wong 2014), but again these papers are largely void of empirical content and may thus get the actual trade-offs wrong.

This chapter proceeds as follows. In the next section, I discuss the data and set up a simple model. In the following section, I discuss the distributional implications of climate change and geoengineering, and suggest a geoengineering policy that is both efficient and equitable. The final section concludes.


## DATA AND MODEL

Tol (2015) reviewed the literature on the total welfare impacts of climate change and conducted a meta-analysis. Twenty-seven estimates of the total welfare impact of climate change were taken from 22 studies. Various impact functions were fitted to the data. A piecewise linear function is, by far, the best fit to the global estimates. This function defines an optimal temperature, the climate at which average welfare is maximized. Welfare falls linearly if the temperature is above or below the optimum.

Ten estimates report regional detail, for six regions or more, and three have results for individual countries. The remaining 14 show only a global total. A weighted regression of the regional estimates on the natural logarithm of per capita income and annual mean temperature, both regionally averaged, suggests that the welfare loss due to a 2.5°C warming is 1.2% of income less, with a standard deviation of 0.6%, for a country that is twice as rich and 0.4% less, with a standard deviation of 0.1%, for a country that is 1°C colder.

The function estimated using the regional results is used to impute national impact estimates. The national imputations are made to add up to the estimated regional and global totals by shifting the imputed values, that is by changing the constant in the linear equation but not its slopes.

Having thus obtained 27 estimates of the national welfare impact of climate change, a piecewise linear impact function is fitted for each country. The global estimates suggest an optimum temperature of 1.0°C above the pre-industrial temperature, or 0.2°C warmer than the average of the last few decades. The national optima are on average 0.3°C—half a degree colder than today—with a standard deviation of 1.3°C. This is if we assume that every country weights equally. If instead we weight every country by its 2005 population, the optimum temperature is on average 0.4°C above pre-industrial with a standard deviation of 1.2°C. If we weight countries by their 2005 GDP (gross domestic product), the average optimum is 1.7°C with a standard deviation of 1.5°C. The different results highlight that the world economy is concentrated in the temperate zone while the world population is concentrated in the tropics and subtropics. The large standard deviations highlight the diversity in the effects of climate change across the world.

The cold slope of the *global* impacts is −0.7% GDP per degree Celsius (%GDP/°C). That is there is a welfare loss equivalent to a 0.7% income loss for every degree Celsius of cooling. This is −7.1(5.4)%GDP/°C averaged over the countries (the number in parentheses is the standard deviation across countries); it is −6.1(5.2)%GDP/°C with population weights and −2.2(3.3)%GDP/°C with GDP weights. The warm slope is −1.4%GDP/°C for the global results: Welfare falls by −1.4%GDP for every degree warming. For the country results, the warm slope is −3.3(1.4)%GDP/°C. With population weights, this is −3.3(1.8)%GDP/°C and with GDP weights this becomes −1.7(1.8)%GDP/°C. The different averages of the slopes deviate from each other for the same reason as the different estimates of the optimum differ.

## RESULTS

Figure 13.1 shows the distribution of the impact of climate change. The top panel shows the Lorenz curves (Lorenz 1905) for the welfare impact if the world would cool by 1, 2 or 3°C. The graph reveals that a 1°C cooling would lead to a welfare loss equivalent to an income loss of 5% or larger for 50% of the world population (in 2005), but a welfare gain for 7% of the people. Greater cooling does not shift the population numbers, but it does increase polarization.

The bottom panel of Figure 13.1 shows the Lorenz curves for the welfare impacts if the world would warm by 1 to 8°C. 92% of the world population would be worse off if the world would warm only by 1°C. This goes up to 99% for 6°C. For a global warming of 1°C, nobody is worse off than the equivalent of a 10% drop in income. At 2°C, 5% of the world population are, and at 3°C, 49% of the world population suffer such a loss. Figure 13.1 thus confirms that climate change would have very different impacts on different people and that even modest climate change would be a serious concern for some.

Figure 13.2 plots the estimated temperature optimum for each country against its current temperature. Colder countries would welcome warming and warmer countries would welcome cooling. Note that the slope of the curve is only −0.1—that is all else being equal, a country with a 1°C higher current temperature would prefer a temperature that is 0.1°C lower.

Figure 13.3 shows the aggregate impact of climate change as a function of climate change. The impact is maximized at a temperature that is slightly below today's, but 0.5°C warmer than the pre-industrial average. Temperatures below pre-industrial times and above 1.1°C above pre-industrial would lead to a net loss of welfare. A warming of 2.0°C—the international policy target—would lead to a welfare loss equivalent to losing 0.8% of income.

The optimum in Figure 13.3 is not a Pareto optimum. It is a Kaldor–Hicks optimum (Kaldor 1939, Hicks 1939): It maximizes total welfare, but some people are clearly made worse off and compensation would be needed for those who lose out. I suggest compensating income transfers below.

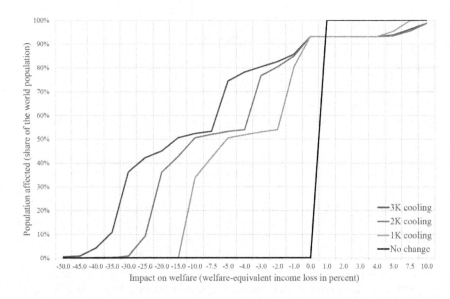

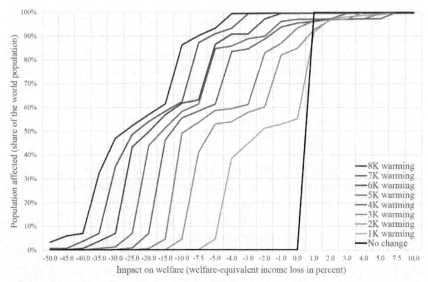

**Figure 13.1** Lorenz curves of the impact for global cooling (top panel) and global warming (bottom panel).

Following Weitzman (2015), Figure 13.3 also shows the fraction of the world population who would prefer to keep the global mean surface air temperature below a certain level, as such climate change would optimize their impacts. Ten per cent of the people would prefer a temperature of 0.1°C or

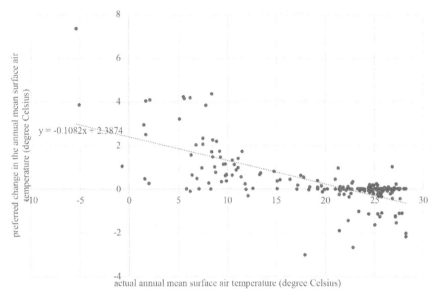

**Figure 13.2   Preferred climate change as a function of the current temperature.**

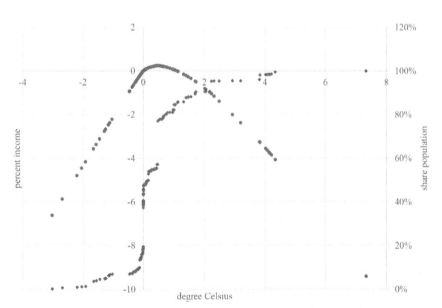

**Figure 13.3   The global total impact of climate change as a function of the change in the global mean surface air temperature relative to pre-industrial times (dots; left axis) and the share of the world population who would prefer this temperature or cooler (diamonds; right axis).**

more below pre-industrial times, 50% would prefer 0.2°C or less above pre-industrial, and 90% 1.7°C or less above pre-industrial.

As geoengineering is so cheap, countries would prefer to geoengineer the climate to match the optima shown in Figure 13.2. There is obvious disagreement on the desired amount of geoengineering. Comparing Figure 13.2 to Figure 13.1 reveals that different degrees of geoengineering would have different effects on different countries.

While geoengineering may be cheap, geoengineering too much entails a cost, namely the welfare loss from a nonoptimal climate (see also Emmerling and Tavoni, this volume). I compute that cost using the Baker–Thompson rule (Fragnelli and Marina 2010, Littlechild and Thompson 1977), an operationalization of the Shapley value (Shapley 1953). That is as geoengineering lowers the temperature from the optimum for Canada, the highest, to the optimum for the United Kingdom, the second highest, only the costs to Canada count. As the temperature is then lowered to the optimum for Switzerland, the third highest, the costs to the Canada and the UK count and are measured relative to their respective optima. The same procedure is applied to the optimum temperature for Lithuania, the fourth highest; for Latvia, the fifth highest; and so on. The curve so derived can be interpreted as the cost curve of geoengineering. Its first partial derivative is displayed in Figure 13.4: It shows the incremental compensation needed if geoengineering pushes the temperature lower.

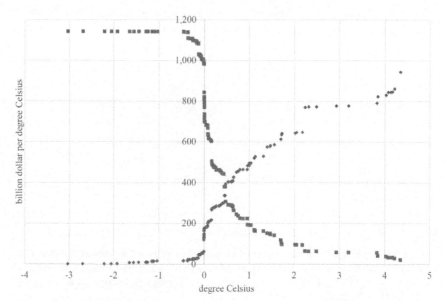

**Figure 13.4** Marginal willingness to pay (squares) and marginal willingness to accept to compensation (diamonds) for geoengineering.

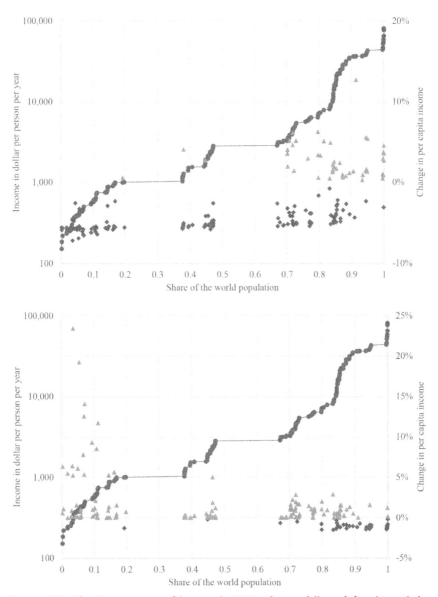

**Figure 13.5  The Lorenz curve of income in 2005 (dots and lines; left axis) and the changes induced by climate change and compensation paid/received (increases in triangles, decreases in diamonds; right axis).** The top panel compensates countries if geoengineering takes climate below their optimum, the bottom panel if the geoengineered climate is above the nation's optimum.

Using the same Baker–Thompson rule, I compute a benefit curve. Only Rwanda is prepared to pay to reduce the temperature from Uganda's optimum, the second lowest, to Rwanda's optimum, the lowest. Both Uganda and Rwanda are willing to pay to reduce the temperature from Mali's optimum, the third lowest, to Uganda's, and so on. The first partial derivative of the willingness-to-pay curve is shown in Figure 13.4.

The marginal costs curve meets the marginal benefits curve at 0.5°C above pre-industrial, a bit cooler than today. This happens to be China's preferred climate. Unsurprisingly (Coase 1960), 0.5°C is the temperature that maximizes the total income (cf. Figure 13.3).

Figure 13.5 shows the distributional implications of this choice. Take the 2005 Lorenz curve of income as a starting point. Assuming countries need to be compensated if geoengineering pushes the climate below their optimum—the intuition behind Figure 13.4—some countries gain. This gain consists of the compensation received and the impacts of climate change. As shown in the top panel of Figure 13.5, these countries tend to be fairly rich already. Other countries, and particularly poorer countries, are doubly hit, first by a climate that is hotter than they want and second by having to compensate the countries that oppose the extent of geoengineering. For the poorest countries, this amounts to a loss of some 5% of an already low income.

Figure 13.4 was set up based on the reasoning that countries would need to be compensated if geoengineering went too far for their taste. This is intuitive as geoengineering is a deliberate act—humans tend to emphasize harmful commission over harmful omission (Spranca, Minsk, and Baron 1991). But one can also argue that countries should be compensated if geoengineering does not go far enough. By the Coase Theorem (Coase 1960), this does not affect Figure 13.4. It does, however, affect the upper panel of Figure 13.5. This is shown in the bottom panel. The compensation flows in the opposite direction. Poor countries tend to gain, some quite a lot. Rich lose out, but only by a little.

## DISCUSSION AND CONCLUSION

I compute the Kaldor–Hicks optimal level of geoengineering and show that is not a Pareto optimal level. There is no Pareto optimal level. I consider two sets of transfers—out of a great many—that compensate the losers of geoengineering to a global mean surface air temperature of 0.5°C. One set of transfers implicitly assumes that people are entitled to unbridled climate change and compensates those that would prefer less-than-globally-optimal geoengineering from the gains of those that would like to see more. These transfer by and large flow from poor to rich. The other set of transfers implicitly assume that people are entitled to their favourite climate change and compensates those that would prefer more-than-globally-optimal geoengineering from the gains of those that would like to see less. These transfers by and large flow from rich to poor. The latter solution thus reduces the disparity of income and may strike many as an acceptable compromise between efficiency and equity.

The analysis here is simple but it shows the basic inequities that come with any choice about geoengineering. If there is an interest in reducing income inequality across the world, then it would be a start to compensate countries for climate change that is greater than they desire. There are obvious shortcomings. The analysis is static, but the problem dynamic. I consider geoengineering in isolation, and omit a comparison to greenhouse gas emission reduction. I assume that there is only one form of geoengineering, that it has a zero cost and that it can perfectly offset greenhouse gas emissions. I ignore uncertainty—about climate change, about its impacts and about geoengineering itself. The welfare analysis is utilitarian with some hand-waving about distribution. All of this can and should be improved.

## BIBLIOGRAPHY

Angel, R. 2006. 'Feasibility of cooling the Earth with a cloud of small spacecraft near the inner Langrange point (L1).' *Proceedings of the National Academy of Sciences of the United States of America* 103 (46): 17184–89. doi: 10.1073/pnas.0608163103.

Bala, G., P. B. Duffy, and K. E. Taylor. 2008. 'Impact of geoengineering schemes on the global hydrological cycle.' *Proceedings of the National Academy of Sciences of the United States of America* 105 (22): 7664–69. doi: 10.1073/pnas.0711648105.

Barrett, S. 2008. 'The Incredible Economics of Geoengineering.' *Environmental and Resource Economics* 39: 45–54.

Barrett, S. 2009. 'The Coming Global Climate-Technology Revolution.' *Journal of Economic Perspectives* 23 (2): 53–75.

Barrett, S. 2014. 'Solar geoengineering's brave new world: Thoughts on the governance of an unprecedented technology.' *Review of Environmental Economics and Policy* 8 (2): 249–69. doi: 10.1093/reep/reu011.

Coase, R. H. 1960. 'The Problem of Social Cost.' *Journal of Law and Economics* 3: 1–21.

Crutzen, P. J. 2006. 'Albedo enhancement by stratospheric sulfur injections: A contribution to resolve a policy dilemma?' *Climatic Change* 77 (3–4): 211–19. doi: 10.1007/s10584-006-9101-y.

Fragnelli, V., and M. E. Marina. 2010. 'An axiomatic characterization of the Baker-Thompson rule.' *Economics Letters* 107 (2): 85–87. doi: 10.1016/j.econlet.2009.12.033.

Gardiner, S. M. 2011. 'Some early ethics of geoengineering the climate: A commentary on the values of the royal society report.' *Environmental Values* 20 (2): 163–88. doi: 10.3197/096327111X12997574391689.

Goes, M., N. Tuana, and K. Keller. 2011. 'The economics (or lack thereof) of aerosol geoengineering.' *Climatic Change* 109 (3–4): 719–44. doi: 10.1007/s10584-010-9961-z.

Govindasamy, B., and K. Caldeira. 2000. 'Geoengineering Earth's radiation balance to mitigate $CO_2$-induced climate change.' *Geophysical Research Letters* 27 (14): 2141–44. doi: 10.1029/1999GL006086.

Hartzell-Nichols, L. 2012. 'Precaution and Solar Radiation Management.' *Ethics, Policy and Environment* 15 (2): 158–71. doi: 10.1080/21550085.2012.685561.

Heckendorn, P., D. Weisenstein, S. Fueglistaler, B. P. Luo, E. Rozanov, M. Schraner, L. W. Thomason, and T. Peter. 2009. 'The impact of geoengineering aerosols on stratospheric temperature and ozone.' *Environmental Research Letters* 4 (4). doi: 10.1088/1748-9326/4/4/045108.

Heyward, C. 2014. 'Benefiting from Climate Geoengineering and Corresponding Remedial Duties: The Case of Unforeseeable Harms.' *Journal of Applied Philosophy* 31 (4): 405–19. doi: 10.1111/japp.12075.

Hicks, John. 1939. 'The Foundations of Welfare Economics.' *Economic Journal* 49 (196): 696–712. doi: 10.2307/2225023.

Hoffert, M. I., K. Caldeira, G. Benford, D. R. Criswell, C. Green, H. Herzog, A. K. Jain, H. S. Kheshgi, K. S. Lackner, J. S. Lewis, H. D. Lightfoot, W. Manheimer, J. C. Mankins, M. E. Mauel, L. J. Perkins, M. E. Schlesinger, T. Volk, and T. M. L. Wigley. 2002. 'Engineering: Advanced technology paths to global climate stability: Energy for a greenhouse planet.' *Science* 298 (5595): 981–87. doi: 10.1126/science.1072357.

Horton, J. 2014. 'Solar Geoengineering: Reassessing Costs, Benefits, and Compensation.' *Ethics, Policy and Environment* 17 (2): 175–77. doi: 10.1080/21550085.2014.926078.

Hulme, M. 2015. 'Better weather?: The cultivation of the sky.' *Cultural Anthropology* 30 (2): 236–44. doi: 10.14506/ca30.2.06.

Irvine, P. J., R. L. Sriver, and K. Keller. 2012. 'Tension between reducing sea-level rise and global warming through solar-radiation management.' *Nature Climate Change* 2 (2): 97–100. doi: 10.1038/nclimate1351.

Jamieson, D. 1996. 'Ethics and intentional climate change.' *Climatic Change* 33 (3): 323–36.

Kaldor, Nicholas. 1939. 'Welfare Propositions in Economics and Interpersonal Comparisons of Utility.' *Economic Journal* 49 (195): 549–52. doi: 10.2307/2224835.

Keith, D. W. 2000. 'Geoengineering the climate: History and prospect.' *Annual Review of Energy and the Environment* 25: 245–84. doi: 10.1146/annurev.energy.25.1.245.

Lenton, T. M., and N. E. Vaughan. 2009. 'The radiative forcing potential of different climate geoengineering options.' *Atmospheric Chemistry and Physics* 9 (15): 5539–61.

Liao, S. M., A. Sandberg, and R. Roache. 2012. 'Human Engineering and Climate Change.' *Ethics, Policy and Environment* 15 (2): 206–21. doi: 10.1080/21550085.2012.685574.

Littlechild, S. C., and G. F. Thompson. 1977. 'Aircraft Landing Fees: A Game Theory Approach.' *Bell Journal of Economics* 8 (1): 186–204.

Lorenz, M. O. 1905. 'Methods of measuring the concentration of wealth.' *Publications of the American Statistical Association* 9 (70): 209–19. doi: 10.2307/2276207.

Matthews, H. D., and K. Caldeira. 2007. 'Transient climate-carbon simulations of planetary geoengineering.' *Proceedings of the National Academy of Sciences of the United States of America* 104 (24): 9949–54. doi: 10.1073/pnas.0700419104.

Moreno-Cruz, J. B. 2015. 'Mitigation and the geoengineering threat.' *Resource and Energy Economics* 41: 248–63. doi: 10.1016/j.reseneeco.2015.06.001.

Preston, C. J. 2011. 'Re-thinking the unthinkable: Environmental ethics and the presumptive argument against geoengineering.' *Environmental Values* 20 (4): 457–79. doi: 10.3197/096327111X13150367351212.

Rasch, P. J., S. Tilmes, R. P. Turco, A. Robock, L. Oman, C. C. Chen, G. L. Stenchikov, and R. R. Garcia. 2008. 'An overview of geoengineering of climate using stratospheric sulphate aerosols.' *Philosophical Transactions of the Royal Society A: Mathematical, Physical and Engineering Sciences* 366 (1882): 4007–37. doi: 10.1098/rsta.2008.0131.

Ricke, K. L., M. G. Morgan, and M. R. Allen. 2010. 'Regional climate response to solar-radiation management.' *Nature Geoscience* 3 (8): 537–41. doi: 10.1038/ngeo915.

Robock, A., L. Oman, and G. L. Stenchikov. 2008. 'Regional climate responses to geoengineering with tropical and Arctic $SO_2$ injections.' *Journal of Geophysical Research Atmospheres* 113 (16). doi: 10.1029/2008JD010050.

Schelling, Thomas C. 1996. 'The Economic Diplomacy of Geoengineering.' *Climatic Change* 33: 303–07.

Shapley, L. S. 1953. 'A value for n-person games.' In *Contributions to the Theory of Games, Volume II*, edited by H. W. Kuhn and A. W. Tucker, 307–17. Princeton: Princeton University Press.

Spranca, M., E. Minsk, and J. Baron. 1991. 'Omission and commission in judgment and choice.' *Journal of Experimental Social Psychology* 27 (1): 76–105. doi: 10.1016/0022-1031(91)90011-T.

Svoboda, T. 2012. 'The ethics of geoengineering: Moral considerability and the convergence hypothesis.' *Journal of Applied Philosophy* 29 (3): 243–56. doi: 10.1111/j.1468-5930.2012.00568.x.

Svoboda, T. 2015. 'Geoengineering, agent-regret, and the Lesser of Two Evils Argument.' *Environmental Ethics* 37 (2): 207–20.

Svoboda, T. 2016. 'Aerosol geoengineering deployment and fairness.' *Environmental Values* 25 (1): 51–68. doi: 10.3197/096327115X14497392134883.

Svoboda, T., and P. Irvine. 2014. 'Ethical and Technical Challenges in Compensating for Harm Due to Solar Radiation Management Geoengineering.' *Ethics, Policy and Environment* 17 (2): 157–74. doi: 10.1080/21550085.2014.927962.

Tol, Richard S. J. 2015. Economic impacts of climate change. In *Working Paper*. Falmer: University of Sussex.

Tuana, N., R. L. Sriver, T. Svoboda, R. Olson, P. J. Irvine, J. Haqq-Misra, and K. Keller. 2012. 'Towards Integrated Ethical and Scientific Analysis of Geoengineering: A Research Agenda.' *Ethics, Policy and Environment* 15 (2): 136–57. doi: 10.1080/21550085.2012.685557.

Urpelainen, J. 2012. 'Geoengineering and global warming: A strategic perspective.' *International Environmental Agreements: Politics, Law and Economics* 12 (4): 375–89. doi: 10.1007/s10784-012-9167-0.

Vaughan, N. E., and T. M. Lenton. 2011. 'A review of climate geoengineering proposals.' *Climatic Change* 109 (3–4): 745–90. doi: 10.1007/s10584-011-0027-7.

Victor, D. G. 2008. 'On the regulation of geoengineering.' *Oxford Review of Economic Policy* 24 (2): 322–36. doi: 10.1093/oxrep/grn018.

Weitzman, M. L. 2015. 'A Voting Architecture for the Governance of Free-Driver Externalities, with Application to Geoengineering.' *Scandinavian Journal of Economics* 117 (4): 1049–68. doi: 10.1111/sjoe.12120.

Wigley, T. M. L. 2006. 'A combined mitigation/geoengineering approach to climate stabilization.' *Science* 314 (5798): 452–54. doi: 10.1126/science.1131728.

Wong, P. H. 2014. 'Maintenance Required: The Ethics of Geoengineering and Post-Implementation Scenarios.' *Ethics, Policy and Environment* 17 (2): 186–91. doi: 10.1080/21550085.2014.926090.

# Index

# Notes on Contributors

**Patrik Baard** holds a PhD in philosophy from the Royal Institute of Technology, Stockholm, Sweden. His doctoral thesis, defended early 2016, was entitled "Cautiously Utopian Goals: Philosophical Analyses of Climate Change Objectives and Sustainability Targets". He is interested in decision-making and planning under epistemic and normative uncertainty and has published papers in journals such as *Ethics & the Environment; Ethics, Policy and Environment* and *Environmental Philosophy*.

**Christian Baatz** has a background in environmental sciences and now is a faculty member of the Department of Philosophy at Kiel University. His research focuses on climate ethics, global justice, environmental ethics and sustainability. He is about to complete his PhD on "Compensating the Victims of Climate Change in Developing Countries—Theoretical Justification and Practical Accomplishment".

**Dzigbodi Adzo Doke** (PhD), a Fulbright from Ghana, is a lecturer at the Department of Environment and Resource Studies of the University for Development Studies (UDS), Ghana. Her main focus is in risk assessment of climate change. She has served as a member in the Upper West Regional Environmental Management Committee, Ghana, providing technical advice on environmental management issues in the northern sector of Ghana.

**Johannes Emmerling** is a senior researcher at Fondazione Eni Enrico Mattei (FEEM), a research institution in Milan devoted to the study of sustainable development and global governance. He holds a PhD from the Toulouse School of Economics, where he worked on welfare economic aspects, namely distributional concerns and intertemporal equity. At FEEM he is co-leading the development of the integrated assessment model WITCH responsible for the economic modelling, risk and uncertainty, and alternative mitigation technologies.

**Augustin Fragnière** is a postdoctoral researcher in the Department of Philosophy at the University of Washington. His research focuses on climate and geoengineering ethics as well as environmental philosophy in the broader sense. Augustin has a PhD in political philosophy from the University of Paris 1—La Sorbonne and the University of Lausanne.

**Stephen M. Gardiner** is a professor of philosophy and Ben Rabinowitz Endowed Professor of the Human Dimensions of the Environment at the University of Washington, Seattle. He is the author of *A Perfect Moral Storm* (Oxford 2011), co-author of *Debating Climate Ethics* (Oxford 2016), editor of *Virtue Ethics, Old and New* (Cornell 2005) and co-editor of the *Oxford Handbook of Environmental Ethics* (Oxford 2016) and *Climate Ethics: Essential Readings* (Oxford 2010). His research focuses on global environmental problems, future generations and virtue ethics.

**Allen Habib** is an assistant professor of philosophy at the University of Calgary, in Alberta, Canada. He works on issues of intergenerational justice, including sustainability, resource distribution and compensation. He also works on promises and voluntary obligations. His work has appeared in *Environmental Values; Ethics, Policy & Environment; the Canadian Journal of Philosophy* and *the Stanford Encyclopedia of Philosophy*.

**Joshua Horton** is a Research Director, Geoengineering at the Harvard Kennedy School's Belfer Center for Science and International Affairs, where he conducts wide-ranging research on multiple governance aspects of geoengineering research and potential deployment. He has published on topics including the risks of unilateralism, liability and compensation mechanisms, and framing effects in decision-making. Before joining the Belfer Center, he worked as an energy consultant for a global consulting firm. He holds a PhD in political science from Johns Hopkins University.

**Marion Hourdequin** is an associate professor of philosophy at Colorado College. She specializes in environmental philosophy, and her recent work focuses on the ethics of climate change and the social and ethical dimensions of ecological restoration. She is the author of *Environmental Ethics: From Theory to Practice* (Bloomsbury 2015) and editor, with David Havlick, of *Restoring Layered Landscapes* (Oxford 2015).

**Frank Jankunis** is an instructor of philosophy at Camosun College. He received his PhD in philosophy in 2016 from the University of Calgary, under the supervision of Allen Habib. His research interests are mainly in environmental philosophy and environmental ethics. His current projects include work on the ethics of geoengineering and an upcoming co-edited volume on Canadian environmental philosophy.

**David Keith** has worked near the interface between climate science, energy technology and public policy for 25 years. His work is focused on the science, technology and public policy of solar geoengineering. He took first prize in Canada's national physics prize exam, won MIT's prize for excellence in experimental physics and was one of *TIME* magazine's Heroes of the Environment. David is a professor of applied physics in the School of Engineering and Applied Sciences, a professor of public policy in the Harvard Kennedy School and founder and chairman at Carbon Engineering, a company developing technology to capture $CO_2$ from ambient air.

**Teea Kortetmäki** is a fourth-year PhD student at the University of Jyväskylä, Finland. Her research interests involve food ethics and environmental ethics. She works in the multidisciplinary Food System Studies Research Group at the Department of Social Sciences and Philosophy, focusing particularly on the ethical aspects of sustainable food systems and food security.

**Jane Long** (PhD) recently retired as the associate director for energy and environment, Lawrence Livermore National Laboratory, and was the dean of the Mackay School of Mines, University of Nevada, Reno, and department chair for the Energy Resources Technology and the Environmental Research Departments at the Lawrence Berkeley National Lab. She was the co-chair of the Task Force on Geoengineering for the Bipartisan Policy Center which made a recommendation to commence research on this topic.

**Cush Ngonzo Luwesi** (PhD) is currently the focal region manager of the CGIAR Research Program on Water, Land and Ecosystems (WLE) for the Volta and Niger basins. He was the 2014 best scholar at Kenyatta University, Kenya. He is spearheading the African geoengineering wing and is a member of the scientific advisory committee on the UN Climate Research for Development (CR4D) in Africa.

**Duncan McLaren** is currently a freelance consultant and researcher, and part-time PhD student at Lancaster University. His research interests include cities, technology, climate change, energy and geoengineering, with a particular focus on issues of justice arising in these areas and the consequences for policy. Previously he worked in environmental research and advocacy, most recently as the chief executive of Friends of the Earth Scotland from 2003 until 2011.

**David R. Morrow** is a visiting fellow at the Institute for Philosophy and Public Policy at George Mason University. A philosopher by training, he has published on climate justice and on the ethics and governance of climate engineering in journals such as *Climatic Change; Environmental Values; Environmental Research Letters* and *Ethics, Policy & Environment.*

**Markku Oksanen** is a senior lecturer in philosophy at the University of Eastern Finland. He has co-edited *Philosophy and Biodiversity* (Cambridge University Press 2004) and *Ethics of Animal Re-creation and Modification* (Palgrave 2014) and published articles on green political theory and environmental ethics.

**Konrad Ott** is full professor for environmental philosophy at Christian-Albrechts-University, Kiel. His fields of research include discourse ethics, environmental ethics, nature conservation, sustainability, nuclear waste deposal and climate ethics. Ott has a background in policy counselling, especially in climate and energy policies (German "Energiewende"). In recent years, he has been engaged in a German research platform on climate engineering.

**Christopher J. Preston** is a full professor in the Department of Philosophy and a research fellow at the Mansfield Center's Program on Ethics and Public Affairs at the University of Montana in Missoula. His work is focused on environmental philosophy, the ethics of emerging technologies, the Anthropocene, and rewilding. He was born and raised in England.

**Toby Svoboda** is an assistant professor of philosophy at Fairfield University. His work on the ethics of climate engineering has appeared in *Environmental Ethics*; *Environmental Values*; *Ethics, Policy & Environment* and *Public Affairs Quarterly*, among other journals. His book, *Duties Regarding Nature: A Kantian Environmental Ethic*, was published by Routledge in 2015.

**Massimo Tavoni** is an associate professor at the School of Management of Politecnico di Milano and coordinator of the Climate Change Mitigation programme at FEEM. He has been fellow at the Center for Advanced Studied in Behavioural Sciences (CASBS) at Stanford University and a postdoctoral fellow at Princeton University. His research is about climate change mitigation policies and has appeared in major scientific journals. He is a lead author of the 5th assessment report of the IPCC, co-director of the International

Energy Workshop and deputy editor for the journal *Climatic Change*. He is the recipient of a starting grant from the European Research Council (ERC).

**Richard S. J. Tol MAE** is a professor of economics at the University of Sussex and a professor of the Economics of Climate Change at the Vrije Universiteit, Amsterdam. He specializes in the economics of energy, environment and climate, and is interested in integrated assessment modelling. He is ranked among the 150 best economists in the world and the 50 most-cited climate scholars. He is the chief editor of *Energy Economics*. He has played an active role in the Stanford Energy Modeling Forum and the Intergovernmental Panel on Climate Change.

**Per Wikman-Svahn** (PhD) is a researcher at the Department of Philosophy and History, Royal Institute of Technology KTH in Stockholm, Sweden. He has published papers on ethics of risk management, scenario planning and adaptation to sea-level rise, and his current research interests include robust decision-making strategies under severe uncertainty applied to climate change and value judgements in assessing extreme scenarios.

CPSIA information can be obtained at www.ICGtesting.com
Printed in the USA
BVOW08s0310120916

461704BV00002B/7/P